VAGRANTS
AND CITIZENS

VAGRANTS
AND CITIZENS

Politics and the Masses in Mexico City from Colony to Republic

RICHARD A. WARREN

SR BOOKS

Lanham • Boulder • New York • Toronto • Oxford

ROWMAN & LITTLEFIELD PUBLISHERS, INC.

Published in the United States of America
by Rowman & Littlefield Publishers, Inc.
A wholly owned subsidary of
The Rowman & Littlefield Publishing Group, Inc.
4501 Forbes Boulevard, Suite 200, Lanham, Maryland 20706
www.rowmanlittlefield.com

Estover Road, Plymouth PL6 7PY, United Kingdom

British Library Cataloguing in Publication Information Available

**The hardback edition of this book was catalogued by the Library of
Congress as follows:**

Warren, Richard A., 1961–
   Vagrants and citizens : politics and the masses in Mexico City from Colony
to Republic / Richard A. Warren
      p. cm.—(Latin American silhouettes)
   Includes bibliographical references.
   1. Mexico City (Mexico)—Politics and government—19th century.
   2. Poor—Mexico—Mexico City—Political activity—History—19th century.
   3. Political participation—Mexico—Mexico City—History—19th century.
   4. Social conflict—Mexico—Mexico City—History—19th century. I. Title.
   II. Series.

   F1386.3 .W37 2007
   972'.5304—dc21

                                                                    2001020990
   ISBN-13: 978-0-8420-2964-3 (cloth : alk. paper)
   ISBN-10: 0-8420-2964-8 (cloth : alk. paper)
   ISBN-13: 978-0-7425-5424-5 (pbk. : alk. paper)
   ISBN-10: 0-7425-5424-4 (pbk. : alk. paper)

Printed in the United States of America

♾™ The paper used in this publication meets the minimum requirements
of American National Standard for Information Sciences—Permanence of
Paper for Printed Library Materials, ANSI/NISO Z39.48-1992.

For my parents,

Florence and George Warren

Acknowledgments

A thorough accounting of the intellectual and personal debts accumulated during the research and writing of this study would certainly rival the rest of the text in length. Most of what may be of value in this book is a result of many gifts that I have received from those I have met along the way. Of necessity, I must limit the acknowledgments to those individuals and organizations that contributed most directly to completion of this work.

Research began at the University of Chicago, where Professors John H. Coatsworth and Friedrich Katz helped shape my understanding of Mexican history and of what it means to be a scholar. They both nurtured a stimulating and comradely intellectual community of Latin Americanists, of which I was lucky to be a part. My fellow graduate students provided encouragement and insight during our years at Chicago and since. Jeremy Baskes, Michael Ducey, Michel Gobat, Laura Gotkowitz, Peter Guardino, Laurie Lewis, and Jane Walter all took time away from their own research and lives to comment on my work as it evolved. Chuck Walker deserves special mention. His careful reading of this manuscript improved the final product in countless ways.

One of the most rewarding results of becoming a historian of Latin America has been the opportunity to meet a group of outstanding international scholars. I have learned much from Bill Beezley, Nils Jacobsen, Vincent Peloso, Barbara Tenenbaum, and Eric Van Young. As I struggled to sort out the complexities of this topic, extensive comments from Silvia Arrom, John Kicza, Pedro Santoni, and Jaime Rodríguez O. pointed in new and rewarding directions. I had the good fortune of conducting my research in Mexico City during a time when Carlos Illades, John Lear, Sonia Pérez Toledo, Ariel Rodríguez Kuri, and Mauricio Tenorio were also in the midst of sifting through the same archives. They shared their findings, their enthusiasm, and their friendship. Subsequently, the participants in the Seminar on the Institutional History of Mexico City provided me with a place to develop a better understanding of the history of one of the world's greatest cities. The anonymous scholars who read the manuscript for Scholarly Resources offered numerous suggestions to improve the book. The editorial and production staff at Scholarly Resources improved the final product in countless ways.

The employees of each of the archives and libraries listed in the notes and bibliography played a crucial role in bringing this project to fruition. The staffs in the Print and Photograph Division and the Map and Geography Division at the Library of Congress helped me to locate the illustrations used in the text. The University of Georgia Press graciously granted permission for the use of materials originally published as part of the essay, "Elections and Popular Participation in Mexico, 1808-1836," in *Liberals, Politics, and Power: State Formation in Nineteenth-Century Latin America*, edited by Vincent C. Peloso and Barbara A. Tenenbaum (Athens: University of Georgia Press, 1996). Over the last five years the staff of the Drexel Library at St. Joseph's University has responded to all of my unusual requests with pleasant professionalism. Support from a Fulbright Fellowship, the American Historical Association, and the Faculty Summer Research Grants Program at St. Joseph's University provided the financial means to complete this book. Dr. Judi Chapman, dean of the College of Arts and Sciences at St. Joseph's, made funds available to enhance the quality of the final product.

Beyond the gifts I have received from each of these individuals lie those of my family. Suzanne Cohen has enriched my life and improved my work with her perceptive mind and generous spirit. Finally, my mother and father, Florence and George Warren, have always inspired me, and it is to them that I owe the greatest debt.

Contents

1

Introduction
Mexico City's Masses and the
Transition from Colony to Nation-State

A poor boy stands outside a church on election day, shouting for all to hear, "Now we rule!" Twenty thousand men descend on the polls, delivering a landslide victory to ambitious political upstarts. Dozens of *léperos*, a disparaging term for the city's ragged masses, storm the congress and refuse to leave until the legislation that they desire is passed. Rumors circulate that a mob plans to celebrate Independence Day by desecrating the tomb of the Spanish conqueror Hernán Cortés. A prominent liberal intellectual blames political instability on the fact that too many poor people had the right to vote. This growing collection of archival evidence convinced me that the relationship between the urban masses and politics was crucial to understanding the transition from Spanish colony to independent nation-state in Mexico. As a result, I decided to write this study of Mexico City during the first tumultuous decades of the nineteenth century, from King Ferdinand VII's abdication of the Spanish crown in 1808 to the end of Mexico's first federal republic in 1836.

"Tumultuous" is a word barely adequate to describe the level of upheaval during this era. Preceded by a half-century of Spanish imperial reform, the Independence War (1810–1821) dragged on for more than a decade, bringing in its wake vast economic, social, and political dislocation. From Independence in 1821 to midcentury, the national executive office changed hands almost fifty times. The constitutional bases of governance fluctuated between federalist and centralist republican models, with an occasional monarchist resurgence. Armed rebellion punctuated political life, accompanied by the ubiquitous *pronunciamientos*, the rebels' mission statements.

For more than fifty years, Mexico failed to construct a peaceful and effective means for the transfer of political power. During the three decades that form the focus of this study, more than twenty different men acted as head of State, holding titles that ranged from viceroy to emperor to president (see Table 1).

Table 1. Acting Heads of State, 1803–1837

Head of State	In Office
José de Iturrigaray	January 4, 1803–September 16, 1808
Pedro de Garibay	September 16, 1808–July 19, 1809
Francisco Javier Lizana y Beaumont	July 19, 1809–May 8, 1810
Pedro Catani	May 8, 1810–September 14, 1810
Francisco Javier Venegas	September 14, 1810–March 4, 1813
Félix María Calleja	March 4, 1813–September 16, 1816
Juan Ruiz de Apodaca	September 16, 1820–July 5, 1821
Francisco Novella	July 8, 1821–September 13, 1821
Juan O'Donoju	August–September 1821
Agustín de Iturbide	September 28, 1821–March 30, 1823
Provisional Executive (Three Men)	March 30, 1823–October 10, 1824
Guadalupe Victoria	October 10, 1824–April 1, 1829
Vicente Guerrero	April 1, 1829–December 19, 1829
José María Bocanegra	December 19–December 23, 1829
Governing Council (Three Men)	December 23–December 31, 1830
Anastasio Bustamante	January 1, 1830–August 14, 1832
Melchor Múzquiz	August 14, 1832–December 24, 1832
Manuel Gómez Pedraza	December 24, 1832–May 16, 1833
Valentín Gómez Farías	June 2, 1833–April 24, 1834
Antonio López de Santa Anna	April 24, 1834–January 28, 1835
Miguel Barragán	January 28, 1835–February 27, 1836
José Justo Corro	February 27, 1836–April 19, 1837

Sources: Timothy E. Anna, *The Fall of the Royal Government in Mexico* (Lincoln: University of Nebraska Press, 1978); Juana Vázquez Gómez, *Prontuario de gobernantes de México, 1325–1989* (Mexico City: Editorial Diana, 1989).

Historians increasingly have focused on the importance of political and ideological disputes in an era too often simply dismissed as the domain of personality conflicts and military chieftains. This study builds upon that foundation as it analyzes the role of Mexico's urban masses, a topic little explored and poorly understood. The evidence demonstrates that the relationship between elites and the urban masses assumed a central role in Mexico's political evolution during the struggle for Independence and in the decades thereafter. Economic stagnation and elite fragmentation contributed motive and opportunity for popular political mobilization. In addition, the protracted struggle to establish a stable, independent nation-state changed perceptions about the relationship between the poor and power. As alternative political models were contested, legitimacy based on willful choice rather than divine providence became the basis for any claim to lasting authority. This material and ideological flux opened a space for Mexico City's poor to clamber onto the political stage, in both traditional and new forms, from riots to electoral campaigns. Their presence at the center of the era's major political upheavals in turn influenced elite perceptions of the new nation's problems and potential solutions.

Long-simmering political, economic, and social conflicts shaped the process of state formation throughout Latin America. These disputes encompassed, but were not limited to, the relationship between capital cities and competing provincial centers; the role of the Catholic Church and other corporate structures and the privileges invested in them; the direction of government economic and fiscal policy, particularly taxation; and the construction of a new body politic, which engendered struggle over the nature of citizenship and political participation. The legacy of militarization during the late-eighteenth and early-nineteenth centuries and a troubled relationship with a changing international political economy exacerbated the arduous transition. A full understanding of this transformation must begin with an assessment of the eighteenth-century Spanish imperial overhaul known as the Bourbon reforms.[1]

The Bourbon Reforms

For almost three hundred years claims to political legitimacy in Mexico were based on the relationship between monarch and subject. Over the course of decades after the Spanish Conquest of the Americas, New Spain became a principal source of revenue for the crown, but local authorities retained relative autonomy in making decisions. By the eighteenth century much of the governance structure had long been under the control of a creole elite, people of Spanish descent born in the colonies and primarily maintaining regional ties and loyalties. This began to change when the House of Bourbon confirmed its claim to the throne as a result of the War of the Spanish Succession (1701–1713). The Bourbons attempted to transform New Spain into a more efficient colony subordinate to imperial fiscal and political necessity. In subsequent years, Spain's ill-fated confrontations with other European powers reinforced the crown's decision to overhaul imperial policies.

Inspired by the ideas of the Enlightenment and fearful of the increased threat of other European powers to the Spanish domain in the Americas, the Bourbon reformers redesigned the bureaucracy, altered appointment policies, and introduced a greater military presence. The crown created two new viceroyalties and additional regional courts (*audiencias*). In an attempt to reduce the number of Creoles in the imperial government and return important political and religious offices to peninsular Spaniards (Peninsulares), new policies replaced the practice of selling bureaucratic appointments. The intendancy system established an entirely new layer of governance for the empire. Based on the French model and implemented at an earlier time in Spain, the monarchy expected intendants to wrest control of revenues and political power from the holders of local sinecures. The Bourbon kings also expelled the Society of Jesus (Jesuits) from Spanish territories. Economic reforms were designed to stimulate trade and mining, while additional taxes and more efficient revenue collection would enhance the crown's share of economic growth.[2]

On the surface, the Bourbon reforms appeared to achieve these goals. Absolute levels of agricultural and livestock production increased. Royal revenues from all sources jumped. These figures, however, masked multiple problems at the economic, political, and social levels. Population growth and government subsidies fueled increases in gross output, but productivity stagnated. By the late eighteenth century, population growth in the countryside began to strain available resources and produce periodic subsistence crises. Migration to cities created a growing urban underclass, with attendant increases in crime and the risk to public health. By the 1790s the Mexico City courts were trying almost ten thousand offenders annually, while five major epidemics in the years from 1761 to 1813 claimed the lives of at least fifty thousand people. New Spain never experienced the outright rebellion that gripped other regions of Latin America during the second half of the eighteenth century, but the Bourbon redirection of the political and economic system, nevertheless, yielded great resentment and resistance.[3]

The Road to Independence and the New Nation

Events between 1808 and 1810 shattered the last vestiges of traditional political arrangements in the Americas and between the colonies and the imperial center. Charles IV, cousin of the ill-fated Louis XVI of France, assumed the Spanish throne in the inauspicious year of 1788. Like most of Europe's leaders, Charles was poorly equipped to respond to the rapidly unfolding events unleashed by the French Revolution and the rise of Napoleon Bonaparte, whose encroachment onto the Iberian peninsula in 1808 precipitated a frantic transfer of the Spanish crown, first between Charles and his son Ferdinand, then to Napoleon's brother, Joseph. These untoward events incited uprisings against the French within Spain. Under English military protection, the Spanish resistance formed a provisional governing body, the Cortes, composed of representatives from all of Spain's dominions. The Cortes hammered out a constitution, implemented in 1812, and called for Ferdinand's restoration. As Napoleon's empire collapsed, Ferdinand VII returned to the throne in 1814 and soon overturned the constitution. A barracks revolt forced the liberal document upon the king and the Spanish population again in 1820.

The Spanish monarchy's roller-coaster ride reverberated throughout the empire, and spurred discontent to action. In the vast Spanish American dominions, diverse economic organization, ethnic composition, geographic location, intra-elite politics, and popular aspirations contributed to divergent outcomes. Some regions, such as the Río de la Plata, achieved effective Independence a full decade earlier than Peru, where loyalists held out until the mid-1820s. In New Spain a massive popular uprising, composed mostly of peasants and mine workers and led by the parish priest Miguel Hidalgo in 1810, frightened as many inhabitants as it attracted and failed to secure early victory. King Ferdinand's return, skillful loyalist politics, and indecision among the discontented delivered a stalemate, broken only in 1820, when ambitious royal officers joined forces with long-term insurgents to sever ties with the unreliable metropolis. An army composed of bitter enemies, agreeing on little other than Spanish futility, took the capital in September 1821.

A rapid succession of governments followed in the years after Independence. A brief creole monarchy under former royal army officer Agustín de Iturbide gave way to a federal republic in 1824.

Partisan political agitation in the second half of the 1820s launched a rancorous debate over the locus of power and which sectors of society should be charged with setting the new nation's political agenda. Ideological and strategic differences soon split federalists into moderate and radical camps. Conservatives lamented the mass mobilizations of the 1820s as a throwback to the days of Hidalgo's marauders. They dreamed of creating a regime controlled by "Hombres de Bien" (Decent Men), property holders of an appropriate class background who could pull the levers of power from Mexico City. By the time of the 1828 presidential election, moderates were increasingly joining their more conservative brethren in condemning mass politics, while radicals were fanning the flames of popular sentiment with an incendiary presidential campaign on behalf of Vicente Guerrero, an Independence War hero. Guerrero's rise to power through insurrection, coupled with the new nation's nagging economic crisis, unified many in the fear that Mexican society verged on a complete breakdown. The backlash culminated with the overthrow of Guerrero in 1829, justified as the first essential step to restore order in Mexican society.

A growing breach between radical federalists and the Decent Men emerged in the early 1830s. The regime of President Anastasio Bustamante implemented a program to reorient politics away from the masses and the radical federalists, although it did not abandon the 1824 Constitution. After Bustamante's regime crumbled under pressure from federalist strongholds and disgruntled military leaders in 1832, new political factions solidified. While President Antonio López de Santa Anna convalesced at his estate in Veracruz, Vice President Valentín Gómez Farías led a faction of radical federalists in the legislature in unprecedented attacks on the privileges of both the Church and the military. Disaffection with these efforts precipitated a more explicit assault on federalism that attracted increasing numbers of citizens. Santa Anna suspended the radical congress and drove Gómez Farías out of office in the spring of 1834. In the midst of a mounting crisis in Texas, a newly installed congress promulgated a series of laws in 1835 and 1836 that dramatically altered the relationship among local, state, and national levels of government and attacked the political rights of the poor. The new regime paraded its constitution through the streets of the capital in January 1837, putting an end to the federal republic, but not the conflict.

At the center of debates over the nation's destiny lay the question of political participation, and what role the masses should play.

Whether one saw them as a scourge, the seed of a new politics—or most likely—some combination of both, the largest concentration of poor folk in the country resided in Mexico City. Any group aspiring to national authority had to control that city and its residents, which was often the final obstacle that would distinguish a provincial uprising from a change in national authority. The city also served as the proving ground of public response to new national policies, as information flowed quickly from the chambers of power through the city's neighborhoods. As capital of both the viceroyalty of New Spain and the independent nation, and the most populous urban center in the western hemisphere at the turn of the nineteenth century, this extraordinarily complex political, economic, and social space and its residents challenged all who aspired to power.

The City and Its Residents

In the fall of 1835 the cosmopolitan entertainer Eugene Robertson brought his hot-air balloon act to the San Pablo bullring, south of the city's center. Large crowds came to see Robertson rise into the clouds, accompanied by a young Mexican woman selected from among the spectators. This airborne odd couple gazed over a city that had changed little in size or design during the last decades. To their north, they could spot Mexico's political, economic, social, and cultural center, the Plaza Mayor, the city's main square. The Metropolitan Cathedral, the National Palace, the municipal council building, other government buildings, and one of the city's principal commercial establishments, the Parián market, pressed up against the vast square. Both foreign visitors and native observers recognized this plaza as the throbbing center of Mexico's universe. They sketched it, painted it, and wrote about the volatile space where the great and varied parade of Mexico's population gathered—and sometimes faced off against one another. As Joel R. Poinsett, the first U.S. representative to republican Mexico noted, each day the plaza provided a "singular exhibition of the busy, the idle and the devout." This activity is readily seen in Pedro Gualdi's lithograph of the Metropolitan Cathedral (see next page). Produced in 1850, the lithograph introduces the viewer to a quiet day in the main plaza, populated with soldiers and dandies, peasants and elegant ladies, and the ubiquitous *aguador*, one of the city's water carriers, burdened with jugs hanging from his head, both front and rear. Another perspective on the main square, originally drawn for

View of the Metropolitan Cathedral and *Plaza Mayor*, ca. 1850. *Source:* Pedro Gualdi, *Views of the City of Mexico* (Mexico City: J. M. Lara, 1850). *Courtesy of the Geography and Map Division, Library of Congress, Washington, D.C.*

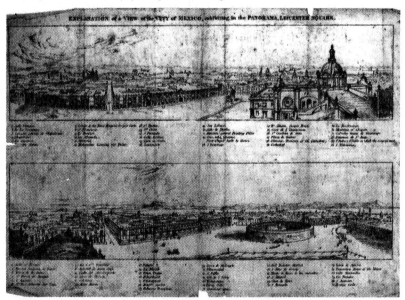

Views of Mexico City from the top of the Metropolitan Cathedral, ca. 1828. *Source:* Description of the Panorama of the Superb City of Mexico and the Surrounding Scenery, Painted on 2700 Square Feet of Canvas, by Robert Buford, Esq., from *Drawings Made on the Spot, at the Request of the Mexican Government* by Mr. William Bullock, Jr., Now Open for Inspection at the Rotunda, New York (New York: E. Conrad, 1828). *Courtesy of the Prints and Photographs Division, Library of Congress, Washington, D.C.*

customers of the Panorama in London, and reproduced here, simultaneously captured some of the different events that brought huge crowds from across the socioeconomic gamut into close contact. The large round structure in the center of the plaza is a temporary bullring constructed for a political celebration. Off to its right a religious procession snakes its way into the plaza.[4]

Emanating from the city's heart, a well-ordered grid of streets stretched in all directions, broken periodically by plazas large and small, such as the Alameda Park in the west or the Santo Domingo Plaza a few blocks north of the cathedral. Most city visitors, like the Englishman Mark Beaufoy, noted the beauty of the center's design, streets "all straight and at right angles to each other." Beaufoy also noted the way the grid gave way to ramshackle improvisations of garbage dumps, cemeteries, and slaughterhouses and tanneries "full of rubbish and filth" on the outskirts of town. Although the periphery remained the distressed and dusty home of the most humble classes, the capital had not yet developed the clear differentiation between rich and poor neighborhoods that later characterized industrial cities. The poor neighborhoods of San Pablo and Salto del Agua lay a few short blocks from the most valuable real estate in the city. Even the historic city center contained a mixture of homes, workshops, and markets, rambling palaces and squalid tenements; the very rich and the unimaginably poor lived side by side. Elites raised a common lament that they lived too close to the unclean, the infirm, and the desperate. "Go where you will in this city, you are haunted by beggars," claimed Brantz Mayer at midcentury. At church services, "the floor was a checkerboard of ladies and *léperos*, of misery and pride."[5]

Mexico City's population grew sharply in the second half of the eighteenth century, largely due to migration from the city's immediate surroundings. Since job opportunities and social mobility were not abundant there, migrants tended to be pushed by rural economic and political distress rather than drawn by the enticements of urban life. During the protracted rural subsistence crisis of the last half-century of Spanish colonial rule, a move to the capital became the last chance for many in dire straits. Although any measure of the city's population during this era is highly suspect, official viceregal documents estimate that the city's population grew approximately 7.6 percent between 1790 and 1811, rising to 113,000. Approximately 43 percent of the population had been born outside the city. In that year, almost 57 percent of the city's inhabitants claimed to be of pure European descent, while "Indians" composed just over 26 percent of the population, and the other approximately 17 percent fell into the category of mixed ethnicity, or *casta*.[6]

The realities of life discredited these discrete census categories. Ample evidence demonstrates the malleability of colonial racial and ethnic terminology and the absence of a fully realized socioeconomic hierarchy based on race and ethnicity. A vast gap in wealth separated the city's elite from the rest of its heterogeneous population. About one hundred Mexico City families controlled assets of one million pesos or more, compared to only twelve families of such wealth in the rest of the viceroyalty. Those who owned their own stores and workshops, as well as teachers, professionals, and some in government service, formed a middle sector whose members were able to maintain crucial distance between themselves and the poor with the capital and other resources at their disposal or the stability of their employment. Wealthy families flaunted their titles and boasted of the purity of their blood, but European descent in reality provided no guarantees of economic success. Among the gamblers, idlers, and other luckless fellows rounded up on the city's street as vagrants and impressed for military service in the last years of imperial rule, almost half identified themselves as Spaniards. The capital's socioeconomic realities blurred racial and ethnic signifiers. Asked to estimate the number of voters from distinct ethnic categories during Mexico City's first elections under the 1812 Spanish Constitution, municipal employees remarked that they just could not tell the difference between one poor man and another.[7]

The impoverished circumstances of its majority did not diminish the city's importance as home to the largest number and greatest variety of workers in New Spain. In the last quarter of the eighteenth century, more than eighteen thousand guild members lived in the city, about 14 percent of its population. Of these, slightly more than half were artisans, and the others belonged to guilds in the service sector, manual labor, and professions that required skills such as literacy or arithmetic. Like their European counterparts, guild members were a strikingly diverse lot. A guild member's status depended on supply and demand, skill level, training, taste, and increasingly, competition from imports. Within each craft, diversity reigned as well. A huge gulf separated the tailor who eked out a living in a small shop that doubled as his home from the fashionable dress designer who catered to the city's wealthiest clients. Most artisans fell into the former category, especially within the most prevalent crafts, such as shoemakers, carpenters, and tailors.

Most toiled in small workshops that employed three or four persons and had little capital invested in tools or materials.[8]

Beyond its small artisanal workshops, the city employed thousands more in a wide variety of poorly remunerated positions. By 1800 only one *obraje*, the infamous colonial manufactories that focused on textile production, remained. The largest single employer in the capital, the royal tobacco monopoly, according to Susan Deans-Smith absorbed between 5,437 and 8,988 workers during this era. Most tobacco workers earned wages comparable to other semiskilled and unskilled workers. The most common of these were bricklayers, porters, domestic servants, and street vendors. Average daily salaries ranged from a half- to one peso per day for skilled workers and a quarter- to a half-peso per day for unskilled workers, barely enough to support an individual and far from adequate for a family. Too many shoemakers scrambled to shoe the few in the city who could afford their goods. Too many carpenters chased after scarce woodworking jobs. Vendors and porters hustled on the streets for their daily pittance. Most of the city's residents barely made ends meet under the best of circumstances, and the worst of circumstances prevailed during the first half of the nineteenth century.[9]

The economic history of the post-Independence era varied from region to region, although national trends were dismal, and the vast majority of Mexico City's population remained mired in poverty.[10] After Independence, population growth in the capital slowed to less than the national average, but migrants still contributed substantially to the population. The 1842 census lists a total population of 121,728, with little change in occupational structure from the turn of the century. Artisanal and other manufacturing jobs accounted for almost 29 percent of the economically active population, with another 24 percent in the service sector, including domestic labor. Small enterprises still characterized the economy, as over 60 percent of the city's units of production were capitalized at a hundred pesos or less, while fewer than 10 percent were capitalized at one thousand pesos or more.[11] Contemporary observers suggested that wages and employment opportunities had not changed significantly from the late colonial period, and meeting basic human needs remained a challenge. At least one-fifth of the city's residents lived in abject poverty, and perhaps only one-half of those of working age had access to stable employment.[12]

This heterogeneous urban underclass was vilified as *léperos* by the press and lambasted in the memoirs of both Mexican and foreign elites, who decried the moral turpitude and easy life of gambling and drinking elected by the city's masses. The liberal poet and newspaper editor Guillermo Prieto lumped masons, carriage drivers, porters, tanners, and pork butchers among those whose love of liquor and pusillanimity absorbed the better part of their days. The German Carl Christian Sartorius seconded the idea that the urban underclass had a congenital aversion to work and property ownership. In 1834, British Minister Richard Pakenham went so far as to report to the Foreign Office in London that the only able-bodied Mexicans without work were those with bad habits. The antidote to these jaundiced observations may be found in other documents that suggest a more complex reality of hand-to-mouth existence and a fine line between the noble laborer and the accused vagrant. One may turn, for example, to the records of the Vagrancy Tribunal, formed in 1828 to address elite concerns with the apparent epidemic of layabouts described by Prieto, Sartorius, and Pakenham. Over 75 percent of the accused dragged before Mexico City's vagrancy court between 1828 and 1850 claimed to have been trained as artisans, and most of them presented witnesses to testify that they were indeed honorable workers who had been temporarily waylaid by hard times. As a result, the conviction rate in the tribunal hovered around 10 percent. The municipal council members who served as judges were roundly criticized for being soft on crime, but their general responsibility for the urban behemoth gave them a clearer perspective on the real opportunities and obstacles faced by the city's population.[13]

Municipal Political Organization

The municipal council or ayuntamiento, with roots in the Iberian political tradition, guarded the "health and comfort" of the city's residents, but the malleable nature of its charge generated a steady debate over the extent of its authority and led to chronic disputes with other bureaucrats who shared similar responsibilities.[14] During most of the colonial period, the municipal council consisted of fifteen hereditary aldermen (*regidores*). Each year, the *regidores* selected two city attorneys (*síndicos*), and two chairmen, or alcaldes. By the mid-eighteenth century, wealthy families who had been in New Spain for generations dominated the ayuntamiento. They had local, rather than imperial, priorities.

During the second half of the eighteenth century, viceroys and other representatives of the monarchy, inspired by the Bourbon reform impulse and Enlightenment concepts of space and order, attempted to rationalize, beautify, and sanitize Mexico City. They began to think of the city as a single entity, rather than a number of ethnically segregated spaces, and incorporated indigenous neighborhoods into a new demarcation of parishes. They also developed a new political organization of the city into major and minor districts (*cuarteles mayors* and *menores*) and established a neighborhood police to enforce a wide variety of new regulations on behavior.[15] Reformers also changed the municipal council structure, adding additional aldermen. The Crown's representatives insisted that a certain number of these seats, as well as one chairmanship, be reserved for Peninsulares. The increased number of Spaniards on the council did little to change the organization's status as the political and administrative arm of Mexico City's creole elite.[16]

As New Spain moved from Spanish colony to Mexican republic, two major changes occurred in the municipal council structure. The first was that all offices on the council became elective rather than hereditary or appointive. The second was that the number of council members changed. Under the Spanish Constitution (in effect during the years 1812 to 1814 and 1820 to 1821), sixteen aldermen served. After Independence, six chairmen served along with eight aldermen and one city attorney. All were elected to two-year terms, with half of the council elected each year.

Other important political actors made their home in the capital. The poorly defined relationship between the ayuntamiento and other officeholders generated great friction. During the colonial era, the viceroy, the Spanish king's representative in New Spain, had his own ideas about how the city should be run. Mexico City also hosted an audiencia, one of the empire's regional high courts. Audiencia judges heard both civil and criminal cases, advised on the correct interpretations of royal policy, and reviewed the decisions of other officeholders. Conflicts also developed periodically between the ayuntamiento and the intendant, the new bureaucratic position created by the Bourbon reforms. The intendant shared responsibility with the council over a wide range of municipal issues, including public safety, during the difficult years of the insurgency.

Independence did little to rectify the ambiguous status and authority of the municipal council. The establishment of Mexico City as the capital of the federal republic in 1824 exacerbated the problem of overlapping authority. Because no founding document delimited the nature of this new political entity, the municipal council was forced to improvise resolutions to jurisdictional disputes with the newly created office of Federal District governor, whose incumbent was a presidential appointee. Confrontations among those responsible for the city's well-being continued, even after more specific operating ordinances for the municipal government were promulgated in 1840. From 1812 on, throughout their conflicts with other authorities, council members argued that they were the elected representatives of the inhabitants of Mexico City and therefore had a role in making policy, not simply in enforcing laws and policies handed down from above. The advent of popular sovereignty unleashed similar confrontations throughout the political system.[17]

The Implications of Popular Sovereignty

Politics engaged the urban masses, and they in turn helped to shape ideas and practices during the first three decades of the nineteenth century. Electoral records, criminal trials, debates in the congress and municipal council, pamphlets, and newspapers reveal that Mexico City's poor were key participants in the era's events and that they increasingly became a focus for elite analysis and a political problem to be solved. The chapters that follow use these sources to analyze the ways in which this relationship influenced the era's political struggles, particularly in regard to such questions as: How will the concept of the sovereign people be defined? How will the people express their will? What is the relationship between popular sovereignty and social control? How will civic virtues be expressed and inculcated in a new body politic?

This enterprise requires an examination of elite and popular discourse and action, particularly the expanded "repertoire of political contention." New rituals and activities draped in the symbols of popular sovereignty provided the opportunity for—or, indeed, required a certain degree of—popular mobilization to meet their designers' goals. In this volatile climate the role of elites remained critical, but ideas and actions often moved beyond their control. Different sectors of Mexico City's heterogeneous population entered the political arena on a regular basis, sometimes to confirm order, at other times as avatars of upheaval. The preparation, execution, and analysis of these activities formed key components of competing narratives about the new nation and the role of the masses within it. They also provided opportunities for communication within the elite, and between elites and masses.[18]

Among these rituals elections assumed a central role. Beginning in 1812, thousands of Mexico City's residents went to the polls periodically to choose electoral delegates who would in turn select municipal council members and legislators. One can only speculate about the exact identity of the tens of thousands of voters shaking the city's political foundations during this era. The franchise incorporated a large and diverse group of adult men in the political process, and, according to every contemporary account, the electorate included thousands of the city's poor. The limited quantitative data available support the conclusion that the urban masses actively participated in the electoral process. The importance of elections went beyond the counting of votes, because elections often triggered general political agitation. The most serious episodes of popular upheaval during this period were connected to electoral contests and the underlying dispute over which sectors of society should have a say in nation-state development. Channels for the peaceful disputation of difference and the incorporation of broad sectors of society into the political process failed to develop. The unpredictability of electoral politics and the general ferment among the masses that elections triggered had a lasting effect on all elite factions in Mexico. Conservatives generally rejected any political formula that mobilized the urban masses for political purposes. For federalists, nascent liberals, and some military officers, the situation was more complicated, as leaders shifted their opinions with changing circumstances. Mexico's quintessential moderate liberal of the era, José María Luis Mora, saw the upheavals that followed Independence as confirmation that citizenship had to be linked to property in order to ensure social stability. Lorenzo de Zavala, alleged mastermind of urban uprising and patron of the poor in the 1820s, asserted in the mid-1830s that Mexico needed to base suffrage on property holding. Both authors laid much of the blame for Mexico's instability on misguided factional efforts to mobilize the poor for political purposes. Over time this interpretation of historical experience led nineteenth-century elites into an implicit social pact to isolate the masses from political participation as much as possible.[19]

The other essential political rituals that emerged in the first half of the nineteenth century, the implementation of new constitutions and Independence Day, also provided the opportunity to acknowledge and symbolically present the place of the masses in the new political formula. Each of these rituals was related in complex ways to the other, and one can limn their meaning only in relation to the broader repertorial and chronological context. Competing elite factions and the masses intermittently employed these opportunities to intervene in politics, to attempt to alter policy, to protest against incumbents, or to express dissatisfaction with the entire state of public affairs. Recalcitrant upstarts in the streets, disgruntled troops, the weather, and the past itself could disrupt the utopian ideals of a ritual's designers and become part of the event and its interpretation. The introduction and reimplementation of three different constitutions in three decades communicated a message of instability and of the plastic nature of all political structures regardless of any ceremony's beauty or grandiosity. The struggle over the appropriate messages and manifestations of Independence Day marked another fissure in Mexico's foundation myth that could ignite popular mobilization. The protracted war and the ambiguous context in which Independence was finally achieved in 1821 contributed to a struggle among moderates, conservatives, and radicals to create heroes and to find lessons in that experience, which then manifested itself in competing celebrations and discourses.

Beyond the grand cyclical events of the political calendar, spontaneous and quotidian encounters also shaped the era's politics. Numerous times during the first half of the nineteenth century, protests broke out over impressment, currency devaluations, or the price of staples. Religious processions sometimes degenerated into political rumbles. Hostile encounters with the police and military provided the opportunity for a dialogue between representatives of the state and the poor. Patterns of motivation, aspiration, and ideology emerge out of these acts as well.

The Elusive Agenda of the Urban Masses

It is notoriously difficult to elucidate the political proclivities of such a heterogeneous group, many of whom were illiterate and left no records of their beliefs and passions. Nonetheless, the archives provide numerous clues to the issues that attracted the attention of large numbers of the poor and the way they understood their political role. Handbills, poems, skits, songs, jokes, and even graffiti suggest the sources of ideas and slogans. Court cases, official correspondence, the minutes of meetings, and reports in the media provide evidence of how thought became action. Most reports note the use of boilerplate sloganeering of the "Long live this " and "Death to that" variety. These accounts often concluded with derisive reference to the ignorance of the masses, but the political savvy of the popular classes cannot be dismissed out of hand. Very sophisticated political ideas were communicated both orally and symbolically. The allegorical dances and allocutions that accompanied public ceremonies may not have been completely transparent or easily accessible, but the ritual elements were often explained and the rules of the political game, including entire constitutions, were recited and discussed over and over in public, providing a language and a set of symbols that "helped shape the perception of interests and hence the development of ideologies."[20]

Even with rote sloganeering, it is not fruitful to ponder for too long over whether or not slogans expressed the true sentiments of the masses, because that is impossible to measure, and sincerity would be a standard placed on the tropes of the masses that is not imposed on elite discourse. Descriptive accounts, bolstered by quantitative data, reveal that sectors within the masses developed affinities for particular persons and movements. They were not indiscriminate in their political passions, and they did not engage solely in hero worship, although their goals were sometimes less clear than those of their rural contemporaries. The issues of taxation and municipal autonomy that dominated *campesino* (countryside) movements during the post-Independence era were obscured in the capital, but both material and ideological objectives may be discerned in some of the actions of the urban poor. The masses also expressed in many ways their loyalties to political movements and particular leaders, to whom they were often linked by local priests, militia and military officers, and other middlemen.[21]

For the city's poor masses, Mexico's post-Independence political problems were symbolized by the Parián market and the Parianistas, the powerful merchants who seemed to dominate Mexico long after the Independence War ended. Mobs tore up the Parián market in an uprising in 1828, but that space had long been a magnet for popular resentment. In 1824 when the leaders of a barracks revolt called for popular support, the municipal council sent loyal troops to protect the Parián. Two years later, members of the York Rite Masonic lodges appealed even to the "most wretched citizen" to use the vote to remove the Parianistas from their privileged positions. Support for protectionist legislation and the movement to deport resident Spaniards also sprang from the concept that control of the country's political economy needed to be removed from the Spanish-affiliated merchant cabal, which focused on the accumulation of wealth through overseas commerce while domestic producers became idle. The heroes and factions that gained popular affection understood the importance of these issues and used related symbols and practices to elicit support from the urban masses. Calls to defend the legacy of Independence and the heroes of the war, to deport the Spanish, and to protect domestic laborers at the polls or in the streets became common during this era. The meaning of popular sovereignty itself rested at the heart of these confrontations.

At Independence, Mexico faced the heritage of three centuries of Spanish colonial rule, the effects of a decade of warfare, and conflicting expectations about what a new nation should be like. A long tug of war between tradition and innovation ensued, during which the lower classes entered the fight to interpret the past and determine the future. The experience of popular political activity in this era influenced both conservative and liberal ideology and action in subsequent decades. The distinct features of Mexican politics in the modern era can only be understood with this crucial piece of the historical puzzle in place.

Notes

1. Frank Safford, "Politics, Ideology and Society in Post-Independence Spanish America," in *The Cambridge History of Latin America*, ed. Leslie Bethell (Cambridge, England: Cambridge University Press, 1985), 3:347–422; Donald Fithian Stevens, *Origins of Instability in Early Republican Mexico* (Durham, N.C.: Duke University Press, 1991), 107–18.

2. Mark A. Burkholder and D. S. Chandler, *From Impotence to Authority: The Spanish Crown and the American Audiencias, 1687–1808* (Columbia: University of Missouri Press, 1977), 89–126; David A. Brading, "Government and Elite in Late Colonial Mexico," *Hispanic American Historical Review* 53, no. 3 (1973): 399–406.

3. Eric Van Young, "The Age of Paradox: Mexican Agriculture at the End of the Colonial Period, 1750–1810," in *The Economies of Mexico and Peru during the Late Colonial Period*, ed. Nils Jacobsen and Hans Jürgen Puhle (Berlin: Colloquium Verlag Bibliotheca Ibero-Americana, 1986), 64, 74; Colin M. MacLachlan and Jaime E. Rodríguez O., *The Forging of the Cosmic Race: A Reinterpretation of Colonial Mexico* (Berkeley: University of California Press, 1980), 264; Stanley J. Stein, "Bureaucracy and Business in the Spanish Empire, 1759–1804: Failure of a Bourbon Reform in Mexico and Peru," *Hispanic American Historical Review* 61, no. 1 (1981): 13; Michael C. Scardaville, "Crime and the Urban Poor: Mexico City in the Late Colonial Period" (Ph.D. diss., University of Florida, 1977), x; Donald B. Cooper, *Epidemic Disease in Mexico City, 1761–1813: An Administrative, Social and Medical Study* (Austin: University of Texas Press, 1965), 186; Pamela Voekel, "Peeing on the Palace: Bodily Resistance to Bourbon Reforms in Mexico City," *Journal of Historical Sociology* 5, no. 2 (June 1992): 183–208; Juan Pedro Viqueira Albán, *Relajados o reprimidos: Diversiones públicas y*

vida social en la Ciudad de México durante el siglo de las luces (Mexico City: Fondo de Cultura Económica, 1987), 261–81.

4. Joel R. Poinsett, *Notes on Mexico, Made in the Autumn of 1822* (1824; reprint ed., New York: Frederick A. Praeger, 1969), 77; Pedro Gualdi, *Views of the City of Mexico* (Mexico City: J. M. Lara, 1850); *Description of the Panorama of the Superb City of Mexico and the Surrounding Scenery, Painted on 2700 Square Feet of Canvas, by Robert Buford, Esq., from Drawings Made on the Spot, at the Request of the Mexican Government by Mr. William Bullock, Jr., Now Open for Inspection at the Rotunda, New-York* (New York: E. Conrad, 1828).

5. Mark Beaufoy, *Mexican Illustrations, Founded upon Facts* (London: Carpenter and Son, 1828), 64; Brantz Mayer, *Mexico as It Was and as It Is* (New York: J. Winchester New World Press, 1844), 55, 152.

6. Eric Van Young, "Islands in the Storm: Quiet Cities and Violent Countrysides in the Mexican Independence Era," *Past and Present* 118 (1988): 151; idem, "The Rich Get Richer and the Poor Get Skewed: Real Wages and Popular Living Standards in Late Colonial Mexico," paper presented to the All-University of California Group in Economic History, California Institute of Technology, May 1987, 15; Herbert S. Klein, "The Demographic Structure of Mexico City in 1811," *Journal of Urban History* 23, no. 1 (November 1996): 67–68, 72. See the excellent discussion of population data in Sonia Pérez Toledo, *Los hijos del trabajo: Los artesanos de la Ciudad de México, 1780–1853* (Mexico City: Universidad Autónoma Metropolitana Iztapalapa–El Colegio de México, 1996), 31–50.

7. R. Douglas Cope, *The Limits of Racial Domination: Plebeian Society in Colonial Mexico City, 1660–1720* (Madison: University of Wisconsin Press, 1994), 162; Rodney Anderson, "Race and Social Stratification: A Comparison of Working-Class Spaniards, Indians and *Castas* in Guadalajara, Mexico in 1821," *Hispanic American Historical Review* 68, no. 2 (1988): 209–43; John E. Kicza, "The Great Families of Mexico: Elite Maintenance and Business Practices in Late Colonial Mexico City," ibid., 62, no. 3 (1982): 432; idem, *Colonial Entrepreneurs: Families and Business in Bourbon Mexico City* (Albuquerque: University of New Mexico Press, 1983), 14–17; idem, "Life Patterns and Social Differentiation among Common People in Late Colonial Mexico City," *Estudios de Historia Novohispana* 11 (1991): 184; Vagrancy Cases, 1797–1798, and 1812, Archivo General de la Nación, Mexico City, Criminal, leg. 556, exp. 1–13; leg. 609, exp. 7–9, 12–18; leg. 675, exp. 8, leg. 462, exp. 6 (hereafter cited as AGN); Electoral Reports, AGN, Historia, vol. 447 (1), 23, 27, 41, 49, 61–64.

8. Pérez Toledo, *Los hijos del trabajo*, 51–103; Ciro F. S. Cardoso, *La industria en México antes del Porfiriato* (Mexico City: Dirección de Investigaciones Históricas, Instituto Nacional de Antropología e Historia, 1978), 21–27; Jorge González Angulo Aguirre, *Artesanado y Ciudad a finales del siglo xviii* (Mexico City: Fondo de Cultura Económica, 1983), 14–15.

9. Richard J. Salvucci, *Textiles and Capitalism in Mexico City: An Economic History of the Obrajes, 1539–1840* (Princeton, N.J.: Princeton University Press, 1987), 138; Susan Deans-Smith, *Bureaucrats, Planters, and Workers: The Making of the Tobacco Monopoly in Bourbon Mexico* (Austin: University of Texas Press, 1992), 176, 197–98; Scardaville, "Crime and the Urban Poor," 66; Van Young, "The Rich," 35–36.

10. Margaret Chowning, "The Contours of the Post-1810 Depression in Mexico: A Reappraisal from a Regional Perspective," *Latin American*

Research Review 27, no. 2 (1992): 119–50; John H. Coatsworth, "Obstacles to Economic Growth in Nineteenth-Century Mexico," *American Historical Review* 83, no. 1 (1978): 83.

11. Pérez Toledo, *Los hijos del trabajo*, 21–22, 45–46, 133–37; Adriana López Monjardín, "El artesano urbano a mediadios del siglo xix," in *Organización de producción y relaciones de trabajo en el siglo xix en México*, ed. Sonia Lombardo (Mexico City: Dirección de Investigaciones Históricas, Instituto Nacional de Antropología e Historia, Cuaderno de Trabajo, 1979), 4.

12. Alejandra Moreno Toscano, "Los trabajadores y el proyecto de industrialización, 1810–1867," in *La clase obrera en la historia de México*, vol. 1, *De la colonia al imperio*, ed. Enrique Florescano (Mexico City: Siglo XXI, 1980), 305, 312.

13. Guillermo Prieto, *Memorias de mis tiempos* (1906; reprint ed., Mexico City: Editorial Porrúa, 1985), 128; Carl Christian Sartorius, *México hacia 1850*, ed., trans., and introduced by Brígida von Mentz (1858; reprint ed., Mexico: Consejo Nacional para la Cultura y las Artes, 1990), 245; N. Ray Gilmore, "The Condition of the Poor in Mexico, 1834," *Hispanic American Historical Review* 32, no. 2 (1957): 213–26; Pérez Toledo, *Los hijos del trabajo*, 251–57; Richard Warren, "Entre la participación política y el control social: La vagancia, las clases pobres de la Ciudad de México y la transición desde la colonia hacia el estado nacional," *Historia y Grafía* 6 (1996): 37–54.

14. Ariel Rodríguez Kuri, "Política e institucionalidad: El ayuntamiento de México y la evolución del conflicto jurisdiccional, 1808–1850," in *La Ciudad de México en la primera mitad del siglo xix*, ed. Regina Hernández Franyuti (Mexico City: Instituto de Investigaciones Dr. José María Luis Mora, 1994), 2:53, 90–91.

15. María Dolores Morales, "Cambios en la traza de la estructura vial de la Ciudad de México," in ibid., 1:162–65; Pérez Toledo, *Los hijos del trabajo*, 32; Voekel, "Peeing on the Palace," 183.

16. Timothy E. Anna, *The Fall of the Royal Government in Mexico City* (Lincoln: University of Nebraska Press, 1978), 26–27.

17. Ariel Rodríguez Kuri, *La experiencia olvidada: El ayuntamiento de México. Política y Gobierno, 1876–1912* (Mexico City: El Colegio de México, Centro de Estudios Históricos–Universidad Autónoma Metropolitana Azcapotzalco, 1996), 53; idem, "Política e institucionalidad," 51–94; Hira de Gortari, "Política y administración en la Ciudad de México: Relaciones entre el Ayuntamiento y el gobierno del Distrito Federal, y el Departamental: 1824–1843," in *La Ciudad de México en la primera mitad del siglo XIX*, ed. Regina Hernández Franyuti (Mexico City: Instituto de Investigaciones Dr. José María Luis Mora, 1994), 2:166–83.

18. Charles Tilly, "Conclusion: Contention and the Urban Poor in Eighteenth- and Nineteenth-Century Latin America," in *Riots in the Cities: Popular Politics and the Urban Poor in Latin America, 1765–1910*, ed. Silvia M. Arrom and Servando Ortoll (Wilmington, Del.: Scholarly Resources, 1996), 228; Silvia M. Arrom, "Introduction: Rethinking Urban Politics in Latin America before the Populist Era," in ibid., 4–8; David Waldstreicher, *In the Midst of Perpetual Fetes: The Making of American Nationalism, 1776–1820* (Chapel Hill: University of North Carolina Press, 1997), 142.

19. Antonio Annino, "El pacto y la norma: Los orígenes de la legalidad oligárquica en México," *Historias* 5 (1984): 3–31.

20. Lynn Hunt, *Politics, Culture, and Class in the French Revolution* (Berkeley: University of California Press, 1984), 24; Mona Ozouf, *Festivals and the French Revolution*, trans. Alan Sheridan (Cambridge, Mass.: Harvard University Press, 1988), 282.

21. On rural movements, see Florencia E. Mallon, *Peasant and Nation: The Making of Postcolonial Mexico and Peru* (Berkeley: University of California Press, 1995); Peter F. Guardino, *Peasants, Politics and the Formation of Mexico's National State: Guerrero 1800–1857* (Stanford, Calif.: Stanford University Press, 1996); Michael T. Ducey, "From Village Riot to Rural Rebellion: Social Protest in the Huasteca, Mexico, 1760–1870" (Ph.D. diss., University of Chicago, 1992); Friedrich Katz, ed., *Riot, Rebellion and Revolution: Rural Social Conflict in Mexico* (Princeton, N.J.: Princeton University Press, 1988). On popular leaders see Torcuato S. Di Tella, *National Popular Politics in Early Independent Mexico, 1820–1847* (Albuquerque: University of New Mexico Press, 1996), 76–87.

2

The Crisis of the
Colonial Order, 1808–1820

The Spanish Empire collapsed during the first two decades of the nineteenth century. Throughout Spanish America the Napoleonic intervention in Iberia triggered confrontation between those seeking greater autonomy from the metropolis and those attempting to preserve colonial order and privilege. Over the following years the crisis sparked theoretical discussions of political authority and practical dilemmas in decision making, as well as armed insurrection. As factions within Spain struggled first to expel the French, then to define the tenor of monarchy, large chunks of the American dominions threatened to break away.

In New Spain, Joseph Bonaparte's coronation in 1808 precipitated first a fiery debate over home rule, then a coup d'état against the viceroy who initiated the discussion. The crisis forced New Spain's rulers to confront questions of legitimacy and sovereignty in a context of increasing popular discontent with local political, economic, and social relations. The conspirators who ruled after the coup alienated Creoles seeking greater autonomy and did little to alleviate the dissatisfaction of the popular classes. Plans to strike against the regime proliferated. Finally, in September 1810, a massive revolt emerged from the agricultural and mining zones of the viceroyalty's heartland. The rebels' ethnic and class composition, amorphous demands, and destructive path added new calculations to the decision-making processes of all elite groups in the years following.

The implementation of a new constitution for the empire in 1812 produced another wrinkle in the conduct of politics amid the armed struggle. The constitution stipulated a dramatic increase in the number of elected offices at the local and imperial levels and also contained a broad definition of citizenship that set the parameters of mass political participation for decades to come. Many loyalists believed that the constitution contained the seeds of destruction. For them the path from abdication to constitution introduced doubts about the efficacy of Spanish rule. Others argued, at least publicly, that the constitution negated many of the current complaints about Spanish rule and could therefore short-circuit the imperial system's opponents. In late 1812 and early 1813 a series of raucous electoral contests, dominated by autonomists and insurgent sympathizers, heartily endorsed by the city's masses and conducted amid an anti-Peninsular media assault protected under the constitution's free press stipulations, seemed to validate the doomsday scenarists. In Mexico City, the center of imperial authority, elections rather than armed insurrection caused the greatest threat to order during the first phase of the Independence War.

Relieved loyalists therefore applauded the return of Ferdinand VII to the throne in 1814 and his suspension of the constitution shortly thereafter. Over the next year, Viceroy Félix María Calleja returned all offices to those who had held them prior to the 1812 elections, while his military officers reduced the insurgency to recalcitrant regional guerrillas. In the capital, disease, economic hardship, and the use of force subverted the political effervescence of 1812. By 1815, with the arrest and execution of rebel leader José María Morelos, much of the viceroyalty seemed subdued, if not completely at peace. Mass politics in Mexico City retreated from the stage for several years, although subsequent events demonstrated the fragility of the apparent rapprochement between the king's representatives and his subjects in the Spanish dominions.

All Change Is Dangerous, 1808–1810

The *Gazeta de México* carried stunning news during the summer of 1808: King Charles abdicates! Ferdinand VII returns the crown to his father! Joseph Bonaparte accepts the mantle of Spanish authority! The Spanish people demand Ferdinand's return! Events on the Iberian peninsula ignited contentious debates about the nature of legitimacy and decision-making authority. For New Spain's elites the asynchronous nature of communications compounded their confusion over how to respond to such rapidly changing circumstances. Readers were acutely aware that the *Gazeta*'s news arrived two months after the events occurred on the continent. As they drafted proposals and adopted strategies, Mexico City's municipal

council, the viceroy, and the audiencia had to anticipate a future
that had already occurred across the Atlantic Ocean.[1]

All the protagonists in this drama attempted to meld Spanish
political traditions and their understanding of contemporary events
throughout the Spanish Empire, in France, the United States, and
Haiti, into effective plans of action.[2] The historical relationship
between Spain and its colonies and the class and ethnic tensions
within the colonies themselves yielded complex alliances as royal
authority disappeared. Two distinct factions emerged in Mexico
City during the summer of 1808. Led by creole members of the
municipal council, one group held that in the king's absence the
municipal councils themselves should become the locus of authority because they alone truly represented the nation. This position
implied dramatically increased autonomy for local decision mak-
ers. On July 19, 1808, the municipal council formally objected to
Joseph Bonaparte's coronation, because only the "universal consent of its peoples" could authorize any nation's ruler. The municipal council's assertion of a nation's right to choose its own ruler
was tempered by the qualification that it could only do so in the
unique case in which the king leaves no legitimate successor to the
crown. This document was not a completely radical claim of popular sovereignty but rather an attempt to assume a practical middle
ground between divine right theory and popular sovereignty. The
autonomist faction argued that the viceroy should convene a governing junta in Mexico similar to those forming throughout Spain.[3]

The other principal faction, represented by members of the
audiencia and leaders of the merchant guild, denounced the statements of the municipal council. In an attempt to defuse the municipal council's initiative, the audiencia asserted that "in the
present circumstances nothing is altered in the legitimately established powers and all should continue" as before.[4] Some proposed
that the viceregal government wait for more definitive news from
Spain before discussing any alteration of government operations.
Others rejected any suggestion of change in the colonial political
order. This intransigence stemmed from the fact that upper-level
bureaucrats and overseas traders were directly dependent on the
favor of the Spanish royal court for the colonial system's greatest
privileges. They understood that a debate over the relationship
between Mexico and Spain could trigger a renegotiation of their
own political and economic advantages.[5]

Viceroy José de Iturrigaray did not enjoy the firm support of
any faction. He began his tour of duty in 1803 and quickly became

a lightning rod for ill will, especially after the implementation of the 1804 Consolidación de Vales Reales. With its coffers depleted and desperate to raise funds, the Spanish crown used this law to transfer major assets from the Catholic Church to the monarchy, which in theory would repay with interest the value of all that it had confiscated. Since most of the capital demanded by the Crown was tied up as church loans on agricultural land and other real estate, the law threatened to bankrupt many and drain vast amounts of capital from the colony at a time of economic slowdown. Initial protests and maneuvering by powerful actors in the colony did not prevent the law's implementation. Some estimate that over 10 million pesos were drained out of New Spain, while at least 2.5 million pesos were collected from the Archbishopric of Mexico alone. Important members of New Spain's merchant guild, like Gabriel de Yermo, claimed to have lost vast fortunes, and blamed Iturrigaray for enforcing the law. Rumors of the viceroy's avarice and corruption compounded their ire.[6]

Unsure of how to proceed amid mutual suspicions and recriminations, in August 1808, Iturrigaray opted to convene several meetings of Mexico City's secular and ecclesiastical corporations, the nobility, and the leaders of the city's indigenous communities. The viceroy asserted that the consent "of the most practical and respectable authorities and persons of all classes of the capital" was the only way for him to remain in control of such a fluid situation. Audiencia officials agreed to attend on the condition that the discussion would not focus on questions of sovereignty or royal authority. Despite the audiencia's conditions, autonomists raised the sovereignty issue in the very first meeting. City Councilor Francisco Primo de Verdad argued that sovereign political authority ultimately resided with "the people." Several members of the audiencia and the chief Inquisitor immediately declared the idea "seditious and subversive." The audiencia judge Guillermo de Aguirre asked exactly who or what constituted "the people." He deemed unacceptable Primo de Verdad's response that the "constituted authorities" of the realm (the municipal councils) embodied the people's sovereignty. Aguirre reported that the autonomists' logic would in fact return control of Mexico to the "*pueblo originario.*" Although Aguirre did not specify his definition of the "original people," the minutes of the meeting noted that debate stopped at this point because leaders of the capital's indigenous communities were in attendance, including a descendant of Moctezuma. By pointing to the obvious dilemma of ruling a colony by popular consensus, the judge attempted to raise fears of the indigenous masses as a means of preempting autonomist machinations. News of this discussion spread through the city and caused an "extraordinary sensation."[7]

The abdication crisis brought dread of an uprising to the surface by reminding the Spanish elite of its tenuous hold on New Spain in legal, military, and demographic terms. It is striking that the above exchange took place two years before the outbreak of armed conflict in Mexico. No part of New Spain had witnessed massive popular mobilization or violence yet, although there had been increasing unrest during the eighteenth century in the form of local revolts, legal disputes, and banditry.[8] Mexico City itself had had a remarkably tranquil colonial history. Riots had broken out in the city periodically, but the last major tumult had occurred more than a century before Ferdinand's abdication. In many ways the city was the most secure place in the colony for loyalists and would remain so during the Independence War.[9] Still, paranoia hung in the air in 1808, a nagging sense that the rousing words of some demagogues or a small gesture of capitulation by the viceroy might symbolize that the staff of power was being wielded less effectively, and anarchy might ensue. Rumors fed the paranoia that summer. Broadsides with anti-European slogans appeared throughout the city shortly after news of the king's abdication circulated in July. Later in the summer, word spread that a descendant of Moctezuma had presented himself to the viceroy demanding his birthright, the throne of Mexico. Another observer reported that European residents had begun to stockpile arms and ammunition in anticipation of ethnic and class warfare.[10]

The viceroy's opponents portrayed him as a major instigator of unrest for his own insidious purposes, which included aspirations to rule Mexico himself. He and his wife were said to court the favor of the plebs by tossing coins to them. Much worse, Iturrigaray apparently combined poor judgment and a leveling impulse when he allowed an "ordinary man" to approach the viceregal coach and speak to him without demanding that the man remove his hat. Later that day, stone-throwing poor folk, emboldened by the viceroy's permissiveness, attacked the coaches of some of the city's principal residents. The connection between Iturrigaray's cavalier attitude toward the social rules of engagement between elites and masses and these subsequent attacks was clear to the audiencia. Its members listed these incidents among the justifications for the coup against Iturrigaray later that year.[11]

Between the first and second meetings organized by the viceroy that summer, a third alternative between autonomy and inaction emerged, as representatives from the Seville resistance arrived to request support. A coalition of Creoles and Peninsulares, who saw that some action had to be taken but were unwilling to join the autonomists, presented a motion at the next meeting to recognize the Seville junta as the legitimate authority in Spain. That very day representatives from another regional junta in Oviedo arrived to solicit support in New Spain as well. The appearance of anarchy on the peninsula destroyed the chances of prompt recognition of any junta as the legitimate authority in Spain, at least until news reached Mexico City of the organization of a central Supreme Governing Junta later that year. On September 1 a majority voted to recognize none of the Spanish juntas, and it appeared that the polar positions of inaction versus autonomy had again solidified.[12]

After this meeting, the head of the Inquisition, Bernardo del Prado y Obejero, warned Viceroy Iturrigaray of the dangers facing the colony. Prado advocated militant inaction, at least until a regency was formed in Spain. For him, the autonomy argument was unacceptable, even immoral. He also argued that quick recognition of a Spanish junta could precipitate a ferment that would play into the hands of seditious elements. Prado conjured a barrage of clumsy images to elaborate his theory of social upheaval and enumerated critical factors that increased the potential for disaster in New Spain: "All peoples are like docile lakes of water [ready] to be shaken if there is a strong wind that blows them. . . . How much more so in New Spain, which can be compared to a body full of many diverse humors that cannot be touched without risk of fatal resistance from the multitude of *castas* and reciprocal rivalry from which even the Spaniards suffer. All change is dangerous."[13]

Shortly after Prado sent his letter, plotters removed the viceroy in a coup d'état. On the night of September 16, 1808, approximately three hundred men, mostly employees of powerful merchants, attacked the viceroy's palace and forced Iturrigaray to resign and replaced him with the octogenarian Peninsular military officer Pedro de Garibay. Gabriel de Yermo and other wealthy merchants were behind the coup, but the action had the support of the audiencia, the archbishop, and other prominent members of the Peninsular elite. In a curious twist, the plotters justified their actions as a response to popular demand.[14] The conspirators' announcement of Iturrigaray's overthrow noted that the coup was carried out for reasons of "utility and general convenience," and the new viceroy wrote that a "popular movement" brought him into office. The audiencia emphasized that the "multitude" enthusiastically affirmed Garibay's appointment and asserted that: "only one reflection would be sufficient to justify [the coup]: the comparison of the situation in the viceroyalty before the viceroy's separation [from power], the fears of the cities and towns in that time, and their later and present satisfaction."[15] This rhetoric of contract and utility underscores the profound crisis of the day, as the self-proclaimed guardians of royal sovereignty in the weeks before the coup had supported extralegal and ostensibly popular action to correct the perceived excesses of the king's duly appointed representative in the colony.

The coup was a blow to the municipal council as well as to Iturrigaray. Numerous people were arrested in the coup's wake, including the municipal councilors Azcárate and Primo de Verdad and the autonomist ideologue Friar Melchor de Talamantes. Fear of a popular backlash led the coup's organizers to close down the city's cafés and to police other potential gathering places carefully. The plotters' program then extended beyond the neutralization of autonomist agitators to encompass a series of fiscal reforms, including suspension of the 1804 Consolidación de Vales Reales and reduction of taxes unpopular with the merchant conspirators.[16]

Apologists for the conspirators denied any connection between the coup and later rebellion. Gabriel de Yermo's allies defended his actions through the next decade.[17] Yet, many others considered Iturrigaray's imprisonment a primary accelerant of upheaval. Far from solidifying the loyalist elite's control of Mexico, the coup became a key element of the autonomists' rallying cry. Mexico City's municipal council denounced the event as an "abominable example" of the overthrow of legitimate authority from within by dissident factions. The council presciently feared repetition in the future.[18]

Between 1808 and 1810, government on both sides of the Atlantic remained in flux. While the masters of New Spain's destiny ultimately recognized the Spanish Central Junta and then the regency when each was formed in turn, the audiencia judges and merchants who had orchestrated Iturrigaray's downfall maintained firm control of the colony's political and economic affairs. They appointed and removed two viceroys within two years, General Garibay and his successor, Archbishop Francisco Javier Lizana y Beaumont, while doing little to address the growing discontent of the creole elite and the poor. Finally, late in the summer of 1810, the regency's viceregal appointment, Francisco Javier Venegas, an experienced army officer and former governor of Cádiz, arrived in New Spain, promising a return to stability. Venegas was feted for several days upon entering Mexico City in mid-September. Optimism trumped fiscal restraint at this moment, as an exuberant welcoming committee overspent its budget by a factor of three. Hopes for the future were dashed quickly. The arrival of Venegas in Mexico City coincided almost exactly with Father Miguel Hidalgo y Costilla's call for the viceregal government's overthrow.[19]

Pretensions of Equality, 1810–1812

Between 1808 and 1810 numerous conspiracies hatched in New Spain, principally the work of creole priests, lower-level bureaucrats, militia officers, and others adversely affected by the Bourbon reforms. They were further stimulated by the opportunity of the imperial crisis and disaffection with the viceregal government. The key conspiracy, which would spark the Independence War, developed in the Bajío, a crucial agricultural and mining region north of the capital. The plot did not develop as planned, since a loyal subject betrayed the conspirators. Warned of the arrest of one of his coconspirators, Father Miguel Hidalgo accelerated the call to rebellion. On September 16, 1810, Hidalgo urged the crowds attending the Sunday market in his hometown to rise up in defense of religion and Ferdinand VII, against the forces of oppression, which included those who overthrew Iturrigaray and those who enforced tribute payments. Hidalgo's followers, primarily indigenous and mestizo peasants, mine workers, and day laborers, responded in huge numbers, quickly outgrowing Hidalgo's ability to lead or form a coherent set of political goals and military strategies. The rebels grew to as many as sixty thousand troops and within six weeks had overrun some of the principal towns of the Bajío and threatened the capital. Shocked at first by the number and passion of the rebels, royalist troops soon regrouped to delay the rebels' advance on Mexico City and then inflicted the first real setback to the rebels in the Battle of Monte de las Cruces. Reinforcements advancing from Querétaro and internal dissension within the rebel camp soon persuaded Hidalgo to withdraw his army from the capital's periphery so that he could rethink his program.[20]

Except for this brief threat to Mexico City in late October 1810 and again for a short time in 1812–13, insurgent armies never posed a serious military threat to the capital, nor did sustained armed conflict erupt inside the city during the war. Rebel machinations were thwarted several times by the apparatus of repression and social control concentrated in the capital, while rudimentary levels of social and economic services in the city continued even at the height of armed conflict, muting some of the rebels' appeal. An effective propaganda campaign turned many of the city's residents against the rebels of 1810–11.

The capital seemed far from a safe place to the loyalists. Serious plots to overthrow the viceregal government were uncovered in April and August 1811. In the wake of these conspiracies, Viceroy Venegas established the Junta of Police and Public Security, which tightly controlled movement in and out of the city and enforced a form of martial law. This combination of factors squelched rebel plans to take the capital through force or intrigue during 1810 and 1811. The greatest threat inside Mexico City came not from armed rebels, but from the Spanish Constitution, which soon opened unprecedented channels for the expression of discontent.[21]

The 1812 Constitution

In its struggle to see Spain survive, the regency revived the institution of the Cortes. When the new Cortes opened in September 1810, it was a far cry from the eleventh-century bodies that had been used by Iberian kings to divide and conquer regional elites. Although the Cortes still consisted of representatives of every province, selected by each provincial capital's municipal council, the kingdom now included vast overseas dominions, each of which would also be represented. Creole representation was guaranteed by the stipulation that delegates had to be natives of the province from which they were selected. Voices from the Americas were heard from the very first sessions, since substitute delegates resident on the peninsula served in the place of elected representatives delayed by the arduous voyage to Cádiz.[22]

The Cortes was charged with simultaneously restructuring the government and prosecuting the war. Representatives converged on Cádiz to deliberate over the very essence of political authority and ultimately to promulgate a new constitution for the empire. The document changed the relationship between residents and state authority, altered the balance of internal power relations in each of the Spanish dominions, and also called into question the relationship between Spain and the Americas. Local, regional, and imperial government structures changed, and elections were called to fill many offices, including those of municipal councils and the Cortes.

The debate on elections and the suffrage was especially contentious, as delegates argued over the definition of citizenship, which would determine three things: the population base for distributing representative offices and structures; the composition of the electorate; and eligibility for employment in the government bureaucracy. Most Peninsular representatives, eager to maintain numerical dominance in the Cortes, argued for a highly restrictive definition of citizenship. Some overseas representatives, hoping to gain more seats in the Cortes, argued for a broad definition of citizenship that included those of all races. Considerations of the racial and ethnic balance of power and access to state employment split the American contingent into opposing camps. One favored broad incorporation while the other backed the narrower definitions supported by the Peninsulares.[23]

The most influential representatives from New Spain argued for a broad definition of citizenship. Miguel Ramos Arizpe, the delegate from Coahuila, asserted that the goal of the constitution "consists in merging all . . . castes, in making one nation, one people, one family." The representatives of other powerful social, regional, and economic interests countered with suggestions for various restrictions on the franchise and a corporatist concept of representation. New Spain's merchant guilds proposed that the Veracruz, Mexico City, and Guadalajara guilds be allocated six Cortes seats for their representatives. They also argued that the suffrage should be severely restricted, because New Spain's population consisted of "five million automatons, one million disloyal subjects, and one hundred thousand citizens addicted to order." The representatives of colonies with large populations of African descent and Andean representatives who carried fresh memories of mass indigenous revolts feared the "pretensions of equality" of blacks and the indigenous population. Many of them joined the movement to restrict the franchise severely. José Miguel Gordoa y Barrios, the delegate from Zacatecas, responded that war was already at hand in the colonies and exclusion of non-Europeans would only exacerbate matters because these groups "would not accept anything less than equality."[24]

After long and rancorous debate, compromise and ambiguity characterized the constitution's definition of citizenship. Peninsular delegates joined in promoting the exclusion of those with African roots, because the Spanish were eager to limit the population base by which the American Cortes seats would be allocated, but ultimately they were unable to exclude the indigenous population from the suffrage. The constitution defined citizens as those who "have their origin in the Spanish dominions of both hemispheres and are settled in any village of the same dominions." The Spanish word *avecinado*, translated as "settled" here, carried important but ambiguous meaning, since it had been equated traditionally with household heads and white Europeans alone, although this was by no means a legally binding definition. Foreigners could be granted certificates of citizenship under certain conditions, including meritorious service to the Spanish crown. Additional caveats muddled the definition of citizenship further. Persons with African blood could obtain citizenship only under certain conditions. Citizenship was suspended for those who were morally or physically impaired, including debtors, the unemployed, and convicts. Domestic servants were considered incapable of forming independent opinions, and their rights were suspended as well. Women were not mentioned; their exclusion from the political process was simply assumed. Finally, no minimum income or age qualifications were specified.[25]

The new constitution was introduced in Mexico City with a series of celebrations in the fall of 1812. As preparations began, the municipal council suggested that the celebration should resemble closely those rituals that marked the succession of a new king, incorporating a number of "differences that the distinct nature of this act demands." The council estimated that it would need nine to ten thousand pesos for the ceremonies and asserted that during more prosperous years they had spent two or three times that on similar celebrations. Funds were approved, and the council and viceroy set about their work, organizing an elaborate procession through the city and demanding that residents decorate the façades of their homes.[26]

According to the *Gaceta de México*, the capital's population received the constitution with "the most energetic enthusiasm" on September 30, 1812. After royal officials swore their allegiance, cannon blasts resounded in the main plaza and all the city's church bells pealed in unison. Military bands played, troops marched, and orators praised "this glorious day that has signaled the epoch of our desired liberty." The viceroy and the municipal councilors enjoyed seats of honor with members of the ecclesiastical hierarchy, the nobility, and the governors of indigenous neighborhoods. The ceremonies included a Mass of Thanksgiving and Te Deum in the

Metropolitan Cathedral. Musical and theatrical performances took place around the city that evening.[27]

The way in which the public itself joined this spectacle provides numerous clues to the tensions present in this moment suspended between tradition and innovation. In keeping with colonial demonstrations of state beneficence, royal officials tossed coins to the crowd several times during the celebration, but the way in which this gesture was executed in 1812 suggested a potential new role for the masses in Mexican political life. For the ceremonies on September 30, three stages were constructed. As the procession passed to each stage, the entire constitution was read, and only then were the coins tossed to the crowd. One thousand pesos rained down on the crowd from the main stage in front of the viceregal palace. Five hundred pesos were showered on the crowds gathered in front of the archbishop's palace and the municipal council building. Prior to the festivities, municipal council members expressed concern about the length of the day's festivities if the constitution were read three times in its entirety, but in the end the organizing committee decided that it was a necessary part of the proceedings. The viceroy did request that the document be read quickly to speed things up a bit.[28]

This pattern of joining the traditional and the new also can be seen in the linkage made among the Church, the new constitutional order, and the place of the public in politics. On October 4 each of the city's parishes celebrated a Mass of Thanksgiving for the new constitution. Prior to the offertory, the congregation listened to the entire constitution yet again, after which a priest offered a brief exhortation to the faithful, and then everyone in the church joined in an oath of allegiance. Other Church institutions repeated this model. On October 6, for example, the students and faculty of the Colegio de San Gregorio took their oath and listened to a royal official inform the audience that they were now Spanish citizens, with all the rights and opportunities afforded to citizens, and that "no one is more than you are, and whoever is equal to you has arrived at the highest [state]."[29]

The first municipal elections under the new constitution occurred on November 29, 1812. For the first time in its history, Mexico City would have popular elections to select representatives to citywide governing bodies. Creole families had purchased most of the council positions long ago, except for the new positions set aside for Peninsulares by the Bourbon reforms. The elections therefore presented a special challenge to Mexico City's loyalists. On the one hand, the elections were sure to became a plebiscite on colonial rule, given the pressing military and ideological conflicts. The circulation of inflammatory materials had escalated under the constitution's freedom of the press statute. On the battlefield, José María Morelos assumed the mantle of armed rebellion in 1811 after Hidalgo's capture and execution. Under his leadership rebel troops had grown more disciplined, and alliances with creole elite factions in the capital appeared stronger than during the Hidalgo phase. On the other hand, the Peninsular strongholds of the viceroy's office and the audiencia remained appointive and not elective posts. Autonomist Creoles already dominated the municipal council, so elections simultaneously presented a threat and an opportunity for the Peninsular-loyalist faction. The electoral process mandated by the constitution could have strengthened the loyalists' position under the proper circumstances. The viceroy and the audiencia worked to create those circumstances.[30]

The Cortes stipulated that a commission of prominent ecclesiastic, audiencia, and municipal officials would draw up more specific rules for the elections, because the constitution contained only vague procedures for their conduct. The commission soon clarified electoral procedures for the capital. Sagrario parish, the largest in the city, was divided into four separate electoral districts, although its residents could vote at any one of the four polls. Each of the thirteen other parishes in the city had one polling place. As the electoral commission deliberated, the audiencia judges issued advisory opinions. Determined to win this electoral battle, they expected that limited voter turnout would be to their advantage and therefore argued that only white male household heads should be able to vote and that the minimum voting age should be at least twenty-one.[31]

The electoral commission rejected the audiencia's opinions. They sent instructions to the city's Intendant Ramón Gutiérrez del Mazo that they understood the concept of citizens to include all Spaniards, "pure Indians and those mixed with the Spanish caste, who are called mestizos and *castizos*," regardless of marital status, as long as they had a settled home and made an honest living. The commission issued no opinion on the voting age.[32] Instead, Intendant Mazo instructed parish priests to explain electoral procedures to their parishioners and help electoral officials determine voter eligibility right at the polls, based on prudent determinations of who should vote, though women and children were prohibited from even visiting the polls.[33] These vague suffrage qualifications and complex electoral rules stand in sharp contrast to the clarity of the electoral outcome. Despite the propagandistic efforts to garner support for the regime with the elaborate ceremonies welcoming the constitution, the populace responded to their first electoral opportunity by completely repudiating the loyalists.

The Entrance Is Wide and Resistance Nil, 1812–1814

The defeat was stunning. No Europeans and no American loyalists won in the primary elections. Not only were all of the victors Creoles but some were also suspected members of the Guadalupes, a clandestine pro-insurgent group operating in the capital. Similar results were reported in Puebla, Toluca, and other towns. An analysis of voting patterns reveals several keys to the process. The presence of prefabricated ballots bearing the names of either pro-insurgent or loyalist candidates and clear factional patterns in the distribution of votes at the parochial level demonstrates that these elections were hotly contested, even though electoral behavior varied widely in different neighborhoods. In the city's primarily indigenous neighborhoods, elections were carried out in much the same way they always had been to select neighborhood leaders. Almost no prefabricated ballots were used, and the election's winners generally were priests or traditional indigenous leaders. In contrast, the poor neighborhoods that were the most diverse ethnically and socially were the places where the most prefabricated ballots were used.[34]

Each side offered its analysis of the results. In a letter to rebel leader José María Morelos, the Guadalupes gloated that their side received twenty-eight to thirty thousand votes, a clear indication of the sentiments of the vast majority of the population. Such a figure is impossible to confirm, but it is difficult to believe, based on available evidence. Because of the way elections were conducted and the results reported, accurate voter turnout is impossible to determine for any election prior to 1830. Each citizen cast votes for the number of delegates granted to each parish, which might be only one delegate for a small parish in a municipal election or more than two dozen for a larger parish in a Cortes or congressional election. From the extant reports of electoral officials, we know the number of votes received by the winner in five of fourteen parishes, though not the number of voters who submitted ballots. This figure totals almost eight thousand and includes the largest parish in the city, Sagrario, where many voters used prefabricated ballots.

Even with such incomplete data, it would be difficult to imagine where tens of thousands of additional votes could come from. While the Guadalupes may have inflated voter turnout in their report, the extant voter returns confirm the great magnitude of victory. In Sagrario parish, cleric José María Alcalá, a Guadalupe and a key figure in organizing the autonomist electoral juggernaut, received 5,392 votes, the highest number of votes for anyone in the city. None of the winning delegates in Sagrario received fewer than five thousand votes, and all were autonomists.[35]

Loyalists scrambled to account for their defeat, since they had gamely participated in the process. As the scope of their loss quickly became clear, they denounced the elections as fraudulent. The audiencia claimed that the turnout was much too high, asserting for example that Sagrario parish did not even have five thousand eligible voters, despite the liberal suffrage granted by the constitution. The use of prefabricated ballots and the mass participation of the poor, ethnically mixed population became key points of inquiry into the legitimacy of the election in the eyes of the losers, whose distress was compounded by the public outbursts that followed the elections. A tumultuous celebration succeeded the announcement of the winners, as crowds carried the victors through the streets, shouting insurgent slogans. These outbursts unnerved the viceroy, who responded immediately by banning public gatherings. By the following night the city was quiet again.[36]

Although their course of action was unclear for the first two weeks of December, loyalist response to these events proved dramatic. The newspaper, *El Amigo de la Patria*, denounced the elections as a scandal and asserted that the large voter turnout was a farce, since "in no other part [of the world] are more residents not citizens" than in Mexico. The editors echoed the plaintive tones used by the chief Inquisitor in 1808 when they suggested that "consenting to one disorder opens the door to one hundred more." Days after the election, Intendant Mazo wrote to the viceroy to express concern about the recent excesses in light of the approaching Cortes elections. Mazo alleged numerous electoral violations, repeating rumors that many noncitizens had voted and that many people had voted more than once. He presented evidence that lists of candidates had been prepared and distributed prior to the elections and asserted that many voters presented prefabricated ballots without knowing for whom they were voting. Mazo concluded with suggested improvements for future elections, including the compilation of an accurate census, the distribution of official ballots to

eligible voters prior to the election, and the threat of severe pun-
ishments for cheaters who mock what was essentially a religious
act. The audiencia in turn decided to question electoral officials
directly. In the meantime, Viceroy Venegas would not let the electoral delegates meet to select a new municipal council.[37]

The reports from electoral officials reveal much about the electoral process as well as the agenda of the royal officials who
launched further investigation. The poll watchers' testimony was
not consistent with the dramatic conclusions drawn by the viceroy
and audiencia, albeit one must bear in mind that many of the electoral officials were autonomists who supported the election's outcome. Twelve of the seventeen officials overseeing the polls reported
absolutely no problems on election day. Manuel de Cuevas Monroy
provided a typical response to the inquiry, stating, "I noted none
of the defects you have indicated in the parish junta over which
I was chosen to preside." Alderman Agustín del Rivero unabash-
edly asserted that he had allowed "all free men settled in the
Spanish dominions" to vote, and he concluded that any attempt
to discern the ethnic backgrounds of voters would be fruitless because the city's black, indigenous, and mestizo populations were
indistinguishable.[38]

Other electoral officials agreed with Rivero's assessment. Most
could not say whether they had allowed anyone of African descent
to vote and simply assumed that some must have voted. José María
Echabe, the electoral official for Santa Veracruz parish, noted that
he could not distinguish voter eligibility by sight, although many
were of "miserable appearance." Intendant Mazo reported that he
himself had encountered a "multitude of individuals of suspicious
color and inferior appearance" at the polls. Juan Antonio Cobián, a
wealthy military officer who had donated 25,000 pesos to the defense of Spain in 1810, dissented from the majority. Charged with
oversight of the polls in poverty-stricken San Pablo parish, Cobián
was sure that the majority of those who voted in his parish should
have been ineligible for one reason or another. Nonetheless, given
the uncertainty of how to enforce the electoral laws, Cobián, like
most electoral officials, accepted every vote cast on November 29.[39]

The role of parish priests was also a source of confusion among
electoral officials and of consternation among loyalists. While a
number of poll watchers praised the priests' extensive knowledge
of their parishioners' social and ethnic origins, at least one electoral official questioned the acts of a parish priest. Alcalde José
Palacios Lanzagorta reported that the priest who served as secre-

tary of San Miguel's electoral junta recruited voters from a group of ragged-looking men, saying, "Come with me, children, I will tell you what to do."[40]

In their reports, electoral officials acknowledged the prominence of prefabricated ballots. Intendant Mazo counted almost six hundred in his own precinct. Although officials questioned the value of these ballots when cast by a largely illiterate electorate, the law stated that voters could "carry in their head or written the name of the person to whom they wanted to give their vote," so they were accepted. Fernando Fernández, one of the electoral officials for Sagrario parish, summarized the election-day problems. He noted that confusion was inevitable in the first elections, because the law left the "entrance wide and resistance nil"; that is, the rules were vague and the means to enforce them practically nonexistent. He captured the feeling of many officials when he concluded that the election process had been marred more by "doubt" than by "tumultuous disturbance or disorder" and recommended that the rules of the electoral process need only be clarified to prevent future problems.[41]

Additional testimony collected during the audiencia's inquiry focused on events after the election. Government officials' reports on postelection exuberance revealed chilling hints of the implications of popular sovereignty. One official reported that a mob of poor folk attempted to dislodge the mules from the coach of some electors so that those who brought them to power could wheel the winners through the streets. When one elector refused to participate, another rebuked him, saying "the people who were present were sovereign and could make whatever demonstration they wanted." He added that their prerogative was even more compelling in these "first moments in which they began to exercise the rights of their sovereignty." That same night, a group of forty to fifty people gathered near the Sagrario church to announce their support for America, the nation, the constitution, the electors, and the Virgin of Guadalupe. During the postelection celebrations, a priest, Juan de Irisarri, caught sight of a poor boy about ten years old playing with the chains surrounding the church's atrium. Caught up in the excitement around him, the boy shouted, "Now we rule!" Overcome with rage at this insolence, Irisarri crowned the boy with his fists, saying as he did, "Take that, swine, so that you may rule!"[42]

In response to these events, and out of fear that they would lead to greater evils, Viceroy Venegas began to censor the press. He still refused to allow the electors to meet and select the new municipal council, despite the electors' repeated petitions and the sitting municipal council's concerns that it no longer had any authority to continue in office. Resolution of these conflicts would be left to a new viceroy, General Félix María Calleja, who had extensive field experience fighting the insurgency before taking over as viceroy in March 1813. During several decades of residence in Mexico, Calleja also had built many important political and social connections. He would need all his political wiles during his first year as viceroy, described by *El Diario de México* as "the most calamitous America has seen since the Conquest." During that year, Calleja faced perhaps the strongest rebel mobilization of the entire war, municipal bankruptcy, hyperinflation, imperial uncertainty, and a deadly epidemic.[43]

To address the political stalemate within the city, Calleja first reinvigorated the constitution and claimed that any excuse to rebel disappeared before the generous stipulations contained therein. The electoral process begun in November 1812 came to a close finally in April 1813. Despite the efforts of the ecclesiastical hierarchy and the audiencia, the electors chose no loyalists to sit on the municipal council. In the aftermath of this temporary setback, Calleja launched efforts to prepare for the July 1813 Cortes elections carefully. He ordered a census to set the number of eligible voters in each parish and divided a number of parishes into smaller electoral units. In addition the elections took place over three successive days to diffuse the tensions evident with the massive turnout on a single election day. The epidemic of 1813, which had affected as many as one-half of the city's inhabitants in the summer of 1813 and had taken over twenty thousand lives, surely curtailed voter turnout as well. On July 4, 1813, Sagrario parish's primary election took place. Slightly more that fifteen hundred votes were cast for the winner, less than one-third of those cast for the winner only eight months earlier. The decline in voter turnout did not have an impact on results. All of Mexico City's primary electors were creole autonomists once again. Lucas Alamán asserted that loyalists, who foresaw the outcome, abstained from voting. He also suggested that disorder similar to that of the 1812 election occurred, although no attempt was made to suspend the electoral process in July 1813. Intendant Mazo reported on July 11 that José María Alcalá and Francisco Manuel Sánchez de Tagle, prominent Creoles, members of the municipal council, and Guadalupes, were selected as Mexico City's representatives to the regional electoral junta. One week later the

Province of Mexico chose its Cortes delegates amid "much applause from the public and admirable quiet and harmony." In contrast to this rosy report, Viceroy Calleja was furious at the outcome and viewed it as a personal affront to his efforts to undermine the insurgency through politics. Convinced that the junta had chosen revolutionaries from Mexico City as delegates, including Alcalá, Calleja ordered several men arrested and attempted to deny Alcalá's passage to Spain.[44]

An audiencia report of November 1813 makes it clear that the loyalists' strong reactions to these first elections derived from the massive voter turnout and the chaotic postelection hubbub as well as the identities of the victors. The audiencia requested permission to suspend the constitution in New Spain because subversive elements had abused the new freedoms and placed the entire colony in danger of disintegration. The report cited electoral activity as a prime example of seditious machinations. Elections, the potential safeguard of civil liberty, had been perverted by the insurgents into "assemblies of confusion and disorder" through the manipulation of the ignorant masses. The audiencia described a vast conspiracy that involved insurgent infiltration, ecclesiastical complicity, and a restless urban underclass. The report summarized the allegations about massive use of prefabricated ballots, multiple votes cast by individuals, and voting by ineligible persons. The audiencia also denounced various clerics whose conduct during the elections was akin to that of the priests leading the armed insurrection. Postelectoral events were enumerated and denounced in similar fashion, such as the dramatic repetition of the news that "even children were saying, 'Now we are in control.' " The report concluded that the elections had been conducted "against the constitution, against justice, and against good order," and the audiencia scorned the idea that the postelection upheaval was an innocent outburst of enthusiasm. After all, they noted, "Innocence disappeared from here long ago." In the context of the Independence War, even young children could be coconspirators. The report also condemned the elections of July 1813 as having the same spirit as those of November 1812, as unqualified voters selected insurgent collaborators. The audiencia ominously warned the Cortes that elections in New Spain under the present circumstances only served as a "school for disgrace," which would lead inevitably to the collapse of society.[45]

Shortly after the audiencia sent its report to Spain, both municipal and Cortes elections occurred again. By December 1813 the pestilence afflicting the city earlier in the year had slowed. Despite the audiencia's histrionic predictions, this election proceeded in "an orderly manner," attributable in part to the repeated use of many of the mechanisms introduced by Calleja in July to increase control over the electoral process. Voter turnout was again much lower than it had been in November 1812. Comparing the four parishes for which there are data from both elections (Sagrario, San José, Santa Cruz y Soledad, and Salto del Agua), votes for the most popular candidates fell from 7,718 in 1812 to 1,617 in 1813. Light turnout did not effect the outcome. Autonomists won another decisive victory. There was little chance for either side to react to the implications of the loyalists' continued electoral failures. These would be the last elections in Mexico for six years. Events across the Atlantic Ocean soon provided the impetus for another change in the rules of the political game.[46]

Loyalist Victory, 1814–1820

Napoleon's disastrous Russian campaign precipitated a dramatic reversal of fortune. Across Europe reinvigorated resistance forces punished French troops, while the emperor's domestic support fizzled out. By December 1813, peace negotiations promised to restore Ferdinand VII to the throne and remove both French and British troops from Spanish territory. In April 1814 the Captain General of Valencia, Francisco Javier Elío, handed Ferdinand VII the baton of authority that Elío himself had been given by the Cortes. As he did so, Elío kissed the monarch's hand, a symbol of the army's renewed subservience to the king. The following month the people of Valencia chose a new name for their central plaza, the third designation in less than five years. The plaza, originally named for the Virgin of the Forsaken, then dedicated to the 1812 Constitution, was rechristened the Royal Plaza of Ferdinand VII. Within weeks in Madrid a mixed crowd of soldiers and civilians gathered at the congressional palace to denounce the Cortes and praise Ferdinand, Catholicism, and the Inquisition. Ferdinand suspended the constitution soon thereafter.[47]

Across the Atlantic Ocean, Viceroy Calleja orchestrated New Spain's return to preconstitutional political and social relations, while his commanders in the field did their best to eliminate the last rebel redoubts. Those who had held office prior to the 1812 elections returned to their positions. The Inquisition opened its doors again. Prominent autonomists did their best to fade into the background, though some, including four elected city council members and three Cortes deputies, could not avoid exile or imprisonment. Rebel troops had already suffered major setbacks in late 1813 and early 1814, and the pattern continued through the following year. The army reduced the insurgency to tenacious, but increasingly isolated, armed bands. In the fall of 1814, rebels meeting in the town of Apatzingán attempted to fashion a constitution establishing an independent republic, but the document was never implemented anywhere, and the congress that formed it disbanded. In November 1815 royal troops captured José María Morelos, inheritor of Padre Hidalgo's insurrectionist mantle. He was tried and executed the next month. By the end of 1815, it appeared that "Spain won the war of Independence."[48]

Juan Ruiz de Apodaca followed Calleja into the viceregal office in 1816. Apodaca employed extensive amnesty provisions and eliminated many war taxes, as carrots to follow Calleja's stick. With each report, Apodaca assured the Crown that a slow economic and political recovery was at hand. All was not well, however. Two significant rebel leaders, Vicente Guerrero and Guadalupe Victoria, remained in the field. Guerrero's troops proved especially resilient. Although they could not win large-scale engagements, they were always able to harass the royal army and prevent it from gaining permanent control of the area southwest of the capital and stretching to the Pacific Coast.[49] Just as important, the battles between 1810 and 1814 wreaked havoc on the economy, destroyed political legitimacy, exposed deep rifts within the colonial elite, and placed military power brokers at the center of the political universe. Neither had the thorny questions about the nature of sovereignty and participation simply disappeared. Events between 1808 and 1814 had changed perceptions of the relationship between the masses and the state for elites as well as the poor. When Spain's corkscrew imperial policies twisted yet again in 1820, the discursive and practical legacy of the previous decade would hang heavily over the ensuing events in New Spain.

Notes

1. M. D. Demélas-Bohy and F.-X. Guerra, "The Hispanic Revolutions: The Adoption of Modern Forms of Representation in Spain and America, 1808–1810," in *Elections before Democracy: The History of Elections in Europe and Latin America*, ed. Eduardo Posada-Carbó (New York: St. Martin's, 1996), 34; François-Xavier Guerra, *Modernidad e independencias: Ensayos sobre las revoluciones hispánicas* (Madrid: Editorial Mapfre, 1992), 127; Anna, *The Fall*, 37.

2. See Luis Villoro, *El proceso ideológico de la revolución de Independencia*, 2d ed. (Mexico: Universidad Nacional Autónoma de México, 1967), 36–37; David A. Brading, *The First America: The Spanish Monarchy, Creole Patriots, and the Liberal State, 1492–1867* (Cambridge, England: Cambridge University Press, 1991), 541–44, 561–62; Charles A. Hale, *Mexican Liberalism in the Age of Mora, 1821–1853* (New Haven, Conn.: Yale University Press, 1968), 64–68; Jaime E. Rodríguez O., "From Royal Subject to Republican Citizen: The Role of the Autonomists in the Independence of Mexico," in *The Independence of Mexico and the Creation of the New Nation*, ed. Jaime E. Rodríguez O. (Los Angeles: UCLA Latin American Center Publications, 1989), 25–29; Brian R. Hamnett, "Mexico's Royalist Coalition: The Response to Revolution, 1808–1821," *Journal of Latin American Studies* 12 (1980): 55–63; Doris M. Ladd, *The Mexican Nobility at Independence, 1780–1826* (Austin: University of Texas Press, 1976), 108.

3. Acta de Cabildo, July 19, 1808, in *Documentos históricos mexicanos: Obra conmemorativa del primer centenario de la Independencia de México*, ed. Genaro García (1910; reprint ed., Nendeln, Leichtenstein: Kraus-Thomson Publishers, 1971), 2: doc. 3; Francisco Primo Verdad y Ramos, "Memoria Póstuma," in ibid., doc. 53; Anna, *The Fall*, 38.

4. "Real acuerdo de México, sobre la representación del Ayuntamiento de 19 de julio de 1808," in ibid., doc. 40; Villoro, *El proceso ideológico*, 33.

5. Romeo Flores Caballero, *Counterrevolution: The Role of the Spaniards in the Independence of Mexico, 1804–1838*, trans. Jaime E. Rodríguez O. (Lincoln: University of Nebraska Press, 1974), 9.

6. Ibid., 17–19, 28; Michael P. Costeloe, *Church Wealth in Mexico: A Study of the "Juzgado de Capellanías" in the Archbishopric of Mexico, 1800–1856* (Cambridge, England: Cambridge University Press, 1967), 113; Anna, *The Fall*, 36–37.

7. *Documentos históricos*, ed. García, 2: doc. 12, 15, 51; Villoro, *El proceso ideológico*, 52; Anna, *The Fall*, 46.

8. Friedrich Katz, "Introduction: Rural Revolts in Mexico," *Riot, Rebellion, and Revolution*, ed. Katz, 6–7.

9. Cope, *Limits of Racial Domination*, 125–60; Chester L. Guthrie, "Riots in Seventeenth-Century Mexico City: A Study of Social and Economic Conditions," in *Greater America: Essays in Honor of Herbert Eugene Bolton*, ed. Adele Ogden and Engel Sluiter (Berkeley: University of California Press, 1945), 243–58; Van Young, "Islands in the Storm," 130–55.

10. *Colección de documentos para la historia de la guerra de Independencia de México de 1808 a 1821*, ed. Juan E. Hernández y Dávalos (1877–1882; reprint ed., Mexico City: Instituto Nacional de Estudios Históricos de la Revolución Mexicana, 1985), 3: doc. 147; Villoro, *El proceso ideológico*, 53; Anna, *The Fall*, 47–48.

11. Municipal Council Report, November 9, 1808, in *Documentos históricos*, ed. García, 2: doc. 124; Lucas Alamán, *Historia de Méjico desde los primeros movimientos que prepararon su Independencia en el año de 1808 hasta la época presente* (Mexico City: Imp. J. M. Lara, 1849), 1:295; Anna, *The Fall*, 39.

12. *Documentos históricos*, ed. García, 2: doc. 51; Jaime E. Rodríguez O., *The Independence of Spanish America* (Cambridge, England: Cambridge University Press, 1998), 54; Anna, *The Fall*, 48.

13. Prado to Iturrigaray, September 4, 1808, in *Documentos históricos*, ed. García, 2: doc. 40.

14. Virginia Guedea, "El pueblo de México y la política capitalina, 1808–1812," *Mexican Studies/Estudios Mexicanos* 10, no. 1 (Winter 1994): 36–37.

15. Audiencia, September 16, 17, and November 9, 1808, in *Documentos históricos*, ed. García, 2: doc. 53, 60, 62, and 124.

16. Anna, *The Fall*, 58; Guerra, *Modernidad y independencies*, 95. Flores Caballero (in *Counterrevolution*, 37) notes that Viceroy Iturrigaray suspended enforcement of the Consolidación shortly before the coup.

17. See Captain of the Provincial Squadron of Mexico José Manuel de Salaverría to Viceroy Felix María Calleja, August 12, 1816, *Documentos históricos*, ed. García, 2: doc. 123.

18. Archivo Histórico del Ex-Ayuntamiento de la Ciudad de México, Mexico City, vol. 870, leg. 9 (hereafter cited as AACM). See W. Woodrow Anderson, "Reform as a Means to Quell Revolution," in *Mexico and the Spanish Cortes, 1810–1822*, ed. Nettie Lee Benson (Austin: University of Texas Press, 1966), 191; Ladd, *Mexican Nobility*, 110; Anna, *The Fall*, 58; Villoro, *El proceso ideológico*, 55–59.

19. Anna, *The Fall*, 59–63; Timothy E. Anna, "The Independence of Mexico City and Central America," in *The Cambridge History of Latin America*, ed. Leslie Bethell (Cambridge, England: Cambridge University Press, 1985), 3:60–61.

20. Hugh M. Hamill Jr., *The Hidalgo Revolt: Prelude to Mexican Independence* (Gainesville: University of Florida Press, 1966), 123–26.

21. Van Young, "Islands in the Storm"; Hugh M. Hamill Jr., "Royalist Propaganda and *la porción humilde del pueblo* during Mexican Independence," *The Americas* 36, no. 4 (1980): 423–44; Anna, *The Fall*, 78–82, 103–5; Virginia Guedea, *En busca de un gobierno alterno: Los Guadalupes de México* (Mexico City: Universidad Nacional Autónoma de México, 1992), 48–57; Hamnett, "Mexico's Royalist Coalition," 64.

22. Nettie Lee Benson, "Introduction," *Mexico and the Spanish Cortes*, ed. Benson, 4; Charles R. Berry, "The Election of the Mexican Deputies to the Spanish Cortes, 1810–1822," in ibid., 14–15.

23. James F. King, "The Colored Castes and the American Representation in the Cortes of Cádiz," *Hispanic American Historical Review* 33, no. 1 (1953): 33–64; María Teresa Berruezo León, "La presencia americana en las Cortes de Cádiz," in *Materiales para el estudio de la constitución de 1812* (Madrid: Editorial Tecnos, 1989), 53–74.

24. Berruezo León, "La presencia americana," 61–66; King, "The Colored Castes," 44, 59; Brading, *First America*, 575–76; Ladd, *Mexican Nobility*, 112; Anderson, "Reform as a Means to Quell Revolution," 192.

25. "Constitución de la monarquía español, promulagada en Cádiz el 19 de marzo de 1812," chap. 4, art. 18, in *Colección de Documentos*, ed. Hernández y Dávalos, 4:50–118; King, "The Colored Castes," 44; Berruezo León, "La presencia americana," 66; Berry, "Election of the Mexican Deputies," 18; Anna, *The Fall*, 111.

26. AACM, vol. 2253, exp. 4, September 22, 1812; Steven Flinchpaugh, "Economic Aspects of the Viceregal Entrance in Mexico City," *The Americas* 52, no. 3 (January 1996): 354; *La constitución de 1812 en la Nueva España*, ed. Rafael de Alba (Mexico City: Secretaría de Relaciones Exteriores, Imp. Guerrero Hermanos, 1912–1913), 1:16–20.

27. *Gaceta de México*, October 3, 1812; Proclamation, September 24, 1812, AACM, vol. 2253, exp. 4,; Anna, *The Fall*, 108.

28. Municipal Council Report, September 28, 1812, AACM, vol. 2253, exp. 4; *Gaceta de México* October 3, 1812; Luis González Obregón, *México viejo* (1895; reprint ed., Mexico City: Patria, 1988), 585–91.

29. Proclamation, September 26, 1812, AACM, vol. 2253, exp. 4; *Gaceta de México*, October 13, 1812.

30. Antonio Annino, "Prácticas criollas y liberalismo en la crisis del espacio urbano colonial: El 29 de noviembre de 1812 en la Ciudad de México," *Secuencia* 24 (September–December 1992): 146; Anna, *The Fall*, 27–28.

31. AGN, Historia, vol. 445, 83, May 23, 1812; Alamán, *Historia de Méjico*, 3:289–90; Anna, *The Fall*, 110.

32. AGN, Historia, vol. 445, 100.

33. Report of Intendente-Corregidor, in *La constitución de 1812*, ed. Alba, 1:227.

34. Ibid., 1:240, 2:263; Virginia Guedea, "Las primeras elecciones populares en la Ciudad de México, 1812–1813," *Mexican Studies/Estudios Mexicanos* 7, no. 1 (Winter 1991): 11–12; Alamán, *Historia de Méjico*, 3:291; Nettie Lee Benson, "The Contested Mexican Election of 1812," *Hispanic American Historical Review* 26, no. 3 (1946): 336–50; Guedea, *En busca de un gobierno alterno*, 142; Annino, "Prácticas criollas," 148–49.

35. Guadalupes to Morelos, December 7, 1812, Benson Latin American Collection, University of Texas at Austin, Genaro García Papers, doc. 348 (hereafter cited as BLAC-UTA, GG); Guedea, *En busca de un gobierno alterno*, 138–39; Wilbert Timmons, "Los Guadalupes: A Secret Society in the Mexican Revolution for Independence," *Hispanic American Historical Review* 30, no. 4 (1950): 453–99.

36. Audiencia Report, in *La constitución de 1812*, ed. Alba, 1:241.

37. *El Amigo de la Patria* 5, in ibid., 1:237, 243–44; Municipal Council Correspondence, December 6, 1808, AACM, vol. 870, exp. 4.

38. Report of Election Officials, AGN, Historia, vol. 447 (1), 23, 49.

39. Report of Election Officials, AGN, Historia, vol. 447 (1), 27, 34, 41, 61–64; Anna, *The Fall*, 152.

40. Report of Election Officials, AGN, Historia, vol. 447 (3), 14–15.

41. Report of Intendente-Corregidor, in *La constitución de 1812*, ed. Alba, 1:227; Report of Election Officials, AGN, Historia, vol. 447 (1), 21–23.

42. Report of Election Officials, AGN, Historia, vol. 447 (3), 14–15, 46–48.

43. Electors to Viceroy, December 27, 1812, and January 3, 1813, in *La constitución de 1812*, ed. Alba, 1:244–46; Ayuntamiento to Viceroy, December 29, 1812, in *Colección de documentos*, ed. Hernández y Dávalos, 4: doc. 228; *El Diario de México*, May 20, 1813; Anna, *The Fall*, 115, 162–78.

44. *Gaceta de México*, April 8, 1813; Primary Election Reports, July 2 and 5, 1813, AGN, Historia, vol. 445, 208–11; Guedea, "Las primeras elecciones," 17; Cooper, *Epidemic Disease*, 171–82; Anna, *The Fall*, 162–72; Alamán, *Historia de Méjico*, 3:421–22; Secondary Election Reports, AGN, Historia, vol. 447, exp. 10 and 12; *La constitución de 1812*, ed. Alba, 1:172–73; Berry, "The Election of the Mexican Deputies," 24; Neill Macaulay, "The Army of New Spain and the Mexican Delegation to the Spanish Cortes," in *Mexico and the Spanish Cortes*, ed. Benson, 144.

45. Carlos María de Bustamante, *Cuadro histórico de la revolución mexicana* (1844; reprint ed., Mexico City: Fondo de Cultura Económica, 1985), 4:91–97, 103–5.

46. *Diario de México*, December 23 and 28, 1813, quoted in Berry, "Election of the Mexican Deputies," 78; Election Reports, AGN, Historia, vol. 445, 211, vol. 447, exp. 4; AGN, Ayuntamientos, vol. 168, exp. 4.

47. Gabriel H. Lovett, *Napoleon and the Birth of Modern Spain* (New York: New York University Press, 1965), 2:812, 829–32; E. Christiansen, *The Origins of Military Power in Spain, 1800–54* (London: Oxford University Press, 1967), 17.

48. Jaime E. Rodríguez O., "The Transition from Colony to Nation: New Spain 1820–21," in *Mexico in the Age of Democratic Revolutions, 1750–1850*, ed. Jaime E. Rodríguez O. (Boulder, Colo.: Lynne Rienner, 1994), 100; Ladd, *Mexican Nobility*, 118–20; Anna, "The Independence," 3:76; Rodríguez O., *Independence of Mexico*, 166–67; Anna, *The Fall*, 179.

49. Guardino, *Peasants, Politics*, 71–72.

3

Three Guarantees, Two Constitutions, One Mexican Caesar, 1820–1824

Within a span of four years, political configurations in Mexico ricocheted from Spanish constitutional monarchy to creole empire to federal republic. The restoration of King Ferdinand failed to produce unity within Spain, while rebellion against the Crown in much of Spanish America continued unabated. Early military and popular enthusiasm for the return of Ferdinand VII did not last. After the king dismissed the Cortes and suspended the constitution, he devoted most of his energies to centralizing authority and purging liberals from their positions. Ongoing economic difficulties, and the Crown's seeming indifference to these, dulled popular feeling for the monarchy. Within the military junior officers from the Napoleon-era resistance bridled under stricter rules of comportment as their rise through the ranks screeched to a halt. Their frustrations resonated with growing numbers of unpaid recruits grabbed from the towns of the peninsula and destined for the ongoing conflicts in the Americas. Several abortive conspiracies against the Crown foreshadowed a major barracks revolt early in 1820, when junior officers rallied the support of the expeditionary force gathering in Cádiz before departing for South America. With Masonic lodges coordinating much of the effort, the revolt gained support around the kingdom from a heterogeneous group of military officers, antimonarchists, and former French collaborators. The rebels wrapped their movement in the respectability of the 1812 Constitution, to which Ferdinand formally subordinated himself in the spring of 1820.[1]

The constitution's restoration provoked frenetic political debate and activity in New Spain. Conservative loyalists, military officers, and liberal autonomists all bristled under rulings of the revived Cortes, which simultaneously attacked corporate privileges and asserted greater peninsular predominance in imperial relations. As a result, many loyalists lost their faith in Spanish colonialism, hard-core insurgents saw no reason to revise their proclivities toward Independence, and autonomists searched for a magical compromise between subordination and social dissolution. By late 1820, autonomists thought they might have found their answer in the disenchanted royalist Colonel Agustín de Iturbide. The ambitious Iturbide had had a checkered career fighting the insurgency and had recently been charged with the impossible task of rooting out Vicente Guerrero's guerrilla troops. Iturbide agreed to sponsor the Iguala Plan and to seek additional adherents to this proposal to end the long stalemate in New Spain. The plan, a complex bit of political legerdemain, contained "Three Guarantees" that promised to preserve privileges for the Church and military hierarchies, to secure equality for all Mexicans and to achieve Mexican autonomy under a Bourbon monarch. In other words, the plan promised every group something, and therefore provided the means for a decisive yet temporary compromise among warring factions. The constituents of this coalition bargained that their designs on power could best be achieved through a strategic alliance with the wayward royalist officer. The "Army of the Three Guarantees" overcame the last royalist military bastions in a matter of months.

On September 27, 1821, Iturbide marched triumphantly into Mexico City at the head of an army that included former royalist forces and the insurgents against whom they had been fighting for over a decade. It seemed that Iturbide had achieved an almost impossible task. He appeared a hero to some, the natural arbiter over competing ideas about what the new nation should be and where political legitimacy should reside. For others, Iturbide quickly exhausted his usefulness. In late 1821 and early 1822, few debates over the nation's future achieved resolution. The nature of the Independence coalition precluded either the unadulterated reconstitution of colonial norms or complete renovation, as those pushing for radical change faced off against those with entrenched interests who hoped to salvage the vestiges of their traditional advantages. A powerful military that had developed over the course of the war added another volatile interest group to the equation. Iturbide's own political aspirations could not rely on the legitimating logics of tradition or divine providence. He sought instead to establish a form of Mexican Caesarism with support from sectors of the Catholic Church, the military, and the masses.

Within a year of his entry into the capital, Iturbide parlayed his popularity into a putsch that proclaimed him Emperor of Mexico. Junior military officers and local priests worked the crowds in Mexico City's neighborhoods, persuading significant numbers of the city's poor to take to the streets in support of the man they called the Liberator. Predictably enough, a coronation based on such actions unleashed dissent, as insurgent caudillos, provincial politicians, and loyal Bourbonists clashed with Iturbide and among themselves. Only months after seizing power, Iturbide was in exile, his experiment in creole monarchy an utter failure. Conservatives with monarchist inclinations considered the Emperor Agustín a reprehensible parody of true royalty and a dangerous symbol of mob rule. Federalists and republicans agitated against Iturbide's claim of sovereign authority and his usurpation of regional prerogatives. Iturbide's failure to reward some officers sufficiently and his interference with the privileges of others pushed key military leaders from discontent into armed uprising. The Emperor then chose to abdicate rather than put his remaining support in the military ranks and the poor neighborhoods of Mexico City to the test.

Iturbide's abdication did not yield the political terrain to a unified republican movement. In an uneasy compromise, a constituent assembly crafted a constitution in 1824 that created a sovereignty shared between the national government and the states. State legislatures gained responsibility for selecting the president and vice president, who were to be chosen for four-year terms with no immediate possibility for reelection. The new constitution also limited to a great degree the powers of the executive branch. Still, far from acceding to an extreme devolution of power to the states, the new constitution and the first government elected under its aegis tempered the federalist impulse.[2]

This short interlude added to the contradictory legacy of law and social practice that formed the primordial soup of Mexico's first federal republic. The compromise that assured Independence settled few of the internal conflicts that had festered over the preceding generation. Iturbide's imperial alchemy created an unstable amalgam of incompatible elements. As his star rose, the franchise moved beyond the last ethnic and social strictures of the colonial era to include, in effect, all men over the age of eighteen. Sectors of urban society had manifested a powerful and deep-seated resentment of the perceived privileges of the Spanish commercial elites. During the years after Iturbide's downfall, radical federalists capitalized on the broad franchise and whipped into a frenzy the incipient popular anti-Spanish feeling that had roused the urban poor in support of the Hero of Iguala. On the other end of the political spectrum, in later years opponents of the most radical federalists rediscovered Iturbide as a friend of the Church and the military who attempted to establish a hierarchical system that preserved corporate privilege and promised unity among disparate constituencies. Subsequent generations of antagonists would try to slice Iturbide's legacy into individual components, preserving the memory of some tenets of this complex leader and discarding others as suited their needs.

The Collapse of Viceregal Government, 1820–1821

In the spring of 1820 the imperial bureaucracy in the American territories still loyal to the Spanish crown dusted off the 1812 Constitution and hoped for the best. Officials in Mexico City swore their allegiance on June 1, 1820, amid ceremonies almost identical to those conducted in 1812. The bill for the festivities reached almost 6,000 pesos.[3] The constitution's free press statutes permitted a lively debate over sovereignty and political participation to reignite. A spate of new pamphlets appeared, while others issued from 1812 to 1814 were reprinted. Some authors contended that Ferdinand VII remained a divinely chosen monarch who simply had volunteered to reinvest the constitution with legitimacy. Others emphasized that all governments were founded on a social pact that could be severed if the government failed to concern itself with the common good.[4] Some of the most interesting pamphlets focused on the lower classes, who once again would have access to politics through the polls. Short dialogues circulated, starring poor artisans who discussed the finer points of constitutional monarchy and the obligations of a responsible citizenry. A series of pamphlets featured "the Puebla weaver" and his associates, who attempted to answer such questions as why the empire needed both a king and a constitution. These pamphlets emphasized deference to the political opinions of men of respect, but they also contained a message of empowerment for the lower classes. The Puebla weaver asserted that in a constitutional system, political legitimacy originated with the "will of a poor artisan." *The Constitutional Indian* suggested that the "sacred code" of 1812, once again in force, held the key to the peaceful liberation of New Spain's indigenous population.[5]

As in 1812, the constitution itself was printed, circulated, and read aloud. Viceroy Apodaca distributed one thousand copies to the cities and towns of New Spain. The *Gazeta del Gobierno* published an order that even schoolchildren should have the constitution explained to them and that the document should be used as a reading primer. Devices to aid in this political pedagogy proliferated. One political catechism, published for the "instruction of youth and use in schools," had the same question-and-answer structure as the catechisms young Catholics used to memorize the tenets of their faith. It began with basic definitions of terms such as "citizen" and "nation" quoted directly from the constitution but went on to address even the most difficult conundrums of Spanish rule. The document emphasized that sovereignty rested with the nation and not the king, who was a respected chief executive, but ultimately just another citizen. The law, therefore, which used to be what the king wanted, now would reflect the general will of the citizens.[6]

Elections measured the temperature of the body politic once again. An electoral council formed and immediately began to mark up a copy of the poster that had announced the 1812 elections, changing only the smallest details, such as the dates on which the elections would occur. For the capital, the documentary sources on results proved more elusive for 1820 and 1821 than for prior elections, but both the qualitative and quantitative evidence suggest that organizational efforts and popular enthusiasm for elections had diminished. Turnout decreased from earlier years, and votes were distributed among large numbers of individuals, which suggests the absence of the large-scale preelectoral organizing practiced in 1812 and 1813. Critics denounced technical infractions of the municipal council elections held on June 19, but Viceroy Apodaca reported that the procedure occurred in an orderly fashion, with no serious complaints over process or outcome.[7] The Cortes elections in August generated little excitement. The largest number of votes received by any individual in Sagrario parish was 822, almost 200 votes less than the winner of the elections conducted during the epidemic of July 1813. At least 119 different men received votes in this election, a far cry from the results produced by the disciplined factional machines that had operated in 1812. Lucas Alamán asserted that these elections triggered urban unrest, though he provided no examples, and later scholars have not been able to document any major incidents. Due to the peculiar timing of the constitution's reimplementation, another round of Cortes elections had to be carried out in December 1820. At this time, the electoral official for San Pablo parish reported that the highest number of votes received by any individual in his district was 38, compared to over 100 votes cast for the winner in the December 1813 election, itself a quiet affair compared to November 1812. Low turnout did not prevent creole autonomists from dominating in all of these elections.[8]

Contemporaries accounted for this lukewarm reception in a number of ways. In one investigation of New Spain's response to the constitution, Francisco Manuel Sánchez de Tagle, long-time autonomist and municipal council member, blamed the increasing disaffection on sermonizing priests. His research revealed that, with each passing day, the constitution lost support among the "feminine sex and the low and middle class in general." He accused the clergy of spreading the false idea that the constitutional system was impious and heretical. One of the city attorneys agreed with Sánchez de Tagle that the common people originally received the constitution with "joy and satisfaction," but that the clergy's activity, based on their fear of continued Cortes attacks on ecclesiastical privilege, had dissuaded the populace. These supporters of constitutionalism agreed that it was "absolutely essential to cut off such an evil with clear, energetic and discreet measures so that we do not see ourselves enveloped in evils of great transcendence." Others attributed popular disaffection to the bitter experiences of 1812 and 1813, when the hopes of many were dashed by the royalist backlash. In one fictionalized account, a barber argued with one of his customers that apathy among the lower classes stemmed from the fact that the constitution had never improved their condition. His customer, obviously a supporter of the constitution, urged the barber—and all citizens—to be patient and to vote for good men when they had the chance.[9]

The constitution reopened avenues for political action in the countryside as well, though here, too, results were mixed. Within months of the constitution's return, cities and towns throughout Mexico swore their allegiance and conducted new elections. In the region that is now the State of Guerrero, between July 1820 and January 1821 over seventy new municipalities formed and elected city councils under the terms of the constitution. In general, however, ambivalence rather than enthusiasm became the primary response to the return of constitutional government and elections. The revived Cortes in Spain undermined the privileges of the

Church and the military, but it took no action on the key issues of autonomy, trade, and expanded citizenship. As a result, clergy preached against the constitution, royalist military leaders on both sides of the Atlantic grew restive with shortages of human and capital resources, and the insurgency continued to advocate a clear break with Spain. Although some argued—and perhaps sincerely believed—that the return of the constitution obviated the need for further agitation, most of the protagonists, whether urban or rural, monarchist or republican, recognized the untenable nature of the compromise of 1820. In the meantime, all jockeyed to make the most of circumstances.[10]

Amid these unsettling conditions, civic, clerical, military, and commercial leaders sought a compromise that might provide a transition to stable home rule without protracted violence. The ambitious creole military officer Agustín de Iturbide emerged as a key figure in these machinations. Iturbide spent the early years of the Independence War fighting against the insurgency in the Bajío, but lost his commission in 1816 in the shadow of a corruption scandal. In a fortuitous twist of fate, he regained a military command in 1820, charged with subduing the south, Vicente Guerrero's home territory. Unable to achieve a quick or convincing victory, Iturbide joined a movement first proposed by members of an elite social group in Mexico City. Their plan sought to preserve monarchy as a legitimizing force in politics and the privileged place of Catholicism as the basis of social cohesion, while also granting greater autonomy to New Spain in recognition of the fact that Spanish politics had again become a destabilizing force in the Americas.[11]

Iturbide attempted to bring the most important of the insurgent military leaders into the fold, but Guerrero rebuked the offer at first. In a letter to Iturbide, written in January 1821, Guerrero explained that the events of the previous decade had convinced the insurgents that no compromise was possible with the Spanish government in either absolutist or constitutional form. Guerrero noted that Spain had continuously "rebuffed with abuse the humble and just representations of our deputies, then they laughed at us and unjustly rejected our other proposals. They did not grant us equality in representation, nor did they wish to cease calling us the infamous name of colonials, in spite of the fact that they declared the Americas were an integral part of the monarchy. A conduct such as this, so contrary to natural law, divine law, and the law of nations, was horrifying." Guerrero ended the letter vowing, "Independence and hatred for those cruel people!"[12]

Within two short months, Guerrero joined forces with Iturbide. This about-face is related to the formal document that Iturbide issued in February, outlining his program. The Iguala Plan incorporated platforms attractive to the ecclesiastical and military elites, but it also promised effective Independence and individual political equality without regard to race or ethnicity, which had been two key sticking points for the guerrillas. The plan's "Three Guarantees"—Long live the holy religion we profess! Long live Northern America, independent from all the nations of the globe! Long live the union that makes our happiness!—were fluid enough to allow Guerrero to sign on with the growing number of Iturbide supporters. Like the other factions in the coalition, circumstances left the insurgency in a position to gamble on a strategic alliance with Iturbide in the short term, while sorting out its options for the longer term.[13]

The Army of the Three Guarantees advanced rapidly in mid-1821. The final months before Iturbide and Guerrero marched into Mexico City presaged events in the post-Independence period. In March 1821 the municipal council still supported the constitutional option and issued a proclamation urging the city's residents to "resist with equal fearlessness the attacks and intrigues of servile despotism and the seductions of anarchy." By June, as Viceroy Apodaca increasingly ceded authority to military officers in the capital, the municipal council grew bolder and more openly critical of viceregal policies. The final push in the council's defection to the Iturbidist cause came with the royalist military coup against Apodaca in July 1821. From that point on, the council's actions bordered on open obstructionism.[14]

General Juan O'Donoju, newly appointed by the Cortes as New Spain's chief political officer, was buffeted by the changing tide shortly after he arrived in Veracruz. O'Donoju met with Iturbide en route to the capital, and the two signed a peace treaty on August 24, 1821. The Treaty of Córdoba confirmed the Iguala Plan's intent to establish Mexico as an autonomous entity within the Spanish Empire and called upon King Ferdinand VII to assume executive authority over the commonwealth or for another member of the House of Bourbon to assume that role. The treaty acknowledged the Spanish Constitution's legitimacy and called for a provisional governing junta to act as a legislature until it could organize election of an assembly along the lines of the Spanish Cortes. The junta would also appoint a regency as interim executive until the Spanish crown responded to the treaty's terms.[15]

Three weeks after O'Donoju signed the treaty, Francisco Novella, the commander of Mexico City's Royal Army contingent who
had led the coup against Viceroy Apodaca, surrendered his troops
and removed the final obstacle to Iturbide's triumph. On September 27, 1821, his thirty-eighth birthday, Agustín de Iturbide marched
triumphantly into Mexico City at the head of an army of more than
sixteen thousand troops. The façade of harmony, however, masked
deeper trouble in the war-weary land. Ominous warnings of future conflicts preceded Iturbide's entry into the city. Two days before the liberating army marched through the city gates, a distressed
municipal council fretted over the disorders unleashed in the city
by Iturbide's advance guard. They expressed grave concern over
the cries of "Death to the *Gachupines*," a derogatory term for Spaniards that lingered in the air, and they desperately hoped that Iturbide would enforce the Three Guarantees and that peace would
reign finally. Subsequent events quickly destroyed that hope.[16]

The Regency and the Constituent Congress, 1821–1822

According to stipulations in the Treaty of Córdoba, while Mexico
waited for the response of the Spanish crown, interim political authority would be exercised by a provisional governing junta, which
would name a regency and then help organize elections for a legislative assembly. Iturbide, chosen—to no one's surprise—as head of
the regency, exercised a strong influence over the provisional junta
as it set about its other tasks. Iturbide proposed that the assembly
consist of representatives of Mexico's estates, weighted according
to their importance. Iturbide did not envision the medieval European model of three estates. His legislature included heavy alloca-
tions for bureaucrats (twenty-four), ecclesiastics (eighteen), and
"men of letters" (eighteen), as well as equal representation for both
artisans and merchants (ten each), with nine seats reserved for representatives of "the people." His proposal attempted to resolve the
problems created by a broad suffrage, the current constellation of
domestic forces, and Iturbide's own desire to determine the composition of this crucial decision-making body.

Pamphlets disseminated arguments in favor of this proposal to
a wide audience. One featured a dialogue between a "simple master carpenter and his friend," who agreed that classes were natural
in all societies and that, therefore, each distinct class should be represented in the assembly. The protagonists reflected on Iturbide's
definition of class, which included social as well as economic roles,

and agreed that a truly representative legislature would have to include clerics and the military as well as artisans and merchants. Far from the political forms of the despotic past, the protagonists described this innovative estates system as a way to promote equality by ensuring representation of all social interests in the congress. The converted concluded that the elimination of all racial exclusions on citizenship signaled clearly that the new system broke with past tyranny.[17]

The contradictions between this proposal and the Spanish Constitution, still allegedly in effect, dominated discussion in the provisional junta and in public. Intense debates over the form and function of government institutions swelled. Flush with enthusiasm for peace after ten years of civil war, some suggested that wide-ranging debate of public issues epitomized a healthy new political culture. Indeed, when the provisional junta received complaints that the record of its sessions was not being published as promised, the members voted that a transcript of its daily sessions would be read publicly so that Mexico City's residents would receive timely word of the junta's deliberations. Months later, the junta published an edict soliciting suggestions from citizens of the empire who wished to contribute ideas to the debate over a new constitution.[18]

Public debate of the junta's tasks featured extended discussions of the theory and practice of popular sovereignty, especially in the numerous proposals about electoral legislation that appeared in newspapers and pamphlets. Most of these proposals contained either explicit or implicit characterizations of Mexico's newly sovereign citizenry. Although some pamphleteers idealized the plebs as the most valuable sector of society, most authors argued that the success of popular government depended on consensus, hierarchy, and deference, not mass mobilization. Many pamphleteers portrayed a common good that was easily seen and could be distinguished from the sectarian interests of party and petty avarice, if only voters would look for true "Fathers of the Nation" to lead them and not cast votes for those who did not have independent financial means and who therefore might use political office for private gain. The poor were advised not to sell their votes, as in previous elections, and to rely on persons of some respect for electoral advice rather than other simple folk. Other writers warned of the dangers of voting from the lists distributed in cafés by factional operatives. Cognizant of the uproar produced by elections during the Independence War, many debaters proposed mechanisms for greater state control over the electoral process, some of which would be implemented in later years, such as conducting a preelectoral census and distributing official ballots to eligible voters before election day. José Joaquín Fernández de Lizardi, the prolific pamphleteer known as "The Mexican Thinker," adopted a contrarian posture, suggesting that voters should elect their representatives directly, but he was pounced upon by others who harped on the importance of indirect elections in an environment in which a generally ignorant population could be trusted to know and select responsible individuals only at the parish level.[19]

After protracted negotiations with Iturbide, the provisional junta published an electoral law for the constituent congress on November 17, 1821. The final product was a legal collage constructed of snippets of the Spanish Constitution splashed against the background of Iturbide's proposals. The end result was described by Lorenzo de Zavala as a "monstrous amalgam of heterogeneous elements." Although the new law stated that elections would be carried out according to the Spanish Cortes ordinance of May 23, 1812, many articles contravened this Spanish precedent. Iturbide's innovative estates system apportioned seats in upper and lower legislative chambers, while outdated colonial demarcations rather than current population determined the geographical distribution of representatives. A further twist in the new law stipulated that there would no longer be separate congressional and municipal elections. Municipal councils, elected indirectly by citizens over the age of eighteen of "all classes and castes, even foreigners," would choose representatives to regional councils, who in turn would select congressional delegates. The new law effectively enfranchised every man over eighteen who had employment of any kind.[20]

As election day approached, street clashes broke out around the city. Iturbide and the junta, concerned with these popular excesses, agreed to crack down on the circulation of allegedly subversive materials shortly before the elections. Election day itself proved tranquil. Conservative standard-bearer Lucas Alamán wrote that the elections went very smoothly, primarily because the bodies in charge of the elections were "very well composed" and had not yet been invaded by the political agitators who came to the fore later in the 1820s. The electoral results were not without controversy, however. Contrary to Iturbide's hopes, the estates structure did not resolve the conflict between a broad suffrage and hopes for limited popular political impact.[21]

Agitation over the electoral results surfaced, primarily over the issue of how to reconcile the paradox of inclusive hierarchy embodied in the law. In one case from the city of Puebla, craft solidarity rather than deference took center stage. The city's primary electors chose a merchant named Francisco Puig to represent Puebla's artisans in the assembly. His election inspired the vociferous protests of some artisans, who complained that it was improper for a rich Spanish merchant to represent them. They argued that there were real artisans who deserved the congressional post and that it was hard to imagine how Puig could represent artisan interests when he did not even know how to card a skein of wool. The pamphlets emphasized that Puig was an import merchant whose interests were diametrically opposed to those of the artisans. The authors pointed out the dangers to artisanal well-being from continued textile imports, which Puig would surely support in congress. Rejoinders followed, signed by artisans from different crafts who supported Puig as a competent representative of the broadest interests of all of Puebla's citizens. Despite the protests, Puig took his seat in congress. The junta, which had already heard the voice of artisans in protectionist appeals directed to it before the elections, confirmed Puig's victory without comment. No member of the elite really expected artisans to be seated in the constituent congress. Rather, they assumed that some respectable members of the elite would be charged with representing the artisans' best interests. The wave of artisans' direct appeals to congress demonstrated that nonelites had held a different expectation of their place in politics. The limits of their role would be tested in more serious confrontations in the coming months.[22]

The general review of delegates' credentials revealed other problems of seating a congress by estates in nineteenth-century Mexico. Many of those elected to the congress had multiple interests and titles that rendered a strict allocation of seats to different estates impossible. The junta argued over the seating of two representatives from Veracruz who were both members of the civic militia. Because the men were not in the regular army, the reviewers decided that they did not exceed the Veracruz allocation of military representatives and awarded them seats. The junta then considered the representatives from the State of Mexico. Junta member José Guridi y Alcocer noted that Mexico had too many magistrates among its representatives. Several others responded that a strict interpretation of the law would require the junta to deny congressional seats to many other representatives as well. One junta mem-

ber added that a reduction in the number of congressional representatives from certain classes, such as the clergy, would leave very
few enlightened subjects of any kind in the chambers. The junta
concluded that the electoral law was designed to prevent control
of the congress by one preponderant class. Since this had been ac-
complished, there was no need to pursue the matter further.[23]

The constituent congress elections represented the first steps
in Iturbide's plan to build a system based on popular consent, while
simultaneously limiting its impact and isolating potential opponents inside a subordinate legislature. Soon after it opened its doors,
the assembly dashed any hope that the electoral law had delivered
a subservient body. A critical mass of delegates showed themselves
completely hostile to Iturbide's ambitions and expected the assembly itself to be the locus of national power and policy making.
Troubles between the congress and Iturbide arose in the very first
sessions in February, ranging from disputes over the minutiae of
seating arrangements in the legislative chamber to the most pressing issues of the day. The new government's fundamental problem
came down to whether Iturbide or the legislature had the principal
authority to make laws. The congress affirmed that Mexico should
indeed have a monarch as stated in the terms of the Treaty of
Córdoba, but asserted that sovereignty resided not with the throne,
but in the congress and the congressional deputies who had been
elected by the people, the true holders of sovereignty. Iturbide had
an ambitious agenda of his own. He wanted veto power over congressional measures, control of Supreme Court appointments, and
extraordinary powers over a larger military. The assembly repeatedly rebuffed these demands. Legislators made several attempts to
curtail Iturbide's power and even tried to appoint new members to
the regency who would be less beholden to the Liberator.[24]

Iturbide faced increasing opposition both within and outside
the legislature. Provincial politicians and dyed-in-the-wool republicans, such as Miguel Ramos Arizpe and José Servando Teresa de
Mier, sought greater regional autonomy. Old-line Mexico City–
based autonomists and Bourbonists supported stricter adherence
to the Treaty of Córdoba. Most insurgent leaders were never inte-
grated into the new regime's military structure and they remained
distrustful of Iturbide. Much of the opposition to Iturbide began to
coalesce within the Scots' Rite Masonic lodge. The Scots' Rite Masons formed their lodges in Mexico originally under the influence
of the liberal Spaniards who arrived with Juan O'Donoju, the last
chief political officer appointed by the Spanish Cortes. The lodge

received a boost from the active participation of republican exiles returning to Mexico after the collapse of the royal government.[25]

Iturbide had the support of key military regiments, many non-commissioned officers, the clergy, and sectors of Mexico City's poor. Mutual accusations of treason, tyranny, and malfeasance were traded throughout the spring of 1822, at which time news of Spain's rejection of the Treaty of Córdoba arrived, bringing the battle between the regency and the congress to a climax. In the wake of that rejection and a congressional attempt to remove him as head of the army, Iturbide turned to the extralegal power of his military supporters to intimidate the opposition. Citing raucous crowds in Mexico City's streets as the sovereign voice of the people, he seized the throne.[26]

Mexican Caesar, 1822–1823

On the night of May 18, 1822, junior officers loyal to Iturbide rose up in the capital. As the evening progressed, the streets swelled with Iturbide supporters who set off fireworks, shot guns in the air, and ran through the streets shouting their endorsement of Iturbide as emperor. Sergeants Pío Marcha and Mariano Prieto recruited a mob from the poor neighborhoods in the south of the city. They received support from small-time merchants such as Luciano Castrejón and a Mercedarian Friar named Aguilar. The whole group converged on Iturbide's home and demanded to see their hero. Iturbide later wrote that he accepted their demand that he make himself emperor because the "will of the people is law." Contemporary accounts asserted that as many as forty thousand people—surely an inflated figure—took to the streets in support of the coronation, but the mob nevertheless created a formidable and frightening sight, especially to Iturbide's congressional opponents who were hearing death threats on the lips of those on the street. The following morning, a crowd wheeled Iturbide's carriage to the congressional chambers, then filled the gallery, shouting threats and insults to the congressmen during a stormy session in which Iturbide was proposed and approved officially as emperor.[27]

Contemporary observers offered various explanations for Iturbide's popularity among the poor: the plebs' personal attachment to the dashing figure of Iturbide, the seductive promises of propagandists, and the influence of pro-Iturbide clergy. Still, the clearest common denominator that links the musings of these writers with the actions of the lower classes as reported in the primary documents is the identification of Iturbide with liberation from the Spanish. As noted above, one of the very first messages that Mexico City's residents received about *Iturbidismo* was from the advance guard of the Army of the Three Guarantees that preceded Iturbide into the capital. This vanguard force marched through the streets with a chorus of "Death to *Gachupines*." The cry echoed in the streets of the capital during the spring and summer of 1822, reaching at least once the point at which a crowd tried to turn word into deed and stoned the homes of two local officials.[28]

Iturbide's enemies emphasized this relationship in their criticisms. One anti-Iturbide pamphlet from early March 1823 took the form of a mock last will and testament. The author lampooned Iturbide's exploitation of the poor's "excessive patriotism" and noted their readiness to sack the Parián market at Iturbide's command. The author concluded that Iturbide ultimately would leave the poor no greater legacy than worthless paper money to "support their indigence," because Iturbide was driving the economy into the ground with his reckless policies. This attack, like many of the diatribes published against Iturbide, emphasized his relationship with the urban poor and the connection between his rise to power and urban unrest to the exclusion of the other constituencies that brought him to power. In fact, Iturbide was concerned as much as any of his predecessors or successors with the problem of social control. Early in 1822, he decried the "enemies of order" and implored the municipal government to use all means at its disposal to clear the streets of the "vagrants and idlers" who preyed on the city's residents. Nonetheless, even Iturbide himself recognized the importance of popular acclaim as a key component of his claims to power. [29]

Iturbide and his supporters constructed an argument that justified the coronation as a humble response to the organic and spontaneous expression of the will of the people, yet its possibility had been debated for months before the first regiments began their machinations on March 18. Iturbide tested the waters in the spring of 1822 by circulating an order to key officials around the country to measure the strength of public sentiment toward both monarchy and republicanism. In the meantime, pro-Iturbide forces published arguments in newspapers and pamphlets that justified the push toward coronation based on a combination of popular sovereignty and hero worship. As these pamphleteers put it, the nation could never have achieved Independence without Iturbide's guidance, and few rewards would be large enough for his sacrifices.

They concluded that since sovereign and legitimate power resided with the nation that Iturbide himself had created, it would only be right for him to lead it.[30] Proponents of this campaign even appealed directly to Iturbide: "If the common view of the people, that is, not of some individuals in particular but of the people in general, fulfilling their duty of gratitude, proclaims Your Excellency as Emperor, . . . how can Your Excellency resist the vote of the nation?"[31]

This sentiment was not universal. Many had argued that Iturbide's coronation would be illegal, a violation of the Spanish Constitution, the Iguala Plan, and the Treaty of Córdoba. Anti-Iturbide forces also feared the strain of Jacobinism in the pro-Iturbide movement, which was only reinforced by the way in which Iturbide took the throne. In response, pro-Iturbide forces argued vociferously that Independence meant Mexico was free to remake its political destiny and that Iturbide was the most deserving and popular leader in the country.[32] Iturbide and his supporters believed that independent Mexico could somehow rest on the cusp of two conflicting visions of state construction. They dreamed of a "moderate monarchy, which by a marvelous union . . . joins together the liberties of a republic with the vigor of monarchic unity, without the dangers which always were exhibited by the democratic governments of antiquity and the absolute monarchies of these last centuries."[33]

Iturbide set out to construct an impressive show to introduce the moderate monarchy officially. He created a new noble order, the Imperial Order of Guadalupe, and filled it with key political, religious, and military figures. Four days of elaborate festivities marked his coronation in July. The ceremonies included heavy martial and religious themes, as well as popular entertainments, such as bullfights conducted in a temporary ring constructed in the central plaza. The coronation ceremony itself lasted five hours. Special coins bearing the imperial seal were minted and tossed to the crowd at the precise moment that Iturbide left the main cathedral and designated shouters commenced the refrain, "Long live the Emperor." A new calendar of imperial holidays soon followed. It included a number of religious feasts, the birthdays of Iturbide and his son, the day congress proclaimed Iturbide Emperor, and the day the Army of the Three Guarantees marched into Mexico City. September 17 became a national day to remember the "Victims of the Fatherland," but the start of the Independence War (September 16) was not included in the official calendar.[34]

In the coming months, some of Iturbide's advisers wondered whether the Emperor had been too successful in winning the support of the masses. They lamented the extent to which the popular classes had embraced the new regime. Manuel López Bueno, who helped to design the imperial symbols, warned Iturbide that reproductions of his coat of arms had turned up all over the city, even in butcher shops and "the most indecent places." The guardians of taste warned the emperor that the proliferation of unauthorized popular versions of the venerated symbols of rule could diminish Mexico in the eyes of the world. They were unaware that U.S. Consul William Taylor, the only foreign diplomat to attend the coronation, had already labeled the regime a clumsy pantomime of true royalty.[35]

The royal seal declared that Iturbide had been selected "by divine providence and by the congress of the nation constitutional emperor of Mexico," yet Iturbide's path to the throne exposed a struggle for dominance rather than a fusion of different kinds of authority in the person of the new emperor. The congress and Iturbide tested the nature and limits of their respective powers, resulting in months of increasingly bitter feuding. The political stalemate broke in August when the emperor discovered a plot to overthrow him. Iturbide retaliated by ordering a large number of arrests, including those of several prominent legislators. With his handling of the crisis, Iturbide lost any remaining congressional support. Legislators argued that Iturbide had trampled on congressional immunity and legal precedent. On October 31, 1822, Iturbide simply dissolved the legislature entirely, saying it was an idle, unrepresentative institution. In its place, Iturbide selected a new Founding Junta, which was supposed to convoke another constitutional congress and resolve the treasury crisis.[36]

By the fall of 1822, Iturbide added military discontent to his mounting political problems. He set off for Veracruz in early November to investigate a number of complaints against Antonio López de Santa Anna, the region's military chief and leader of the battle against the remaining Spanish troops in the area. Unimpressed by Santa Anna in a personal meeting, the emperor decided to relieve the officer of his military command. Santa Anna responded by rebelling. Guadalupe Victoria, who would become first president of the republic, joined the uprising. Shortly thereafter the old insurgents Vicente Guerrero and Nicolás Bravo added a southern front to the revolt. In February 1823, General José Antonio Echávarri, whom Iturbide had sent to Veracruz to squash the revolt, switched sides. The rebels then issued the Casa Mata Plan, which called for the restoration of the congress, more provincial autonomy, and a decentralized army. The plan did not demand Iturbide's overthrow, but the idea of a powerful congress, regional autonomy, and a decentralized military clearly were incompatible with Iturbide's ambitions. Iturbide attempted to sidetrack the revolt by reinstalling the congress on March 4.[37]

Tensions only increased in Mexico City after congress reconvened. Many businesses in the city had already shuttered their doors in February out of fear of popular commotion. Unsure of his future, Iturbide tested his remaining strength in the early days of March. Once again, he allowed himself to be wheeled through the streets in a carriage propelled by his poor supporters, while rumors abounded of plots to make him a dictator through the promotion of a mass uprising. Congressional deputy Carlos María de Bustamante and others reported hearing cries in the streets of "Death to the congress" and "Long live the absolute emperor." Although opposition factions gained control of key regions, this did little to quell the fears of those politicians who lived in the capital, surrounded by vocal armed supporters of the emperor. The congress requested that Iturbide take decisive action to avoid bloodshed in the city by disarming the popular militias that had formed in the city's poor neighborhoods. Other government officials expressed concern that a plot was being hatched to "put in movement the inhabitants of the barrios for sinister ends" and asked if Iturbide had forgotten the lessons of the Independence War and the damage the masses can do to property and all decent folk when they are unleashed. Captain General José Antonio de Andrade, a staunch supporter of Iturbide, replied in wounded tones to this alleged calumny. Andrade argued that the honorable citizens of the impoverished southern neighborhoods of San Pablo, Santo Tomás la Palma, Salto del Agua, and Santa Cruz Acatlán had simply formed their own "Provincial Police Regiment of the Four Barrios" to preserve order, not to upset it. Iturbide ultimately decided to distance himself from this support and issued a proclamation on March 13 prohibiting groups from gathering in the streets and insulting the authorities. Less than a week later, he abdicated, unwilling to lead an ill-equipped, disorganized force of poor avengers against his former allies.[38]

On the day before Iturbide left for exile, the victorious congress and its military supporters reiterated the ban on public gatherings of more than ten people, ordered the popular militia disarmed, and made special note that every effort should be made to keep "all domestic servants, artisans, and manual laborers of every profession" off the streets at night. Some people who fell into these categories had their own plans. The self-proclaimed "liberating army" had difficulty persuading die-hard Iturbide supporters to accept their version of liberation. The troops faced major resistance from the "Battalion of the Four Barrios," which met the new arrivals at the city gates and opened fire. Dispersed by a retaliatory volley, mobs continued to harass the invading troops for days. On March 29, responding to the continued unrest, the occupation army's leader in Mexico City drafted a decree with a long preface that asserted that the anti-Iturbide forces had not come as enemies of the people but as guarantors of a return to the rule of law. The commander felt compelled to assure the city's residents that in fact the "entire army is American" and that, while they had come to "erase despotism," the short-term goals of squelching anarchy and bloodshed required the imposition of a nightly curfew, limitations on public gatherings, and the confiscation of all weapons held by private citizens.[39]

The Genesis of the Republic, 1823–1824

The restored congress first declared the Treaty of Córdoba and Iturbide's coronation void, then formed a three-person executive authority. During its brief existence, insurgent leaders such as Nicolás Bravo, Guadalupe Victoria, Vicente Guerrero, José Mariano Michelena, and Miguel Domínguez all served in the triumvirate. The provincial governments insisted that elections for a new constituent congress be called quickly under legislation that eliminated the peculiarities of Iturbidist precedent. The new law, passed in June 1823, apportioned representatives by population, resumed separate elections for municipal and congressional offices, and eliminated the estates system. It maintained the extensive suffrage of the Iturbide law and did nothing to resolve the problem of identifying eligible voters.[40] Still, the electoral process seemed to run relatively smoothly. There were small confusions at times over which laws applied to municipal versus federal elections, but overall, between 1823 and 1825, elections proved to be relatively tranquil affairs, especially compared to the upheavals of 1812 and 1813.

In December 1823, elections were held to replace the entire Mexico City municipal council. The total number of votes cast in all parishes barely passed 1,100. The following August approximately

1,300 votes were cast in Mexico City's congressional primary elections. Writing of these elections years later, the conservative Francisco de Paula de Arrangoiz echoed Lucas Alamán's assessment of the 1822 elections, noting that men of "order and property" were elected and that, as long as elections remained the preserve of the elites, they were a fine thing. The periodicals of the day had little to say about the elections except to report the results—and even those only occasionally. In contrast, the acerbic Carlos María de Bustamante, never at a loss for words, yet again captured telling detail beneath the public reports. In his diary, Bustamante noted that the secondary congressional elections of 1823 played out like a cockfight, attended as they were by every class of person. Much to Bustamante's chagrin, some "jokers" nominated hard-core Iturbide supporters such as Pío Marcha and Juan Gómez Navarrete for seats in the congress.[41]

During these months of transition, the streets reflected social tensions more often than the polls. In the fall of 1823 the constituent congress declared over a dozen Independence War heroes "Glorious Sons of the Fatherland" and decided to transfer the remains of a number of them to the capital for reinterment. A commemorative mass was scheduled for September 17 to honor these heroes. Amid the preparations for this event, popular anti-Spanish sentiment erupted, stoked by inflammatory pamphlets and newspaper articles. Rumors circulated of a plot to use the symbol of Hidalgo's cry for Independence on September 16 as a launching pad for a mob attack on the tomb of Hernán Cortés. Minister of Interior and External Relations Lucas Alamán stepped in to whisk Cortés's remains from their resting place in the Hospital de Jesús, and the uprising never materialized. The commemorative festivities continued as planned, culminating with a solemn ceremony on September 27, remembered still as the day when "all were one."[42]

A more serious threat to political stability occurred the following January, when José María Lobato, a former shoemaker and mixed-race military officer, declared his regiment in revolt. His two major demands were to remove all Spaniards from public posts and to force moderates José Mariano Michelena and Miguel Domínguez from the executive triumvirate. The debate in Mexico City's municipal council over what the revolt meant and what to do about it foreshadowed subsequent political fault lines. One council member argued that the movement consisted solely of "seditious members of the plebs who only rebel to get jobs that they do not deserve." Another council member retorted that the revolt had some merit, because Spanish residents' support for Independence was "not so absolute and general as is said." Ultimately, the council issued a decree that condemned the revolt and supported equality for all before the law. At the same time, it assigned additional police to the Parián market to prevent looting and anarchy.[43]

Lobato's revolt failed to win any adherents among the major military or political players of the time, and its leader surrendered. Although the revolt had a negligible immediate impact, it captured the attention of politicians, the press, and the public. The doubts that Lobato raised about Spanish domination of Mexican political and economic affairs returned with a vengeance soon thereafter. In the meantime, the constituent congress, charged with drafting a new constitution, went about its work. This body had a more equitable regional representation than the congress that met under Iturbide, and one of the major debates in framing a new constitution became the balance of power between the states and the national government. Many of the deputies arrived with strict limits placed on their mandate by their provincial deputations, most of which wanted the congress to adopt an extreme federalist constitution with a very weak national government. The efforts of a vocal centralist minority and a commitment to preserve national unity even among the radical federalists provided a countervailing force, which led to compromises in the 1824 Constitution and a shared sovereignty between the states and the national government. The fiscal situation, which had improved as a result of several loans negotiated in London, abetted the air of compromise and contributed to the optimism that greeted the republic's early days. The cash flow allowed the government to meet its operating costs in the short term. Many people both within and outside Mexico expected the economy to recover further with peace and stability seemingly at hand.[44]

The congress passed the new constitution in the fall. The public received the document with "the solemnity that has been customary in acts of this type." The ceremonies mirrored in many ways the celebrations that had greeted the 1812 Constitution and other recent political events. As part of the festivities, each parish in the city held a mass and a swearing-in ceremony. The affair's organizers recruited two hundred people of "all classes and ages" to participate in the pledge of allegiance ceremony in the city's largest parish, Sagrario. During the procession, acolytes met representatives of the government bearing the constitution at the back of the church and escorted them to a place of honor. A priest delivered a homily extolling the advantages of the constitution and admonishing members of the congregation that they were obliged to obey it. At the end of the mass, the new constitution was read and those in attendance stood and swore their allegiance.[45]

According to the new constitution, the president and vice president would be elected by the state legislatures. All of the top candidates were heroes of the Independence Wars. Veracruz native Guadalupe Victoria, known more for his indefatigable allegiance to the Independence movement than his current political proclivities, won a clear majority that assured him the executive office. Two very different men from the south split the runner-up position that determined the vice presidency. Nicolás Bravo came from a prominent landowning family near Chilpancingo; Vicente Guerrero had less prestigious family roots as a muleteer in the region near Tixtla. Both had joined the insurgency early in the struggle for Independence, but their paths split dramatically in the 1820s, when Bravo emerged as a centralist stalwart and Grand Master of the Scots' Rite Masons, while Guerrero became the standard-bearer for egalitarian federalism and Bravo's counterpart in a different Masonic lodge. With neither candidate having a clear majority from the state legislatures, the national congress was responsibile for the decision. The congress chose Bravo, who soon became a consistent critic of the new president. President Victoria, who took office in October 1824, reflected in his decisions the air of compromise represented by the constitution. Throughout his term, Victoria populated his cabinet with representatives of each major political current, including the conservative centralist Lucas Alamán as Minister of Interior and External Relations, the Iturbidist Manuel Gómez Pedraza as Minister of War, and the federalist José Ignacio Esteva as Minister of the Treasury. The period during which it appeared that the consensus around the 1824 Constitution might bring an end to factional strife was brief. The struggle for hegemony among uncompromising elite factions resumed quickly. In the following months and years, the urban poor came to play a larger role in the turmoil than they ever had before. The consequent impact on Mexican political development would be profound.[46]

Notes

1. Lovett, *Napoleon*, 2:841; Christiansen, *The Origins*, 17–21; Anna, "The Independence," 3:82–84; Rodríguez O., *The Independence*, 240–41.

2. Jaime E. Rodríguez O., "La Independencia de la América española: Una reinterpretación," *Historia Mexicana* 42, no. 3 (1993): 571–620; Timothy E. Anna, *Forging Mexico, 1821–1835* (Lincoln: University of Nebraska Press, 1998), 167–75.

3. Proclamation and Municipal Council Reports, AACM, vol. 2253, exp. 9 and 12.

4. *Ideas sobre el ciudadano en diálogo* (1814; reprint ed., Mexico City: Imp. Alejandro Valdes, 1820); *El Fernandino constitucional al sr. ex-Diputado de Cortes* (Mexico City: Imp. Mariano Ontiveros, 1820); *El Fernandino constitucional a los fidelísimos mexicanos* (Mexico City: Imp. Arizpe, 1820); *Parabien al Fernandino arrepentido, por el colegial* (Mexico City: Imp. Alejandro Valdes, 1820).

5. *El tejedor poblano y su compadre: Plática familiar entre éstos y su aprendiz* (Puebla, Mexico: Imp. Mariano Ontiveros, 1820); *Segunda plática del tejedor y su compadre* (Puebla, Mexico: Imp. Mariano Ontiveros, 1820); *El indio constitucional* (Mexico City: Imp. Alejandro Valdes, 1820).

6. Rodríguez O., *Independence of Mexico*, 197; D. J. C., *Catecismo político arreglado a la constitución de la monarquía española; Para ilustración del pueblo, instrucción de la juventud, y uso de las escuelas de primeras letras* (Puebla, Mexico: Imp. San Felipe Neri, 1820).

7. AGN, Ayuntamientos, vol. 168, exp. 3; *Abusos de las elecciones populares* (Mexico City: Imp. Alejandro Valdes, 1820); Viceroy letter, June 21, 1820, AGN, Ayuntamientos, vol. 193.

8. San Pablo Report, AGN, Ayuntamientos, vol. 168, exp. 4; Berry, "The Election of the Mexican Deputies," 32–33; Election Report, AACM, vol. 870, exp. 20; Anna, *The Fall*, 194.

9. Municipal Council Reports, January 9, 1821, AGN, Ayuntamientos, vol. 179; January 11, 1821, AGN, Ayuntamientos, vol. 178; *Conversación del barbero y su marchante* (Mexico City: Imp. Alejandro Valdes, 1820).

10. Guardino, *Peasants, Politics*, 75–77; Hamnett, "Mexico's Royalist Coalition," 74–75; Anna, "The Independence," 85; Rodríguez O., "The Transition," 105–6; *Ataque a los hipócritas que seducen el pueblo* (Mexico City: Imp. Alejandro Valdes, 1820).

11. Rodríguez O., *Independence of Mexico*, 206.

12. Guerrero to Iturbide, January 20, 1821; reprinted in William Forrest Sprague, *Vicente Guerrero, Mexican Liberator: A Study in Patriotism* (Chicago: R. R. Donnelly and Sons, 1939), 153.

13. Guardino, *Peasants, Politics*, 77; Timothy E. Anna, *The Mexican Empire of Iturbide* (Lincoln: University of Nebraska Press, 1990), 5; Hamnett, "Mexico's Royalist Coalition," 76–79.

14. Municipal Council Minutes, March 3 and June 14, 1821, AACM, vol. 670a; Timothy E. Anna, "Francisco Novella and the Last Stand of the Royal Army in New Spain," *Hispanic American Historical Review* 51, no. 1 (1971): 92–111.

15. Anna, *Mexican Empire*, 12, 50; Jaime E. Rodríguez O., "The Struggle for Dominance: The Legislature versus the Executive in Early Mexico," paper presented at the conference "The Mexican Wars of Independence, the Empire, and the Early Republic," University of Calgary, Canada, April 1991, 7–14.

16. "Orden general del 25 de septiembre de 1821, disponiendo la entrada del ejército a la Ciudad de México," BLAC-UTA, GG, vol. 338, Iturbide

Papers, folder 1; Municipal Council Minutes, September 25, 1821, AACM, vol. 670a.

17. Anna, *Mexican Empire*, 12; Agustín de Iturbide, *Pensamiento que en grande ha propuesto el que subscribe como un particular, para la pronta convocatoria de las próximas Cortes, bajo el concepto de que se podrá aumentar o disminuir el número de representantes de cada clase, conforme acuerde la Junta Soberana con el Congreso de Regencia* (Mexico City: Imp. Don Alejandro Valdes, 1821); Karl Schmitt, "Church and State in Mexico: A Corporatist Relationship," *The Americas* 40, no. 3 (January 1984): 355; J. M. R., *Lo que interesa a la patria, por el artesano y su amigo* (Mexico City: Imp. Americana de José María Betancourt, 1821).

18. Congressional minutes, October 11, 1821, in *Historia parlamentaria de los congresos mexicanos de 1821 a 1857*, ed. Juan Antonio Mateos (Mexico City: U. S. Reyes, 1877), 1:79; "Oficio de la Soberana Junta Provisional Gubernativa del Imperio, excitando al público a presentar planes para la constitución del Imperio (January 21, 1822)," in *Planes en la nación mexicana*, vol. 1, *1808–1830* (Mexico City: Senado de la República, 1987), 133.

19. J. M. R., *Lo que interesa a la patria*; *El tribuno de la plebe, o escritor de los pelados, número uno* (Mexico City: Imp. D.J.M. Benavente y Socios, 1821); *El tribuno de la plebe: Diálogo entre el tribuno y el vulgo, número dos* (Mexico City: Imp. D.J.M. Benavente y Socios, 1821); *Consejos y bigotes ya no se usan, pero si advertencias* (Mexico City: Imp. Doña Herculana del Villar, 1822); *A perro viejo no hay tus tus: O sea diálogo entre un zapatero y su marchante* (Mexico City: Imp. Mariano Ontiveros, 1821); Antonio Mateos, *Proyecto acerca de elecciones de Diputados . . . al enhornarse tuerce el pan* (Mexico City: Imp. Alejandro Valdes, 1821); D.J.E.F., *Proyecto de nuevo reglamento para las elecciones* (Mexico City: Imp. D.J.M. Benavente y Socios, 1821); José de San Martín, *Cuestiones importantes sobre las Cortes, número uno* (Mexico City: Imp. D.J.M. Benavente y Socios, 1822); El Pensador Mexicano [José Joaquín Fernández de Lizardi], *Ideas políticas y liberales* (Mexico City: Imp. Imperial, 1821); D.J.E.F, *Busca-pies al Pensador Mexicano* (Mexico City: Imp. Mariano Ontiveros, 1821).

20. Lorenzo de Zavala, *Ensayo histórico de las revoluciones de México desde 1808 hasta 1830* (1831–32; reprint ed., ed. Manuel González Ramírez, Mexico City: Porrúa, 1969), 102; Minutes of the Soberana Junta Provisional, November 1821, in *Historia parlamentaria*, ed. Mateos, 1:99–131; Antonio García Orozco, ed., *Legislación electoral mexicana, 1812–1977*, 2d ed. (Mexico City: Comisión Federal Electoral, 1978), 25–28; Rodríguez O., "The Struggle for Dominance," 10–14; Anna, *Mexican Empire*, 52; Schmitt, "Church and State," 355.

21. Superior Order, December 10, 1821, AGN, Gobernación, Sin Sección, caja 34, exp. 9; Junta Minutes, December 11–12, 1821, *Historia parlamentaria*, ed. Mateos, 1:140–43; Alamán, *Historia de Méjico*, 5:481; Vicente Riva Palacio et al., *México a través de los siglos* (1889; reprint ed., Mexico City: Editorial Cumbre, 1980), 7:52–53.

22. *Para estos lances sirve la imprenta: Diálogo: un zapatero y un tejedor* (Puebla, Mexico: Imp. Liberal de Moreno Hermanos, 1822); R. H., *Al tejedor y el zapatero* (Puebla, Mexico: Imp. Pedro de la Rosa, 1822); *Satisfacción que los artesanos de esta Ciudad abajo suscritos dan al señor su Diputado don Francisco de Paula Puig, por las expresiones que vierte en el diálogo del tejedor y el zapatero* (Puebla, Mexico: Imp. Don Pedro de la Rosa, 1822); Juan Nepomuceno Estevez Ravanillo, *Vindicación de señor Diputado de Cortes don*

Francisco de Paula Puig, por la parte en que lo injuria el diálogo entre el tejedor y el zapatero (Puebla, Mexico: Imp. Don Pedro de la Rosa, 1822); Junta Minutes, December 4, 1821, in *Historia parlamentaria*, ed. Mateos, 1:134; Junta Minutes, February 22, 1822, in *Actas constitucionales mexicanas* (1821–1824; reprint ed., Mexico City: Universidad Nacional Autónoma de México, 1980), 1:338.

23. Junta Minutes, February 22, 1822, in *Actas constitucionales*, 1:340–43.

24. "Constitutional Bases: Second Mexican Congress (February 24, 1822)," in *The Political Plans of Mexico*, ed. Thomas B. Davis and Amado Ricon Virulegio (Lanham, Md.: University Press of America, 1987), 159.

25. Anna, *Mexican Empire*, 55, 88.

26. Rodríguez O., "Struggle for Dominance," 18–22, 26–31; Anna, *Mexican Empire*, 58–59, 88–94; Alamán, *Historia de Méjico*, 5:411–12, 588–91; Zavala, *Ensayo histórico*, 110; Torcuato S. Di Tella, *Iturbide y el cesarismo popular* (Buenos Aires: Cuadernos Simón Rodríguez, Editorial Biblos, n.d.), 31; Riva Palacios et al., *México a través*, 7:65–75.

27. Di Tella, *National Popular Politics*, 87, 112; "Lista de individuos que acompañaron a don Luciano Castrejón la noche del 18 de mayo 1822," BLAC-UTA, Hernández y Davalos Papers, 15–4.1812 (hereafter cited as HyD); Unsigned Correspondence, n/a, n/d [May 1822], BLAC-UTA, GG, vol. 338, Iturbide Papers, folder 1; Francisco de Paula de Arrangoiz, *México desde 1808 hasta 1867* (1871–72; reprint ed., Mexico City: Porrúa, 1968), 313–34; Zavala, *Ensayo histórico*, 128.

28. Alamán, *Historia de Méjico*, 5:590, 605; Zavala, *Ensayo histórico*, 121; Police Report, July 5, 1822, AGN, Gobernación, leg. 23 (1), caja 46, exp. 9.

29. *Ya agoniza el despotismo y otorga su testamento* (1823; reprint ed., Mexico City: Imprenta Nacional, 1823); Municipal Council Minutes, January 4, 1822, AACM, vol. 696a.

30. Superior Order, March 27, 1822, and Responses, BLAC-UTA, GG, vol. 388, Iturbide Papers, folders 1–4; *Cada cual piensa en su cabeza* (Mexico City: Imp. D.J.M. Betancourt, 1821); *Legitimidad de la elección de nuestro Emperador* (Mexico City: Imp. de Doña Herculana del Villar y Socios, 1822); *Derechos convincentes para elegir Emperador Americano* (Mexico City: Imp. Don Alejandro Valdes, 1821); E. A., *Derecho del pueblo mexicano para elegir Emperador* (Mexico City: Imp. D.J.M. Benavente y Socios, 1821).

31. *Contestación de un americano al Manifiesto del Señor D. Agustín de Iturbide* (Mexico City, 1821), quoted in Anna, *Mexican Empire*, 35.

32. M. G. de V., *El importante voto de un ciudadano* (Mexico City: Imp. de José María Benavente y Socios, 1821); *Reflexiones políticas sobre la elección de Emperador* (Mexico City: Imp. Americana de José María Betancourt, 1821); "Quilibet," *El más sublime heroísmo del exmo. Sr. Iturbide y sus dignos compañeros de armas, contra el llamado importante voto de un ciudadano* (Mexico City: Imp. Mariano Ontiveros, 1821).

33. *Extracto del noticioso general de México, del lunes 22 de julio de 1822, segundo de nuestra Independencia* (Puebla: Imp. Don Pedro de la Rosa, 1822).

34. Proclamation, AACM, vol. 1058, exp. 2; *Proyecto del ceremonial que para la inauguración, consagración y coronación de su magestad el Emperador Agustín Primero se presentó por la comisión encargada de formarlo, al Soberano Congreso en 17 de junio de 1822* (Mexico City: Imp. José Ma. Ramos Palomera, 1822).

35. Manuel López Bueno to Iturbide, June 8, 1822, BLAC-UTA, HyD, 16-1.3141; Anna, *Mexican Empire*, 80–81.

36. Designs for Royal Seal, BLAC-UTA, HyD, 16-3150; Alamán, *Historia de Méjico*, 5:602; Anna, *Mexican Empire*, 76, 110–18, 125; Rodríguez O., "Struggle for Dominance," 31–33.

37. Anna, *The Mexican Empire*, 169–71, 201–10; Arrangoiz, *México desde 1808*, 320; Di Tella, *Iturbide*, 45–46.

38. Zavala, *Ensayo histórico*, 165; Minutes of Congressional Session, March 11, 1823, in, *Historia parlamentaria*, ed. Mateos, 2:125; Anna, *Mexican Empire*, 191; Di Tella, *Iturbide*, 49; Congress to Iturbide, March 7, 1823, AGN, Gobernación, Casa Amarilla, leg. 1586 (1), exp. 2; Provincial Deputation to Captain General Andrade, March 1, 1823, BLAC-UTA, GG, vol. 338, Iturbide Papers, folder 3; Andrade to Provincial Deputation and Municipal Council, March 2, 1823, BLAC-UTA, GG, vol. 338, Iturbide Papers, folder 3; Di Tella, *Iturbide*, 17, n. 27; Alamán, *Historia de Méjico*, 5:744; Frederick J. Shaw, "Poverty and Politics in Mexico City, 1824–1854" (Ph.D. diss., University of Florida, 1975), 15; Superior Order, March 13, 1823, AGN, Gobernación, Sin Sección, caja 51, exp. 4.

39. Congressional Minutes, March 30, 1823, in *Historia parlamentaria*, ed. Mateos, 2:172; Di Tella, *Iturbide*, 17, n. 27; Alamán, *Historia de Méjico*, 5:744; Di Tella, *National Popular Politics*, 130; Proclamation, March 30, 1823, AGN, Gobernación, Sin Sección, caja 39, exp. 4.

40. "Bases para las elecciones del nuevo Congreso (June 17, 1823)," in *Legislación electoral mexicana*, ed. Garcíca Orozco, 33–41.

41. Municipal Election Reports, AACM, vol. 862, exp. 9–10; Congressional Election Reports, AACM, vol. 873, exp. 2; Arrangoiz, *México desde 1808*, 341; *El Sol*, August 23 and December 9, 1824; Carlos María de Bustamante, "Diario histórico," entry for August 18, 1823, microfilm, roll 2, Biblioteca National de Antropología y Historia, Mexico City (hereafter cited as BNAH).

42. Arrangoiz, *México desde 1808*, 334; Riva Palacio et al., *México a través*, 7:206; Hale, *Mexican Liberalism*, 99; Francisco de la Maza, "Los restos de Hernán Cortés," *Cuadernos Americanos* 32 (1947): 153–74; Civic Oration, September 27, 1823, quoted in Bustamante, *Cuadro histórico*, 6:181.

43. Arrangoiz, *México desde 1808*, 326; Municipal Council Minutes, January 24, 1823, AACM, vol. 288a.

44. Jaime E. Rodríguez O., "The Struggle for the Nation: The First Centralist-Federalist Conflict in Mexico," *The Americas* 44, no. 1 (July 1992): 1–22; Michael P. Costeloe, *La primera República federal de México (1824–1835): Un estudio de los partidos políticos en el México independiente* (Mexico City: Fondo de Cultura Económica, 1975), 23–24, 32; Barbara A. Tenenbaum, *The Politics of Penury: Debts and Taxes in Mexico, 1821–1856* (Albuquerque: University of New Mexico Press, 1986), 22.

45. Proclamations on Constitutional Ceremonies, AACM, vol. 2253, exp. 19 and 20.

46. Guardino, *Peasants, Politics*, 54–57; Anna, *Forging Mexico*, 178–79; Costeloe, *La primera República*, 32, 46–47; Arrangoiz, *México desde 1808*, 340; Zavala, *Ensayo histórico*, 222.

4

The Rise of Republican
Mass Politics, 1824–1830

During the second half of the 1820s, Mexico experienced an explosion of popular political organizing and activity, as competing factions attempted to gain office at the national, state, and local levels through alliances with the urban masses. Masonic lodges took the lead, generating partisan propaganda and recruiting unprecedented numbers of people into the political process. In a context of highly competitive electoral politics, all parties attempted to spin their discourse for mass consumption. Although each faction's positions were in a high degree of flux and often focused on the politics of personality, serious debate still occurred over the locus of political power and which sectors of society would be charged with setting the political agenda. In the mid-1820s, followers of the York Rite lodge (Yorkinos) appeared to be on their way to domination of Mexico City, and perhaps the entire nation, based on their ability to capitalize on mass politics. The Yorkinos achieved convincing victories in their first electoral contests in the capital, including a landslide in the 1826 congressional elections. At approximately the same time the followers of the Scots' Rite lodge (Escoseses) were discredited when a number of the lodge's key figures participated in an ill-fated conspiracy to return Mexico to the Spanish crown.

Instead of achieving political hegemony, the Yorkinos split in 1827, as one group within the movement saw dangers of mob rule and anarchy emanating from the new political culture. In the 1828 presidential race, moderates from the York lodge joined many Escoseses in advocating the candidacy of the reconstructed Iturbide supporter and current Minister of War Manuel Gómez Pedraza, while radicals fanned the flames of popular sentiment even more with an incendiary campaign on behalf of the Independence War hero Vicente Guerrero. Although both groups draped themselves in the banners of nationalism and federalism, moderates joined their more conservative brethren in condemning the political tactics that had been so successful for the Yorkinos from 1825 to 1828. In contrast, when the radicals chose armed insurrection to place Vicente Guerrero in office in 1828, they pointed to Guerrero's popularity with the masses as evidence that Gómez Pedraza's selection as president by the state legislatures violated the popular will.

These events, coupled with the new nation's nagging economic crisis, which was exacerbated by default on British loans in 1827, produced a reaction that unified conservatives and moderates in the fear that Mexican society was on the verge of a breakdown. Measures suggested to rein in anarchy ranged from calls for electoral reform to the establishment of a special vagrancy court. This backlash peaked when the coalition of moderates and conservatives, known as "Hombres de Bien" (Decent Men), overthrew Guerrero in 1829 and justified the revolt as the first essential step to put Mexican society back in order.

Yorkinos versus Escoseses, 1824–1826

Beneath the harmonious appearances of reconciliation that marked the birth of the republic in 1824, discontent had grown among provincial political brokers, hard-core federalist ideologues, and some ambitious souls whose search for economic and social mobility in post-Independence Mexico had not yet been realized. These groups complained that men such as the conservative Lucas Alamán dominated the Victoria government. Critics accused Alamán and others of harboring nostalgia for the colonial era and preserving too many structures that centralized power and decision making. A number of Alamán's allies, including cabinet ministers Pablo de la Llave and Sebastián Camacho, belonged to the Scots' Rite Masons. By the mid-1820s, all of those accused of harboring pro-Spanish, centralist tendencies were branded Escoseses whether they were lodge members or not.

To provide an organizational boost to their own activities, in mid-1825 Senators José María Alpuche and Lorenzo de Zavala, Minister of the Treasury José Ignacio Esteva, and Miguel Ramos Arizpe, who had played a major role in the constitutional congress, formed a new Masonic lodge with the help of Joel R. Poinsett, the U.S. minister plenipotentiary. The York Rite Masons soon attracted additional members, such as José María Tornel, who was at the time

President Victoria's secretary, and Vicente Guerrero. Lorenzo de Zavala estimated that the Yorkinos founded 130 lodges all over the country within months of the rite's formation. According to Zavala, the movement attracted "every class of citizen" who wished to organize against the privileged classes, to dislodge the Spanish monopoly on the country's wealth, and to use lodge connections to secure patronage jobs.[1]

Given that the Masonic lodges were secret societies and that few of their internal documents have entered the public realm, there are no reliable membership lists from which to ascertain the relative size of either the York Rite or Scots' Rite lodges. Available sources do indicate that membership was a luxury beyond the means of most Mexicans. The York lodge "Mexican Independence" had an initiation fee of thirty-two pesos, a sum equal to more than one month's salary for most workers in the capital. In addition, the lodge collected monthly dues of one peso, one-third of the median monthly rent for a house in the city. The lodge rules stated clearly that no member could have these fees waived.[2] The lodges were much more than fraternal organizations, however, and their impact went beyond the networking done by members at lodge meetings. They were political movements, whose leaders advocated public positions clearly stated within the pages of periodicals affiliated with the lodges. The lodges printed and distributed electoral propaganda and sample ballots, and the Yorkinos in particular developed an outreach strategy to "incorporate in a more rational political form the enormous potential force of the masses."[3]

One of the very first things the Yorkinos did to appeal to the masses was to tap into popular anti-Spanish sentiment with a campaign to transform September 16 from a quietly acknowledged day of remembrance into a rousing spectacle. In 1824 there were no major Independence Day activities in the capital, and neither *El Sol* (The Sun), the Scots' Rite mouthpiece, nor *El Aguila Mexicana* (The Mexican Eagle), which became the York Rite standard-bearer, devoted a single line to Hidalgo's uprising. In contrast, in 1825 the Yorkinos actively campaigned for appropriate festivities in mid-September to commemorate such a momentous national event. Juan Wenceslao Barquera, a former Guadalupe and current Yorkino and municipal attorney, became the driving force within the government to organize the celebration. A patriotic organizing committee envisioned a dramatic fireworks display on the night of September 15, followed the next day by a grand procession, speeches, orchestral music, dancing, and patriotic allegories. The committee argued that Mexico needed an antidote to the "lukewarm civic enthusiasm" that currently afflicted the republic. In a telling response to these suggestions, Minister of Interior and External Relations Lucas Alamán expressed concern for the preservation of public order. After all, Alamán had been the man to rescue Cortés's bones on September 16 only two years before. His ministry demanded that the municipal council limit the scope of the festivities and ban the sale of alcohol on the night of the celebrations, and the Federal District governor deployed extra troops in the city center.[4]

The civic exercises, as finally agreed upon, contained a number of elements borrowed from the standard ritual repertoire, including fireworks, music, and the construction of public ephemeral art, which became regular features of the annual patriotic celebrations. A pompous allegorical dance featured America oppressed by Despotism, Discord, and Envy. Liberty, with the aid of War and Glory, subdued these evils and released the Mexican Eagle in a grand finale. Another feature added a special character to this year's celebration. The organizers paid for the liberation of a group of slaves. Manumission was incorporated as part of the day's public events, and would be again later in the decade, although it became increasingly difficult to find donors in the area. By 1828, the patriotic commission could locate only one slave in the capital to manumit. The following year, President Guerrero abolished slavery outright, which eliminated this feature from future ceremonies.[5]

The 1825 patriotic oration, given by Juan Wenceslao Barquera, the event's principal promoter, elided all references to Iturbide in its narrative of the path to Independence. Barquera spoke of the discord and costly errors that precluded a quick victory after the glorious early days of the uprising. He noted the constancy of Guerrero and Victoria, "faithful depositories of the precious seed" planted by Hidalgo and "irrigated with the blood of so many martyrs," but the hero of Iguala received only brief reference as a proponent of the "Three Guarantees" and was never mentioned by name. Literary works produced for the occasion displayed equal discretion. One short poem contained a line of praise for the "caudillo of Iguala," but the author felt compelled to include a footnote explaining that he admired only "Iturbide, liberator of the country, not Agustín I, Emperor of Mexico." Independence Day orators later in the decade grew bolder in mentioning Iturbide by name, but they, too, were quick to preserve their republican credentials and emphasized only his service to the cause of Independence, not his later activities.[6]

Each lodge's newspaper devoted significant space to commemorate the day. Perhaps in response to the perceived ground-
swell of patriotic sentiment and the machinations of their rivals,
the editors of *El Sol* ran a long, upbeat story under the headline
"Anniversary of Independence" in their edition of September 16.
Not to be outdone, *El Aguila Mexicana* devoted three days to news,
prose, and poetry on the subject, under such headlines as "Long
Live the Fatherland." Among other items, they reported for pos-
terity and national consumption that, in spite of an afternoon rain,
the Yorkinos' efforts had succeeded. The citizens of Mexico City
had "manifested anew the sincerity of their patriotic sentiments."[7]

In addition to their campaign to foment a particular brand of
patriotic sentiment, the Yorkinos developed a two-tiered strategy
of political activity. The first wave applied pressure on President
Guadalupe Victoria directly to remove their opponents from his
cabinet, which met with only limited success. More important for
the long term, the Yorkinos began to leverage the peculiarities of
the electoral system (a broad suffrage, the absence of census rolls,
and Mexico City's huge electoral districts) into a means to achieve
power. The Escoseses responded to some extent, but their political
program did not generate so much popular enthusiasm, nor were
party militants willing and able to engage in the same level of street
politics as the Yorkinos. [8]

A Dangerous Liberty, 1826–1828

The first major electoral confrontation between Yorkinos and
Escoseses occurred in the 1826 congressional election in late summer. It replaced half the Senate and the entire Chamber of Deputies and also determined who would control many state legislatures.
The latter elections were crucial because the constitution stipulated
that each state legislature would have one vote in selecting the next
president in 1828. Many participants in these events would soon
lament the overheated personal attacks that then characterized
political discourse, but beyond the mutual recriminations hurled
about by the political factions, serious political discussion took place
as well. The principal debates addressed the essence of political
practice, a crucial issue for the early years after Independence, when
Mexico took its first tentative steps toward establishing a system
of governance. The roles of patronage and parties, appropriate campaign tactics, and the way balloting should occur took center stage
in the debate over these elections.

The partisan attacks took place mainly within the pages of *El Aguila Mexicana* and *El Sol*. The papers expressed very different views on the role of the popular classes in politics. *El Sol* accused the Yorkinos of using politics merely as a way to secure patronage for lodge members, while they simultaneously promoted a malignant spirit of class conflict and anarchy. The editors of *El Aguila Mexicana* responded that the Escoseses promoted apathy because they could not attract popular support. As the elections approached, articles in *El Aguila Mexicana* returned again and again to this distinction between the two lodges as they encouraged a large voter turnout. As *El Sol's* pages filled with complaints about the flaws in the electoral process and the low-class composition of the York lodges, writers for *El Aguila Mexicana* embraced the inclusive nature of the political process and proudly accepted the idea that Yorkinos were egalitarian. Two days before the elections, one letter to the editors of *El Aguila Mexicana* stated unequivocally, "The people prefer a dangerous liberty to tranquil slavery." The author asked, "Do we want only those [who run] the Parián to be voters and electoral delegates?" His reply: "We want even the most wretched citizen to be able to use his rights."[9]

These short phrases summarized the Yorkinos' strategy heading into the 1826 election. They pursued a broad constituency based primarily on the assertion that wealthy Spanish merchants and their lackeys had dominated the political process since the fall of Iturbide. The Parián market still sat in the very heart of the capital to symbolize this. In other words, they tried to tap into the class and colonial resentments that had arisen over the city periodically since 1808.

The Escoseses' response to the anti-Spanish campaign took an interesting twist. *El Sol* defended the Spaniards on constitutional grounds, but simultaneously attacked the Yorkinos as false patriots, who "did no more than kiss the chains of Spanish oppression" during the Independence War.[10] The tactic of trying to separate nationalist fervor from increasing anti-Spanish sentiment and denying nationalism as the exclusive realm of the radicals surfaced again during the 1828 presidential campaign.

Congressional primary elections took place in all fourteen Mexico City parishes on August 20, 1826. Voter turnout reached an all-time high. The official government report noted that more than thirty thousand votes were cast, although one press report claimed that more than forty thousand people voted in Sagrario parish alone. The lower official figure was still approximately twenty-three times greater than the number of votes received by the winners of the 1824 congressional elections. Both Escoseses and Yorkinos had distributed prefabricated ballots. The Escoseses complained that the Yorkinos bought Scots' Rite sample ballots and destroyed them at the same time that other Yorkinos paid poor folks to vote more than once. One writer claimed that, in the parish of Salto del Agua, the number of votes cast exceeded the population of eligible voters by sixfold. The Scots' Rite press further argued that the Yorkinos intimidated voters by recruiting crowds to shout that the Scots' Rite lodge was filled with Bourbonists. Accusations of Yorkino mob actions and malfeasance spilled over into Mexico State, where critics claimed that Lorenzo de Zavala personally escorted vagrants to the polls and physically intimidated his opponents' partisans. The controversy ultimately reached the national congress, which dismissed the charges.[11]

The Yorkinos did not let these accusations remain unanswered. The electoral official who presided over the Yorkino landslide in Santa María la Redonda parish defended the fairness of electoral procedures in a letter to the editors of *El Sol*. Others wrote to *El Aguila Mexicana* to praise the unprecedented voter turnout as a further step toward the perfection of civil society. The Yorkinos had good reason for their sanguine assessment. In January 1827 more than one-half of the delegates who took their seats in the Chamber of Deputies had York sympathies, although the Escoseses still controlled the Senate and many state legislatures. The 1826 election turned out to be only the first salvo in a protracted war that grew more divisive and complex over the next two years.[12]

In the aftermath of the 1826 elections, sensing the political pendulum's swing toward York hegemony, anti-Yorkinos of all stripes launched a campaign to reduce Yorkino influence. This movement included a press and pamphlet campaign and harangues from the pulpit, as well as an investigation by the Escoseses in the Senate into the influence of secret societies on Mexican life.[13] There had been a debate in Mexico over the Masons soon after the very first Scots' Rite lodges emerged, but the original objection to the lodges was based mostly on Catholic opposition to their alleged freethinking nature. Although this accusation surfaced again in 1826, conservative centralists and even some moderate federalists increasingly denounced secret societies on political rather than moral grounds. The major accusations launched against the Yorkinos in 1826–27 grew from the seeds planted during the 1826 congressional campaign. Opponents argued principally that

Yorkinos were not true patriots because they emphasized special interests and personal ambition over the national well-being. The Yorkinos' political tactics were roundly condemned as promising to precipitate a French-style reign of terror if their flirtations with mob rule were not checked.[14]

Although the opposition consistently condemned York political tactics, it often adapted those tactics to its own ends, a strategy amply evident in the 1826 election campaigns. Anti-York discourse also adopted the nationalist rhetoric that the Yorkinos used so successfully, except that anti-York writers argued that the York lodges were controlled not by Spain, but by the United States through Minister Joel R. Poinsett. Another tactic that the anti-Yorkinos condemned in print but put into practice themselves was to stir popular passions in dramatic public displays. In 1827, Escoseses participated in the processions during the annual feast of María Santísima de la Merced. At one point during the festival, the Escoseses threw flyers calling the Yorkinos heretics and anarchists into the crowd. The Yorkinos had prepared retaliatory propaganda, but before they could act, the ecclesiastic authorities barred all of the lodges from further participation in the feast.[15]

The Yorkinos defended themselves both in the congress and in public with the argument that voluntary associations were always acceptable in free countries. They painted themselves as patriotic, egalitarian, devout Catholics, versus the aristocratic, Spanish-influenced Escoseses. Pablo Villavicencio, the radical pamphleteer who published under the pen name "El Payo de Rosario," put it succinctly. He wrote that Mexico had two parties. The Yorkinos represented general public opinion and the Escoseses did not. The choice was simple: the party of the homeland stood against that of the oppressors. Would Mexicans prefer federalists or Bourbonists, Americans or Spaniards, to lead them?[16]

The 1826 Senate investigation of secret societies did little damage to the Yorkinos, who continued to capitalize on popular anti-Spanish sentiment. York legislators introduced anti-Spanish proposals in several states and the national congress. This campaign accelerated in early 1827, as an ill-fated scheme to return Mexico to the Bourbon dynasty surfaced. The Arenas Conspiracy, named after the fanatical Spanish priest who had inadvertently betrayed the plot, implicated a number of priests and others in several states, but the real extent of the scheme was never discovered, as Yorkinos and Escoseses turned the investigation into a game. *El Sol* downplayed the entire series of events, while the new York periodical, *El Correo de la Federación Mexicana*, devoted much coverage to the plot and the subsequent government investigation. The Scots' Rite strategy backfired, as the lodge became even more closely associated with the Spanish, and radical Yorkinos seized the initiative to push more aggressively for anti-Spanish sanctions.[17] The first of several prejudicial laws against resident Spaniards passed through the congress in May 1827. When news reached the city's neighborhoods that the Chamber of Deputies had approved the law, crowds rushed to the city center, stormed the cathedral, and rang the church bells all night. The Senate soon concurred on the legislation as a large group anxiously waited outside its doors and hecklers operated inside the room. When opponents of the law accused the Yorkinos of exploiting lower-class prejudices in pushing its passage, they embraced the accusation. One author remarked that if anti-Spaniard fever struck only Yorkinos, then almost everyone in Mexico was a Yorkino in 1827.[18]

The events of 1827 exposed tensions within the Yorkinos' movement over strategy and goals. As the year wore on, the group split into moderate and radical elements based on political strategy and ideology. Moderates mustered less enthusiasm for the growing expulsion movement and the radicals' involvement with the masses. Mexico's continued economic decline, accelerated by its default on large British loans in August 1827, also caused many to reassess Mexico's political direction and to place blame on incompetent radical "employment-maniacs," patronage appointees who were ruining the country.[19]

El Aguila Mexicana took up the moderate cause in 1827. In June, its editors asserted that the newspaper favored no political faction. As moderates took the reins at *El Aguila Mexicana*, radicals turned to other periodicals to disseminate their opinions, including *El Correo de la Federación Mexicana* and *El Amigo del Pueblo*. As *El Correo* and *El Amigo* pushed the radical agenda ever further, moderates and conservatives rediscovered the message of patriotic reconciliation represented by the moribund holiday of September 27. In an editorial almost identical to one that appeared in *El Sol*, the editors of *El Aguila Mexicana* reminded their readers that independent Mexico had been founded in the spirit of the Three Guarantees, one of which was the equality of Mexicans and Spaniards. Still, though both newspapers honored his triumphant day, they did not mention Iturbide by name, because his ambiguous legacy posed a dilemma. Opponents of the radicals in the mid-1820s might hark back to the Three Guarantees, but too close an association with

Iturbide might lead to accusations of disguised monarchist sentiment. Their ambivalence about Iturbide's flirtations with mobs also
tempered their embrace of the dead emperor.[20]

The Escoseses' political fortunes declined further in late 1827
as a result of a poorly coordinated armed revolt against the Victoria
government. Known as the Montaño Revolt, its instigators sought
the elimination of secret societies, the complete renovation of the
president's cabinet, and the expulsion of U.S. Minister Joel R.
Poinsett. The Escoseses had advocated all these actions in the congress and the press for months before the rebellion. Although the
rebels stated explicitly that they supported the present system of
government, the radical press made much of the fact that the rebellion coincided with the promulgation of further anti-Spanish legislation and they accused the rebels of monarchist objectives. The
revolt attracted few adherents in the army and received little popular support, despite the participation of the Independence War hero,
Vice President Nicolás Bravo. It lasted only several weeks, but the
revolt was nonetheless the most serious armed threat the new republic had seen so far. In its aftermath, the exile of forty-three leaders associated with the Escoseses dealt the movement a serious
setback.[21]

Mexico City buzzed with bitter debates over the fate of the
Montaño rebels and resident Spaniards in late 1827 and early 1828.
The moderate-radical schism widened to overshadow earlier lodge-
based affiliations. As the rancor spilled over from the press into
the streets, the city's officials grew concerned about the mobilizing
masses. In December 1827, reports reached the municipal council
that some individuals had incited the inhabitants of the small towns
around the capital to take up arms in support of a complete expulsion of all Spaniards. In February 1828, the Federal District governor asked the municipal council to organize a series of "honest
distractions" to "maintain tranquility" in the city during the upcoming Lenten season.[22]

In this intensifying partisan strife, the relative quiescence of
municipal elections remains a curious phenomenon that requires
exploration. After the exceedingly contentious congressional elections of 1826, it is striking to read reports in the major newspapers
that "tranquility reigned" in the December municipal elections and
that "the elections the day before yesterday have been the coldest
thing in the world." The following year voter turnout surpassed
twenty-seven thousand, a record for municipal elections, and radical hero Vicente Guerrero received more votes than any other can-

didate. Yet both *El Aguila Mexicana* and *El Sol* reported simply that the elections produced no controversies.[23]

Privately, some observers expressed greater concern. Carlos María de Bustamante noted in his diary that the election results provided great pleasure to the Yorkinos, and while all was calm on the outside, "God knows what will happen" when the primary electors met to select the new municipal council. Days later, after the incoming council members were chosen, Bustamante wrote that they were such indecent men that he would not sully his journal by writing their names. Worst of all, in their Jacobin impudence, the electors even considered appointing as alderman a black horse breaker who had admitted he would never be able to do the job. This was the most histrionic assessment of any municipal election during the second half of the decade, but its vitriol, unlike much of Bustamante's other caustic prose, did not seep into the public domain at the time.[24]

A number of factors explain this sharp contrast between municipal elections and the national political climate. The simplest explanation came from the editors of the partisan periodicals, who accounted for the municipal elections' tranquility in terms of greed. *El Sol* bluntly stated that congressional deputies received a salary of 3,000 pesos, while municipal council members did not, so none of the desperate climbers who heated up the congressional elections wanted to serve on the municipal council. *El Aguila Mexicana* agreed, noting that "when one does not want [something], two do not fight." Further explanation for the contrast between Mexico City's municipal and congressional elections lies in the nature of the two institutions themselves. The role of this institution in the capital stood in sharp contrast to the place of municipal office in smaller towns, where control of the municipal council meant the ability to direct community resources. In Mexico City, the municipal council had a vastly complex relationship with resources and other authorities. After the formation of the Federal District in 1824, the council then had to negotiate over key issues with the Federal District governor, a presidential appointee, who often had his own agenda. Furthermore, the municipal council had a dizzying array of administrative duties in this megalopolis, including law enforcement, hospital administration, and market oversight, and its members had few resources with which to comply with their mandate or with which they could build a political empire or a personal fortune. Their actions were under the constant and often antagonistic gaze of the governor or national political figures resident in the capital. As a result, many citizens hesitated to pursue council seats and often rejected the call to serve, insisting that financial, family, or medical problems outweighed their civic duties. When the municipal council got sucked further into the whirlpool of national politics in the 1830s, the national government's increasing interference in local affairs exacerbated the reluctance to serve.[25]

The relatively smooth functioning of municipal elections, even with huge voter turnout, attracted little comment at the time. Instead, moderates increasingly joined conservatives in advocating new legislation to fight growing mob rule, exemplified by the congressional elections and the expulsion campaign. Congressional deputies entertained and defeated proposed electoral reforms for the Federal District during the summer of 1828, eliciting cries that the incoming legislature would have to revisit the issue immediately upon assuming office. *El Aguila Mexicana's* editors conceded that elections expressed popular sovereignty most directly, but they demanded that the new legislature coming to office in 1829 take the necessary steps "to purify and characterize the voting mass, registering those who compose it, and giving some document or signal to individuals with which they could prove that they were in the free use of their citizens' rights."[26]

Calls for electoral reform joined other programs with roots in the increasing concern that the poor had declared a war against polite society. In contrast to the ill-fated electoral reform proposal, in the spring of 1828 the congress passed legislation to form a special tribunal to combat the capital's allegedly growing epidemic of vagrancy. Although complaints about the city's abundance of rogues and layabouts had a long history, it was only in the middle of the political mobilization of the city's masses that this separate legal institution was established. Vagrancy was a nebulous legal concept that could be applied in theory to any able-bodied man who refused to be a productive member of society. Used properly, the legislation could be directed precisely against the sector of the city's population that opponents thought provided the Yorkinos' electoral shock troops. In the early days of the new tribunal, it was expected that accused vagrants would be rounded up in raids on the city's saloons and gambling dens, which were seen as breeding grounds of vice and recruiting stations for the radicals. Vagrancy convictions would deny these folks the right to vote.[27]

The Vagrancy Tribunal failed to achieve these goals. The pursuit of vagrants was left to neighborhood officials who had conflicts of interest. As one alderman reported to the municipal council,

"Of my three auxiliaries, one has a café and the other a wine shop, and one cannot expect them to denounce those who contribute to their subsistence." The alderman also pointed out the ambiguity of the very concept of vagrancy. He noted that many of those arrested claimed to be skilled artisans suffering from an economic slump and not sloth. The low conviction rate for vagrants during this period, around 10 percent, reflected the contradictions of the entire enterprise. Sincere efforts to reduce crime were inextricably mixed with the political and social connections between city officials and the masses. As a result, the antivagrancy campaign was stillborn, and after several months, the tribunal stopped meeting regularly. Events during the next eighteen months would steel the resolve of the Decent Men to take control of the political process and the streets. Both electoral reform and antivagrancy measures emerged repeatedly in the following years.[28]

The Radicals' Pyrrhic Victory, 1828–29

As the summer of 1828 approached, all other issues facing the republic took a back seat to the upcoming presidential succession. Before the August congressional elections, both *El Sol* and *El Correo de la Federación Mexicana* endorsed candidates and excoriated their rivals' endorsements, but after the elections the papers published few comments on the incoming congressional personnel or the election results themselves. In contrast, the republic's first presidential succession consumed public attention and generated reams of commentary and hostile partisan rhetoric. Radicals rallied around the Independence War hero Vicente Guerrero, while disaffected Yorkinos and former Escoseses supported Minister of War Manuel Gómez Pedraza. A clear class and ethnic schism opened between supporters of the two candidates. In the woefully racist view of English visitor Mark Beaufoy, "All the Indians and Sambos and darker races of the Creoles, comprising at least eight-tenths of the nation, consider [Guerrero] as one of themselves, and look up to him as an idol." Gómez Pedraza's domestic partisans used explicit appeals to class fears and labeled Guerrero "the blind executor of the precepts of a mob of vile parasites," a gambler, and a thief. Moderates also portrayed radical leaders around Guerrero as selfish political climbers who placed their own ambition ahead of the common good and rewarded faithful lackeys with patronage positions to the detriment of national development.[29]

For their part, Guerrero's supporters expressed concern that a victory for Manuel Gómez Pedraza would paralyze the workshops of Mexico's artisans and destroy all hopes of prosperity for "sons of the Mexican nation." Most of their rhetoric was even more colorful. They portrayed Gómez Pedraza as an aspiring second emperor and a man unfit to shine Guerrero's boots. The rabidly pro-Guerrero *El Amigo del Pueblo* played the nationalist and populist cards simultaneously. Several weeks before the election, the paper's editors asserted that those who were anti-Guerrero "ceased to be Mexicans." They concluded that if the presidential election were determined by popular sentiment rather than the state legislatures, Guerrero, a distinguished hero of the Independence War, would be the next chief executive without a doubt.[30]

The way in which moderates attempted to invert the popular postures of the radicals provides an interesting caveat to any generalizations that can be made about factional discourse during the presidential campaign. Blunt anti-Spanish rhetoric was the forte of the radicals. Spanish money and opinion supported Gómez Pedraza, but in the heat of the partisan battle for hearts and minds in mid-1828, moderates also attempted to exploit popular anti-Spanish passions, albeit in subtler ways than the radicals. One pro–Gómez Pedraza pamphlet asserted that the Spanish secretly supported Guerrero because they knew he would cause much harm as president of Mexico. Some moderates also contested radical claims to a monopoly on federalism. The moderate press accused the radicals of betraying true federalism, since the York lodge operated as a centralized organism, dictating strategy to the provinces from the capital's grand lodge.[31]

During the preelection mudslinging, moderates began to lament the decline of genteel political discourse, even as their propagandists continued to produce ever more vituperation. Radicals, confident of their popularity, praised the torrid debate's salubrious effect on the national spirit. As the election approached, Mexico City's municipal council, the guardians of public order, grew increasingly concerned with the potential for unrest resulting from these intense animosities. On August 14, one council member reported that a "scandalous effervescence" permeated the city, produced, he claimed, by the journalistic rabble-rousing. His suggestion to introduce rigorous press censorship went unheeded, but his warning about the direction in which the conflict was moving proved prescient. Within days, Guerrero's supporters attempted to impose their own brand of censorship, as hundreds gathered at the offices of *El Aguila Mexicana* and *El Sol*, threatening to destroy the presses of both papers for their insults to Guerrero. A detachment of troops, whose commander told those gathered that they would achieve their goals only over his dead body, dispersed the crowd.[32]

With the support of provincial moderates and the old Scots' Rite coalition, Manuel Gómez Pedraza received a majority of votes in eleven state legislatures, while Guerrero won nine. Many of the legislatures voting for Gómez Pedraza had been formed prior to the major organizing efforts of the Yorkinos. The Federal District did not get a vote in the presidential succession. Even before the tally became official, reports that Gómez Pedraza had won circulated in the press. Within days of the election, General Antonio López de Santa Anna took up arms to protest the results. Santa Anna's reasons remain unclear, although many observers attributed the act to personal animosity between the president-elect and Santa Anna.

In most of the country, including the capital, a tense but generally quiet atmosphere prevailed in the first weeks of September. The first postelection disturbance of the peace in Mexico City looked as if it might occur on Independence Day. On September 15, the municipal council moved into secret sessions to discuss the trouble they saw brewing. Although the Santa Anna rebellion had not spread to the city, the council requested extra troops to keep order, because a rumor had reached them that the radicals had distributed money in the notoriously volatile San Pablo neighborhood in the hopes of organizing a crowd to run through the city shouting "Death to Guerrero and long live Viceroy Pedraza of Mexico and Ferdinand VII." Extra troops again ensured a tranquil Independence Day, but their presence only delayed the turmoil. While the old Scots' Rite Mason Pablo de la Llave announced in his surreal patriotic discourse that "all is peace, union, fraternity, and contentment," *El Sol* lamented that the dead heroes of the Independence War could only look down from heaven and weep over the sorry state of current affairs.[33]

Santa Anna slowly recruited adherents as the moderates attempted to solidify their victory. Santa Anna's revolt gave them a vehicle to label all radicals as traitors against the constitution. In the fall of 1828, the congress banned secret societies, then proceeded to trump up charges against José María Tornel, the York Federal District governor and Santa Anna ally who had played a central role in anti-Spanish agitation. Lorenzo de Zavala, then governor of

Mexico State, was also accused of subversion and went into hiding. The radical press responded with a reignited campaign against the Parianistas' victory. When President Victoria tried to use the threat of a Spanish invasion to unite the warring factions, his plan backfired, as radicals accused the Gómez Pedraza faction of complicity in the Spanish machinations. Armed revolt finally exploded in the capital at the end of November, as Lorenzo de Zavala reappeared and pro-Guerrero troops took the Acordada barracks, with its store of arms. It was only at this very late date that Vicente Guerrero himself joined the movement conducted in his name. After several brief skirmishes in the city, Gómez Pedraza chose to flee rather than defend his right to the presidency. The future of the government was in the hands of the rebels, who insisted that Guerrero be chosen by the incoming congress as the legitimate president.[34]

On December 4, in the shadow of Gómez Pedraza's capitulation and in a frenzy of popular and military resentment against the Spaniards and their alleged Mexican front men, a mob descended on the Parián market and pillaged its shops as well as a number of homes and businesses elsewhere in the city's center. Estimates of the number of participants in the riot range up to several thousand. The upheaval drove most people of means off the streets for several days, including the municipal council officers who were supposed to preserve public tranquility. Sporadic looting, particularly by the military detachment deployed to restore order, continued well after the riot subsided.[35]

The Parián riot became the great symbol of 1820s popular radicalism. Conservatives claimed that the Parián booty was offered as a reward to the poor for supporting the Acordada Revolt. The looting itself confirmed conservative fears of the relationship between popular political participation and social dissolution. Radicals on the other hand referred to the event as an understandable response to three hundred years of Spanish oppression and the repeated aristocratic conspiracies of the post-Independence era promulgated by those who survived off the sweat of the Mexican people. Zavala wrote a lengthy defense of himself, in which he denied accusations that he instigated the riot and maintained that the conservatives, who overestimated the size of the mob and the amount of property damage, had blown the entire event out of proportion.[36]

Assessing the events surrounding the Parián riot is made particularly difficult by the lack of primary documents that address the topic. No government investigations probed the event, and the municipal council records during the most heated period of conflict yield virtually nothing about the riot.[37] From the paltry data, confusion, and partisan accusations, several points do stand out. Most important, Mexico City's largest uprising in over one hundred years came about directly as a result of partisan politics. Material circumstances, such as the poor state of the economy, contributed to the frustration, as did longer-term resentments of the Spaniards and the merchant class, but these were all constants for most of the nineteenth century. Many among the elite saw the Parián riot as the inevitable culmination of the political enfranchisement of the urban poor. Regardless of their position on other issues, many of them resolved to reclaim the political realm for the country's Decent Men.

The riot and its aftermath unnerved the capital's municipal council members. Seeing a return to normal commerce as one way to move toward stability, the council ordered the city's taverns to reopen during the second week of December and they requested that merchants return immediately to their regular business practices. In February 1829 the council presented an alarming report to the Federal District governor describing the capital's fearful population, still hounded by thieves and rogue military regiments. The report explained that the justice system was completely ineffective. The courts were achieving only a 10 percent conviction rate, and the Vagrancy Tribunal did not even function. The city had no regular police patrols, leaving all decent residents at the mercy of criminals. The council presented a twenty-four-point plan of action that called for judicial and police reform, a version of urban renewal that required tearing down notorious dens of thieves, and the completion of the city's first census since Independence, so that the government might have some idea of what it was up against.[38] An elaborate plan to recapture the city, which included many of these reforms, was introduced after Guerrero was driven from office at the end of 1829. In the meantime, Guerrero's brief reign was marked by a severe fiscal crisis, constant grumbling from unpaid military regiments and allegedly overtaxed property holders and merchants, the continuing dilemma of the expulsion conflict, and the general crisis caused by polarized, class-based politics.

The class and racial composition of the president's support and the growing hostility his supporters displayed to Spaniards and the wealthy scandalized Guerrero's opponents. Amid rumors of an impending *lépero* revolt, the congress passed another expulsion decree, asserting that public opinion demanded it. As after the earlier expulsion decrees, the number of Spaniards forced from Mexico was limited. The large number of exemptions granted by the government caused a popular outcry and threats of violence, even against Guerrero. Pamphlets began to appear with such titles as "Either the Gachupines Go or Guerrero Will Fall," "Signal Agreed to for a General Riot and Massacre of Coyotes," "Now There Is No Remedy but to Put the Gachupines to the Knife," and "The Congress' Treason Will Be Avenged in Blood."[39]

Conversely, the new regime's economic policies garnered the resentment of the wealthy and contributed to fiscal uncertainty. In May 1829, Guerrero signed into law new tariff legislation, which included an outright ban on imports of inexpensive cotton textiles. His plan to solve the severe treasury crisis, designed by none other than Lorenzo de Zavala, proposed progressive taxes on property owners and merchants, demanded a forced loan of three million pesos from the state governments, and proposed a salary reduction for high-level civil and military employees.[40]

To further complicate matters, after years of speculation and rumors, Spanish troops invaded Mexico in the summer of 1829. The congress awarded Guerrero extraordinary powers during the invasion. For a short while, partisan strife subsided while the extent of the Spanish threat was assessed on all sides. As Independence Day approached, the fate of Santa Anna's expedition against the Spanish invaders was still unknown. Anti-Spanish violence had broken out in the city just prior to the invasion and threatened to accelerate, while Guerrero partisans wished to regain greater social peace in the capital now that they controlled the national government. On September 13, Federal District Governor Tornel published a decree noting the importance of the upcoming Independence Day festivities, given that "the execrable Spaniards have returned to profane the sacred ground of the republic." Tornel asserted that the invaders needed to see evidence of "the inextinguishable hatred" that the Mexican people felt for them. With the events of the last twelve months in mind, however, security precautions were foremost even for Tornel, who promised that the police would accept no alterations of public order under any pretext.[41]

The year's Independence Day speaker, Minister of Justice José Manuel de Herrera, suggested that he would like to address only the great events of the struggle for Independence, but this was impossible, since Mexico currently was threatened by a repeat of the atrocious offenses of Hernán Cortés. Herrera proceeded to enumerate a list of Spanish crimes against the Mexican people over the course of three hundred years and ended his short speech with praise for Guerrero and Santa Anna, assuring the crowd that they would emerge victorious in their struggle for federation or death. In fact, the Spanish expedition was small and unprepared for the travails that awaited them on the coast during the height of the fever season. Mexican troops defeated the Spaniards handily, and Santa Anna became a national hero.[42]

While anti-Spanish passions still burned brightly among the city's masses, Guerrero's opposition grew braver as it became clear that the reconquest was a fiasco. *El Sol's* columns maintained a relentless campaign against the rising anarchy they saw under Guerrero, claiming that the terrorists who led the mobs in December 1828 acted as dictators now and grabbed the country's wealth. Lorenzo de Zavala, Guerrero's finance minister, was the most common object of attack because of his alleged role in the Parián riot and his unpopular proposals to put the government's fiscal house in order, but radicals in other prominent positions were reviled as well. The opposition press constantly reminded the public that Mexico was now run by "mixed-race, illiterate whoremongers" and that there were only three types of radicals: "bad, worse, and the worst."[43]

Guerrero's opponents achieved partial victories in the fall of 1829, driving Zavala from office and forcing Guerrero to request that U.S. Minister Joel Poinsett leave the country. These achievements were small compared to the broader goals of remaking Mexican politics in a less radical-popular mold. Efforts to do so grew in intensity after Guerrero received extraordinary powers during the Spanish invasion. The malcontents, led by recently returned exiles from the Montaño Revolt, coalesced into armed pronouncements against the government in mid-November. Their troops took to the field with cries of "Long live centralism" and "Death to the *negro* Guerrero." By early December, Guerrero's opponents published the Jalapa Plan and invited Santa Anna and Vice President Anastasio Bustamante to lead the revolt. Santa Anna demurred, but Bustamante accepted the charge. The rebels publicly proclaimed allegiance to the 1824 Constitution, although the rebellion's leaders had conservative and centralist tendencies.[44]

Even during the revolt, municipal elections sparked few outcries over breaches of decorum. The only complaint sent to the municipal council after the elections involved the campaign tactics of one over-zealous candidate in Santa Ana parish. The parish electoral official reported that this candidate had pursued office through subterfuge and distributed brandy to the voters. In this, the last election before a major reform designed to keep the masses away from the polls, neither electoral officials nor the press had any harsher criticisms, in spite of the size of the turnout, which, at about thirteen thousand votes, was more than twice the number of votes cast in any municipal elections in the years prior to the rise of the Yorkinos.[45] National political upheaval obscured this impressive feat.

President Guerrero requested and received permission to lead government troops against the rebellion. He left Mexico City in early December. The Senate, in which a majority now supported the rebels, refused to meet in special session, but the Chamber of Deputies convened to elect José María Bocanegra as interim President.[46] Shortly after Guerrero's departure, the capital appeared to be on the verge of class warfare. According to the minutes of a secret municipal council meeting on December 13, some councilors expressed fear that events reminiscent of the Parián riot would occur. The city government designated a secure meeting place from which "honorable citizens" could defend themselves in the event that the masses rose up.[47] Military action preempted the popular movement. While Guerrero led his troops off to engage his opponents, a garrison inside the city, led by General Luis Quintanar, attacked the National Palace, declared the present government illegally constituted, and secured the city for the rebels. With the congress out of session, the Government Council, composed primarily of pro-rebel senators, claimed constitutional authority and quickly named a three-person interim executive, whose most prominent member was conservative stalwart Lucas Alamán. With most of the army and the elite now against him, Guerrero chose to return to his hacienda in the countryside rather than to engage his opponents. On December 31, 1829, Vice President Anastasio Bustamante entered Mexico City to take over the government. Soon thereafter the Senate and Chamber of Deputies proclaimed Guerrero incapable of governing, Bustamante assumed the presidency, and the campaign of the Decent Men began in earnest.

Notes

1. Zavala, *Ensayo histórico*, 257–64.
2. *Reglamentos de la r.l. # 3, titulada la independencia mexicana* (Mexico City: n.p., 1826).

3. Luis Alberto de la Garza, "Hombres de bien, demagogos y revolución social en la primera República," *Historias* 15 (October–December 1986): 49.

4. *El Aguila Mexicana*, August 27, 1825; "Cómo se celebró la primera vez el aniversario de la Independencia," *El Nacional*, September 16, 1893, reprinted in *Boletín Oficial del Consejo Superior de Gobierno del Distrito Federal*, vol. 13, no. 22 (September 14, 1909); Interior Ministry to Municipal Council, AACM, vol. 1067, exp. 2.

5. "Cómo se celebró"; *El Aguila Mexicana*, September 17, 1828.

6. Juan Wenceslao Barquera, "Oración patriótica," in *La conciencia nacional y su formación: Discursos cívicos septembrinos (1825–1871)*, ed. Ernesto de la Torre Villar (Mexico City: Universidad Nacional Autónoma de México, 1988), 21–30; *El grito de libertad en el pueblo de Dolores* (Mexico City, 1825); Enrique Plasencia de la Parra, *Independencia y nacionalismo a la luz del discurso conmemorativo (1825–1867)* (Mexico City: Consejo Nacional para la Cultura y las Artes, 1991), 39–40.

7. *El Sol*, September 16, 1825; *El Aguila Mexicana*, September 16–18, 1825.

8. Costeloe, *La primera República*, 63–66.

9. *El Aguila Mexicana*, August 18, 1826.

10. *El Sol*, July 1, 1826.

11. *Representación de varios electores a la Junta General hecha al Congreso de Estado* (n.p. [1826]); Costeloe, *La primera República*, 81–86; Hale, *Mexican Liberalism*, 85, 101–3.

12. *El Sol*, August 21, 22, and 28, September 1, 1826; *La Verdad Desnuda*, no. 2, March 1833; *El Aguila Mexicana*, August 23, 1826; *La Voz de la Patria*, March 15, 1830; Zavala, *Ensayo histórico*, 317, 326; Costeloe, *La primera República*, 81; Harold Dana Sims, *The Expulsion of Mexico's Spaniards* (Pittsburgh: University of Pittsburgh Press, 1990), 8.

13. Records of Investigation, AGN, Gobernación (Casa Amarilla), leg. 55, exp. 4; AGN, Gobernación, Sin Sección, leg. 1586 (2), exp. 1.

14. *Ilustración sobre la sociedad de francmasones* (Mexico City: Imp. Mariano Ontiveros, 1822); *Acábense los yorkinos y salvemos a la patria* (Mexico City: Imp. Mariano Ontiveros, 1827); Juan Ignacio Villaseñor Cervantes, *Algo de masones, o sea diálogo entre un filósofo y una maestra de amiga* (Mexico City: Imp. del Aguila, 1826); idem, *Algo de masones, o sea segunda parte del diálogo entre Doña Tecla y Don Canuto* (Mexico City: Imp. del Aguila, 1827); *Se denuncian al buen juicio las sociedades secretas y caballeros masones* (Mexico City: Imp. Alejandro Valdes, 1826); *En nuestras instituciones no caben los francmasones* (Mexico City: Imp. por José Ximeno, 1826).

15. *El Aguila Mexicana*, October 8, 1827.

16. *Discurso pronunciado en el Senado por el ciudadano Cañedo, en la sesión del 24 de abril, contra el proyecto de ley que presentó el ciudadano Cevallos para la estinción de las juntas secretas* (Mexico City: Imp. del Aguila, 1826); L. C., *Un nuevo plan de revolución: Infamias de los escoseses que conspiran en la patria, o sea, respuesta al impreso titulado infamias de los yorkinos* (Mexico City: Imp. de la ex-Inquisición, 1827); Joel R. Poinsett, *Esposición de la conducta política de los Estados Unidos, para con las nuevas repúblicas de América* (Mexico City: Imp. de la ex-Inquisición, 1827); *El Aguila Mexicana*, August 25, 29, and September 5, 1826; "El Payo de Rosario" [Pablo Villavicencio], *Manifiesto del payo de Rosario a sus compatriotas, o sea suplemento a la memoria del Señor Iturbide* (Mexico City: Imp. de la ex-Inquisición, 1827).

17. Sims, *The Expulsion*, 19–31; Flores Caballero, *Counterrevolution*, 96; Costeloe, *La primera República*, 87–113, 92–96.

18. "An Impartial British Observer," *A Letter to a Member of the British Parliament, on Events Civil and Military of the Past and Present Year in Mexico, to the Period of the Banishment of General Bravo, Ex-Vice President of the Mexican Republic* (n.p.: Imp. Cornelius C. Sebring, 1828); L. C., *Un nuevo plan de revolución*.

19. Tenenbaum, *Politics of Penury*, 29.

20. *El Sol*, September 27, 1827; *El Aguila Mexicana*, September 27, 1827; Costeloe, *La primera República*, 131–32, 157–58.

21 . Costeloe, *La primera República*, 117, 137–66; Flores Caballero, *Counterrevolution*, 116–17; Sims, *The Expulsion*, 27; Arrangoiz, *México desde 1808*, 346–47.

22. Municipal Council Secret Session, December 18, 1827, AACM, vol. 289a; Municipal Council Minutes, February 6, 1828, AACM, vol. 148a.

23. *El Aguila Mexicana*, December 10 and 16, 1826; *El Sol*, December 10 and 12, 1826.

24. Bustamante, "Diario Histórico," entries for December 9 and 13, 1827, BNAH, microfilm, roll 4.

25. *El Sol*, December 9 and 12, 1826; *El Aguila Mexicana*, December 16, 1826; Rodríguez Kuri, "Política e institucionalidad," 51–94; Gortari, "Políitica y administración," 166–83.

26. *El Aguila Mexicana*, July 9, 1828.

27. Most of the records of the Vagrancy Tribunal are located in AACM, vol. 4151–4155. For discussions of vagrancy law and its application during this period, see Shaw, "Poverty and Politics," 266–309; Frederick J. Shaw, "The Artisan in Mexico City," in *El trabajo y los trabajadores en la historia de México*, ed. E. C. Frost, M. C. Meyer, and J. Z. Vázquez (Mexico City: El Colegio de México, 1979), 399–418; Silva M. Arrom, "Vagos y méndigos en la legislación mexicana, 1745–1845," in *Memoria del IV Congreso de Historia del Derecho Mexicano* (Mexico City: Universidad Nacional Autónoma de México, 1988), 1:71–87; idem, "Documentos para el estudio del Tribunal de Vagos, 1828–1848: Respuesta a una problemática sin solución," *Anuario Mexicano de Historia del Derecho* 1 (1989): 215–35; José Antonio Serrano Ortega, "Levas, Tribunal de Vagos y Ayuntamiento: La Ciudad de México, 1825–1835," in *Ciudad de México: Instituciones, actores sociales, y conflicto político, 1774–1932*, ed. Carlos Illades and Ariel Rodríguez Kuri (Mexico City: El Colegio de Michoacán and Universidad Autónoma Metropolitana, 1996): 131–54; Sonia Pérez Toledo, "Los vagos de la Ciudad de México y el Tribunal de Vagos en la primera mitad del siglo xix," *Secuencia* 27 (1993): 27–42; Warren, "Entre la participación," 37–54.

28. Alderman to Municipal Council, AACM, vol. 4151, exp. 5.

29. *El Sol*, August 1, 1828; *El Sol* did not report the electoral turnout, for example. Beaufoy, *Mexican Illustrations*, 127; Flores Caballero, *Counterrevolution*, 118; *Oigan las legislaturas los proyectos de Madrid* (Mexico City: Imp. José Márquez, 1828); *Estado político de la República al tiempo de la elección del Presidente* (Mexico City: Imp. de Galván, 1828); *Colección de artículos selectos sobre política, sacados del Aguila Mexicana del año de 1828* (Mexico City: Imprenta de Galván, 1828).

30. José Antonio Mejía to Manuel Reyes Veramendi, August 3, 1828, BNAH, Bustamante Collection, vol. 21, doc. 54; El Coyote Manso, *Manuel*

Gómez Pedraza, segundo Emperador de los mexicanos (Mexico City: Imp. de las Escalerillas, 1828); *El Amigo del Pueblo*, August 6, 1828.
31. Sims, *The Expulsion*, 43–44; *Oigan las legislatures*; *El Aguila Mexicana*, August 14 and 22, 1828, quoted in Costeloe, *La primera República*, 180.
32. *El Amigo del Pueblo*, August 6, 1828; Municipal Council Minutes, August 14, 1828, AACM, vol. 148a; Federal District Governor to Secretary of Interior and External Relations, August 17, 1828, AGN, Gobernación 1-79, caja 1, exp. 3.
33. Sims, *The Expulsion*, 44; Costeloe, *La primera República*, 189; Municipal Council Minutes, September 15, 1828, AACM, vol. 148a; Municipal Council Secret Sessions, September 15, 1828, AACM, vol. 290a; Pablo de la Llave, "Discurso Patriótico . . . de 1828," in *La conciencia nacional*, ed. Torre Villar, 53–62.
34. Costeloe, *La primera República*, 199–205.
35. Municipal Council Minutes, December 9 and 13, 1828, AACM, vol. 148a; Silvia M. Arrom, "Popular Politics in Mexico City: The Parián Riot, 1828," *Hispanic American Historical Review* 68, no. 2 (May 1988): 245–68.
36. José Ignacio Paz, *Estupendo grito en la Acordada* (Mexico City: Imp. del Correo, 1829); Lorenzo de Zavala, *Juicio imparcial sobre los acontecimientos de México en 1828 y 1829* (New York: C. S. Winkle, n.d.; reprint ed., Mexico City: Imp. de Galván, n.d.); Sims, *The Expulsion*, 51; *Representación del comercio solicitando una indemnización de las pérdidas que sufrió en los primeros días de diciembre de 1828, por conducto y con el correspondiente apoyo del exmo. Ayuntamiento, del Gobierno del Distrito y del Supremo Gobierno, al Congreso general de los Estados Unidos Mexicanos* (Mexico City: Imp. del Correo, 1829). Twenty years later, some merchants were still fighting for compensation. See the reprint of the above document, entitled *Primera representación del comercio solicitando . . .* (Mexico City: Imp. Vicente García Torres, 1849).
37. Arrom, "Popular Politics," 250.
38. Proclamation, December 14, 1828, AGN, Gobernación, Sin Sección, leg. 107, exp. 7; Municipal Council Secret Sessions, February 13 and 14, 1829, AACM, vol. 291a.
39. Yorkinos suggested that "popular agitation" against Guerrero, including these pamphlets, was part of a Spanish plot. See Sims, *The Expulsion*, 60, 72, 104–7; Costeloe, *La primera República*, 220.
40. Robert A. Potash, *Mexican Government and Industrial Development in the Early Republic: The Banco de Avío* (Amherst: University of Massachusetts Press, 1983), 28–31; Tenenbaum, *Politics of Penury*, 35; Costeloe, *La primera República*, 235.
41. Sims, *The Expulsion*, 142–143; AACM, vol. 1067, exp. 6, September 13, 1829.
42. J. M. Herrera, "Oración patriótica . . . de 1829," in *La conciencia nacional*, ed. Torre Villar, 63–70; Wilfrid Hardy Calcott, *Santa Anna: The Story of an Enigma Who Once Was Mexico* (Norman: University of Oklahoma Press, 1936), 76; Costeloe, *La primera República*, 223–24.
43. Costeloe, *La primera República*, 238; *Nuevos diálogos entre el cohetero y el tamborillero* (Mexico City: Imp. Alejandro Valdés, 1829).
44. Guardino, *Peasants, Politics*, 130; Costeloe, *La primera República*, 242–47; Anna, *Forging Mexico*, 228; Calcott, *Santa Anna*, 82.

45. Santa Anna parish report, December 4, 1829, AGN, Ayuntamientos, vol. 13, 247; Election Returns, December 6, 1829, AACM, vol. 862, exp. 12.

46. Costeloe, *La primera República*, 244–45; Arrangoiz, *México desde 1808*, 353.

47. Municipal Council Secret Sessions, December 13, 1829, AACM, vol. 291a.

5

Decent Men and Jacobins, 1830–1834

The leaders of the movement that unseated Vicente Guerrero developed a critique of Mexico's political system based on the premise that instability, crime, and fiscal uncertainty were all linked to radical politics. The Bustamante administration turned this supposition into a reform program, placing a high priority on centralizing decision making and cordoning off the political arena from popular agitation. These efforts were limited at first, because many who had opposed the Guerrero regime had not yet abandoned their support of the 1824 federalist Constitution. After Bustamante's regime crumbled under pressure from federalist strongholds and disaffected military leaders in 1832, political factions mutated once again. In 1833, acting President Valentín Gómez Farías, supported by a newly elected congress, tried to rekindle radical politics. The new generation of federalists also incorporated into their program liberal objectives that encompassed unprecedented attacks on the privileges of both the Church and the military.

Disaffection with these reformist efforts precipitated a renewed and more explicit assault on federalism and the 1824 Constitution. Chastened by the experiences of 1828–29 and 1833–34, many formerly moderate federalists distanced themselves from the radicals and the popular classes, embracing a discourse positing that order preceded progress. These moderates joined more conservative elements in creating new political structures based on the assumption that the popular political mobilizations of the previous two decades had been an obstacle to both order and progress. The new rules of contention were formalized into a constitution written over the course of 1836 and introduced with great fanfare in the early days of 1837, but the process began in the spring of 1834, when Antonio López de Santa Anna suspended the radical congress and drove Valentín Gómez Farías from office.

Anastasio Bustamante and the
Decent Men, 1830–1832

A new U.S. chargé d'affaires, Anthony Butler, arrived in Mexico
during the upheavals of December 1829. Six months later, he delivered a favorable assessment of the new regime. Butler had quickly
overcome his fears that the Bustamante regime would be more in-
clined toward British interests than those of the United States. He
grew confident that the administration would favor the United
States in its commercial relations and would perhaps even be willing to discuss terms for the cession of Texas. By June 1830, Butler
reported that the national government had secured control of the
political situation, principally as a result of the efforts of Lucas
Alamán, "one of the ablest men in the republic."[1]

Mexican observers also emphasized the role of individuals and
the intense personal rivalries of these years, but social and political factors also contributed to outcomes. Although there were no
durable party structures or discipline, and individuals often
changed beliefs and affinities, it is still possible to discern ideological tendencies that transcended personality and historical forces
at work beyond ego clashes. The ascendant Bustamante regime,
led by Minister of External and Interior Relations Alamán, argued
that radicals had trampled on the new nation's social contract by
unleashing the rabble, purchasing votes, and placing shortsighted
partisan candidates in office. According to this reasoning, construction of political order and social peace required a stronger central
government and greater efforts to remove the mob from politics.
To label this faction simply "centralist" or "conservative" would
be problematic, since the regime had never proposed a complete
overhaul of federalist institutions.[2] Supporters of the regime generally did not couch their appeal in terms of political systems, but
in terms of culture and class, "a war of civilization against barbar-
ism, of property against thieves, of order against anarchy."[3] This
language potentially could attract the majority of Mexico's elite,
most of whom had grown cautious over the extent of popular mobilization, the accelerated pace of change, and the chronic difficulties in transferring national authority peacefully. The early successes
of the Bustamante regime were based on the complex relationship
between federalists and the Guerrero legacy. While radicals cried
out that Guerrero's opponents, "the miserable usurpers," had to
be removed from power by armed force if necessary, many moderates accepted the Bustamante regime tentatively as an alternative

to the economic difficulties and popular upheaval of the past five years.[4]

Aware of this ambivalence, pro-Bustamante propagandists walked a fine line. They pledged the regime's commitment to the 1824 Constitution, yet excoriated Guerrero's anarchist partisans for sullying federalism. They urged caution on the expulsion issue, although they were quick to defend themselves from charges that they were "*Gachupín*-ized." At times, they even employed the popular rhetorical devices of their opponents. Lucas Alamán himself attacked one of the regime's loudest critics as an inferior, "adopted Mexican," who had served the country poorly. Another Bustamante supporter appealed to the "noble artisan class" and honest workers to defend the regime against the plague threatened by the radicals. Progovernment supporters plastered buildings around town with signs that railed, "Death to Yorkinos."[5]

In general, though, most Bustamante supporters would recoil at the suggestion that the regime had close ties to the masses, and the new regime was confident that it could sway key moderates with its appeal to a politics of class affinities, the cohesion among Decent Men. Early in 1830, Lucas Alamán wrote that "bad [deputies in the congress] are few, and it would not be impossible to convert them all into good ones." This conversion process proceeded through early policies appealing to those who associated the Guerrero years with economic and social uncertainty. Military spending increased and promotions were lavished on the officer corps. Taxes on property and luxury items decreased. The congress established the national Banco de Avío to promote industrialization by providing loans at favorable interest rates to the administration's supporters. The Bustamante government also attempted to dampen political effervescence and consolidate its control for the longer term through electoral reform, administrative centralization, and a renewed campaign in the capital against vagrancy.[6]

After the overheated politics of the Guerrero era, odds increased dramatically that electoral reform would pass the congress. José María Luis Mora, in some ways the quintessence of moderate liberal thought in the pre-Reform era, expressed his position on elections in an article for the newspaper *El Observador* in April 1830. Mora blamed Mexico's instability in part on the misguided notion of equality that dominated radical politics. He wrote that the worst manifestation of the 1820s political debacle was the "scandalous profusion" of rights that had brought "even the lowest classes of society" into the political process and produced "horrible elections."

Mora demanded that the eligibility to vote and hold office be restricted to a much smaller segment of the population by means of
an income requirement for the suffrage and office holding. The
editors of conservative periodicals echoed Mora's appeal. Even
Lorenzo de Zavala, champion of the popular classes in the 1820s,
by the early 1830s had become convinced of the need for a more
restrictive franchise. To emphasize the priority that electoral reform
should occupy in the spring congressional session, one periodical
rehearsed the alleged Yorkino excesses of the 1826 Mexico City elections in all their sordid details of bribery, intimidation, and fraud.[7]

In July 1830, congress passed a major electoral reform for the
Federal District and territories, designed to serve as a model for
state legislation. The suggestion that the suffrage be restricted by
property or income was not implemented at this time. The reasons
for this decision are still a mystery, given the lack of both public
and private accounts of the deliberation process, although other
innovations were implemented to restrict access to the ballot box.
These restrictions held the potential to change electoral politics significantly. The basic electoral unit for the Federal District was
changed from the fourteen parishes to 245 city wards (*manzanas*) of
approximately four to eight hundred inhabitants each. The municipal council would designate an electoral commissioner for each
ward to conduct a neighborhood census, distribute ballots to eligible voters, and supervise the polls on election day. The Church
and its priests remained a major presence in elections and broader
politics, and little in the new regime's other measures would suggest that the reform was designed as a way to secularize the election process. Rather, the major goal of the reform was to short-circuit
the mass electoral politics of the 1820s. Parish-based elections meant
that political factions could rally large numbers of people to a small
group of candidates by printing reams of prefabricated ballots and
recruiting election day mobs. Under the new system, each of the
245 wards would have its own primary election, which effectively
prevented the mass production of printed candidate lists and the
possibility of gathering large groups at the polls. The commissioners were charged with reducing multiple voting by individuals and
weeding out ineligible voters. They easily could deny ballots to
whomever they chose using the law's vague statement that the suffrage was open only to those men who made an honest living and
who had been residents of the ward for more than one year. The
distribution of ballots well before election day meant that electoral
officials were no longer making decisions about voter eligibility

amid the election-day chaos at the polls. Anyone denied a ballot had the right to appeal, but great individual initiative and bureaucratic wrangling were required to overcome an electoral official's decision.[8]

The *Registro Oficial*, the government newspaper controlled by Lucas Alamán, proclaimed that the new law would render it difficult for parties to gain control of the polls through the use of printed lists and mobs. The proregime press joined the chorus of praise for the reform. *El Sol* noted that the new legislation ended with "one blow the vices and scandalous abuses" of the old electoral system and suggested that order and decency might now replace the "sordid intrigues and dark tricks" of the past. This upbeat assessment was repeated after the fall's congressional elections, in which all the seats in the Chamber of Deputies and one-half the Senate were contested. The *Registro Oficial* of October 2 reported the results of the primary elections ward by ward, noting both the total number of votes cast at most wards and the number of votes received by the winners. The editors argued that the number of votes cast for a wide variety of losers clearly indicated that the elections were free and open. The regime's supporters lauded the results, although they suggested that, because of the complexity of the new system and the ambiguity of certain aspects of the law, a degree of fine-tuning was still necessary. Government officials and others offered suggestions for altering the demarcation of electoral precincts, the order of voting for secondary elections, and the language used to define voter eligibility.[9]

The limited quantitative data on voter turnout in Mexico City provide some clues to the early satisfactions of the Decent Men. For these first congressional elections, the number of votes reported for 200 of the city's 245 wards totaled close to 12,500, a dramatic reduction in the number of votes compared to the congressional elections at the height of Yorkino mobilization in the 1820s. Bustamante's supporters, including a substantial number of clergy, won most of the congressional seats. Municipal elections continued to follow their own trajectory and logic. The number of votes cast in the 1830 municipal council elections (12,218) approached that of the congressional elections a few months earlier. Turnout was only 6 percent lower than that in the municipal elections of 1829 (13,028). By 1831, turnout increased to 12,581, only 3.5 percent lower than for 1829. Each time, the elections ran very smoothly. In 1830 only 14 wards did not hold elections. It is unclear why there were no elections in these wards, but the municipal council fined at least one electoral commissioner for failing to do his job properly. The following year, only 7 wards failed to hold elections. After the 1830 municipal council elections, the *Registro Oficial* noted that the new electoral system had indeed produced great order, although the editors cautioned that the public seemed increasingly apathetic about the electoral process itself. The editors suggested that this might have been due to the public's sense that the municipal council was primarily an administrative institution rather than a representative legislative body, and hence less worthy of attention. Readers were then reminded of the importance of good administration and encouraged to take an interest in municipal affairs and elections, but it was reiterated that the municipal council was in fact an institution with a highly restricted mandate.[10]

In an unsuspected way, the new electoral law dramatically changed the role of the municipal council in national politics, which contributed in the coming years to a growing crisis of legitimacy and increased tensions between the municipal and national governments. Since the advent of popular elections in Mexico City in 1812, the municipal council had been responsible for organizing elections, but the 1830 law shifted its role in the process, because the council members were now responsible for selecting the 245 electoral commissioners who served as key political brokers in national as well as local elections. Shortly after the first municipal elections under the 1830 law, the Federal District governor reported that in many wards the commissioners served as directors of the polls on election day and coincidentally won the elections. The following year, at least 45 percent of the primary election winners had been electoral commissioners. Year after year, the sources reveal the commissioners' role in influencing electoral outcomes. Their importance was not lost on factional leaders. As a result, the selection of commissioners became a hotly contested issue, and the potential role of the municipal council in national political affairs increased. In later years, the vision of the municipal council as an administrative body somehow shielded from broader political turmoil was shattered completely.[11]

Tensions between the municipal council elected before the fall of Guerrero and the national government expressed themselves as the Bustamante regime moved to centralize state functions further, and both the regime and the military hierarchy questioned the municipal government's dedication on a number of fronts more openly. Minister of External and Interior Relations Lucas Alamán denounced the municipal councils of the 1820s for their role in "having converted Mexico City into an asylum and shield for criminals." Alamán promised that his government would always be steadfast in its campaign to eliminate the criminal element, even if faced with resistance from city officials. A national government interested in centralizing authority and controlling the masses joined forces with a military hungry for recruits to pressure the municipal council for an increase in the yield of poor residents for the military levy and allowing the military and national government to participate directly in the recruitment of idlers for the ranks of the army. The disdain with which national figures held local officeholders filtered into the quotidian interactions among military officers, the Federal District governor, and council members. The latter were insulted regularly and their authority as legal and political figures questioned. Chronic fiscal problems brought threats of work stoppages from unpaid public employees, increasing tensions within the city and raising further cries of municipal incompetence or malfeasance. Broader economic malaise and a lack of confidence in the public treasury worried both producers and consumers in the spring of 1830, as merchants threatened to refuse copper coin as payment for goods. The Federal District governor reported to the municipal council his sense that "los miserables" threatened to upset public order and demanded prompt action to defuse any trouble.[12]

As the Decent Men began their efforts to rewire the circuitry of political practice, the themes of reconciliation, continuity, and order emerged as their leitmotivs in the public discourse over the national holidays of 1830 to 1832. Although the program of events in 1830 contained no great innovations, the progovernment press admonished Mexicans to maintain their maturity during the celebrations. The presence of several patrols of regular army troops precluded any attempts to seize the occasion for radical rabble-rousing. On the afternoon of September 16, Francisco Manuel Sánchez de Tagle, who soon became the soul of the centralist reform program, stepped forward to deliver a civic sermon. The recent debacle of the 1829 Spanish invasion still fresh in his mind, Sánchez de Tagle delivered a harsh condemnation of Spanish colonial rule, and called Mexico's Independence an end to "slavery." Then he skillfully limned the goals of Mexico's heroes, who "wanted us to be free, but not libertines or anarchists." He continued with a veiled critique of the expulsion movement and made a direct attack on radical patronage fever. He ended with a plea for union, morality, and civic virtue and suggested that Independence Day be known henceforth as the "Day of Fraternal Reconciliation."[13]

In keeping with this theme of reconciliation, the patriotic commission of 1830 collected funds to pay for the return passage to Mexico of the widows and children of exiled Spaniards. Also at this time, the figure of Agustín de Iturbide began to creep into the festivities again as a symbol of reconciliation and order, although events in 1831 revealed the volatility of public rituals. During the 1831 celebrations of September 16, a portrait of Iturbide appeared along with a poem demanding justice for his memory. When rains forced the cancellation of the fireworks scheduled for that afternoon, the organizing committee announced that they would be rescheduled for September 27, the day that the Army of the Three Guarantees marched into Mexico City in 1821. The decision provoked disturbances throughout the city by those who interpreted the decision as an insult to Father Hidalgo's memory. The fireworks display was canceled again, and finally occurred in October. A small group gathered unofficially on September 27 to raise their voices to the memory of the deceased creole Emperor. By the next year, the featured Independence Day orator completely removed the veil of silence about Iturbide's role and legacy. José Domínguez Manso was a Supreme Court justice and an Iturbidist who, like many other former supporters of the hero of Iguala, had abandoned the popular wing of that coalition. Domínguez devoted a large part of his oration to justifying Iturbide's return to the patriotic pantheon. He departed from the standards of recent orations, which made from time to time passing references to the hero of Iguala who went astray. Instead, in this short discourse, references to Iturbide's achievements occupy almost one-third of the printed text. The speaker noted that, although Hidalgo had sown the seeds of Independence, Iturbide had nourished the crop. He concluded that the "memory of September 16, 1810, united to that of the 27 of that same month of the year 1821" should be the bond that holds the nation together.[14]

Although Independence Day orators might speak of shared purpose, actions revealed these as empty words. Armed resistance movements broke out in the months after Bustamante took office, as local populations responded to the new regime's ongoing interventions in state and local political affairs. The most important of these occurred in Michoacán and in the south, where a guerrilla war, led primarily by Juan Alvarez and Isidro Montes de Oca, delayed the new regime's consolidation for over a year. In early 1831, events took a dramatic turn, as Francisco Picaluga, an Italian merchant in the government's employ, kidnapped Vicente Guerrero and delivered him to military authorities, who tried, condemned, and executed the Independence War hero and former president in a speedy and suspicious court-martial. The circumstances under which Guerrero was captured and executed would return to haunt the regime's key figures for years to come, and his death became a rallying cry for radicals in the opposition. In the short term, the regime bought some time, as the war in the south stalled after the Guerrero assassination and most of the key rebel leaders accepted amnesties. Juan José Codallos, leader of the rebel movement in Michoacán, did not. He, too, was captured and executed.[15]

In 1831, a vocal opposition coalesced on a different front. Inside the legislative chambers, Andrés Quintana Roo and Manuel Crescencio Rejón attempted to reorganize old Yorkinos into a more effective opposition. In addition, to combat the proregime media, several antigovernment periodicals opened, including *El Fénix de la Libertad* (The Phoenix of Liberty), which began publication in December 1831. The opposition held some hope that legislative pressure and the electoral process could achieve their goals, even though the Bustamante government employed subterfuge and repression to counter parliamentary efforts to block its program. It harassed radical leaders, suppressed the federalist press, and formed a spy network to monitor opposition political activities. The regime also purged Yorkinos at the state level. Eleven states saw all or part of their legislatures removed, several governors were forced from office, state employees were dismissed, and attempts were made to suppress the civic militias, the armed bastions of federalism.[16]

At the end of 1831, key federalist politicians decided to pursue a new strategy. They approached regular military officers, who they hoped would join the struggle against Bustamante for reasons of institutional, political, or personal interest. In early January 1832, Antonio López de Santa Anna accepted the call to arms in Veracruz, although much of the financing for the revolt came from the federalist stronghold of Zacatecas. In correspondence with Bustamante, Santa Anna argued that he entered the fray only as a mediator who wanted to avoid wider upheaval by persuading Bustamante to shuffle his cabinet, which would help all of Mexico to avoid a repeat of 1829, "when the perverse ministers of President Guerrero brought the country to ruin." Others in the opposition had a more ambitious agenda, so that even when the Bustamante government attempted to preempt the rebellion by jettisoning cabinet members, including the key conservative Lucas Alamán, the uprising did not cease. As summer approached, some in the opposition hung their hopes on a constitutional transfer of power through the presidential elections scheduled for that fall. A potential political rapprochement might have been achieved then, as a coalition from various factions began to rally around the former Scots' Rite moderate, General Manuel Mier y Terán. His suicide in early July, which many blamed at least in part on his depression over Mexico's political situation, shattered this hope.[17]

In the fall of 1832, the armed conflict intensified. President Bustamante himself assumed control of the military effort to crush the rebellion, while in the capital the government's political opponents were harassed, arrested, even killed. The editors of *El Fénix de la Libertad* held on long enough to condemn the theft of the fall's congressional elections by "Picaluganos," that is, Guerrero's assassins. They described one of the newly elected deputies from the Federal District as a priest who should have remained "on the grounds of his parish, preaching, teaching Christian doctrine to children, and confessing nuns." The other deputy "is a poor man who has elected the path of hypocrisy in search of fortune: a plebeian with aristocratic aspirations, an ignoramus with pretensions of being a learned man of letters." Four days later, "tyranny's henchmen arrived with an order from the governor to turn over our keys," and publication was suspended.[18]

In the provinces, opposition forces won a string of victories, culminating in Bustamante's defeat in early December. Later that month, the principal battlefield protagonists signed the Treaty of Zavaleta. Although the agreement called for Manuel Gómez Pedraza to return as interim president until new elections were called early in 1833, the treaty was primarily an agreement among military factions. Santa Anna, with a strong armed following and continued popular acclaim as the hero of Tampico, was clearly the country's most important political figure at the time, and as much as some in the civilian opposition might not entirely trust Santa Anna, more of them felt that once peace and federalism were restored, they would be able to control the military and the increasingly influential Veracruz caudillo. [19]

The Radical Experiment, 1833–1834

In January 1833, Santa Anna entered Mexico City, greeted by an elaborate procession. Several large floats carried symbols of the victorious coalition: anti-Spanish fervor, federalism, and military heroism. One float depicted Santa Anna's triumph against the Spanish at Tampico. A second float anthropomorphized the Homeland clasping the 1824 Constitution. A third paid tribute to "Honor, Fame, and Abundance." The fourth float reinforced the theme of federalism, carrying twenty-one young women who represented the twenty states, and yet one nation, which constituted Mexico.[20] Popular music and verse reinforced the messages:

> Play the drums and bugles
> Santa Anna's armies
> If they don't leave today, then they will tomorrow
> And who? The *Gachupines*[21]

Santa Anna, at the peak of his popularity, easily won the support of enough state legislatures to secure the presidency in early March, while the radical federalist Valentín Gómez Farías won enough votes for the vice presidency. Even before the final results were announced, Santa Anna decided that poor health would prevent him from taking office at once, and he communicated to Gómez Farías the expectation that the vice president would assume executive duties while Santa Anna recovered in Veracruz.[22]

Elections around the country that spring also produced a new congress, "dominated by ardent progressives." In the days leading up to the elections, the radical press laid the groundwork for a juggernaut. In early January, *El Fénix de la Libertad* proclaimed, "The war has ended but not the revolution." Two days later the same periodical printed the names of all legislators from the 1831–32 congress and warned readers to withhold their votes from these "villains." Attacks on these congressmen continued through election day. The radical press kept the pressure on in other ways as well. *El Fénix de la Libertad* printed a letter to the editor from "The anti-Spaniard," in which the author lambasted the electoral commissioners for handing out ballots to *Gachupines*. The author made clear that he referred not only to those born in Spain but also to those born in Mexico who should be too ashamed to vote because of their prior support for the "Picalugana Administration." The paper's editors took up this theme in their postelection analysis, when they argued that many Spaniards indeed had voted and that some "aristocrats" would not even stoop to attend the polls, but instead sent servants to deliver their ballots. The article advised secondary electors to rectify any infractions by rejecting the credentials of those elected from suspicious wards.[23]

At the other end of the political spectrum, a new periodical, *La Verdad Desnuda* (The Naked Truth), appeared in late February primarily to attack the return to Yorkino-style politics heralded by the recent elections. According to this paper's editors, the elections of January 27 had all of the elements of the mid-1820s, with the added twist that the radicals now had to contend with the electoral law of 1830. In contrast to the mass assaults on the parishes, according to *La Verdad Desnuda*, this time the "Parián patriots" intimidated the commissioners of electoral wards that were not already secured by the radicals, forcing them to withhold ballots from eligible voters. Then, on election day, the radicals engineered coups of the polling stations around the city, hired groups of *léperos* to descend on key electoral wards to demand ballots on site, stuff these bogus ballots into the electoral urns, and unfairly nullify any votes for other candidates. In wards where even these tactics might not work, the radicals simply created chaos enough to cause elections to be canceled. Other observers were somewhat less histrionic, but indicated major problems with the elections. According to José María Luis Mora, moderates wanted to distance themselves from the inevitable tumult and opted out of the electoral process from the start, thus opening the way for the radicals to seize the day. Miguel Santa María, of the old Scots' Rite faction, simply called the elections "a joke."[24]

The controversy did not end at the ballot box. Many critics, including Mora, Santa María, and José Ramón Pacheco, delivered harsh assessments of the newly elected congressmen. They asked how Mexico's future could be entrusted to men who could not even run their own personal affairs? *La Verdad Desnuda* warned that the worst nightmares of the Decent Men were about to come true, based on an assessment of the two new congressional representatives for the Federal District, Mariano Riva Palacio and Juan Rodríguez Puebla. Riva Palacio, according to the writers for this periodical, was a man of "very little intelligence and less prudence," who had received his seat in congress as a reward for marrying the late Vicente Guerrero's daughter. Even more dangerous was Rodríguez Puebla, who was described as a race baiter. Readers were reminded that Rodríguez Puebla had made a speech in 1827 (or maybe 1828—

the editors confessed their confusion) in which he called for a restoration of the "rights of the ancient Mexicans, usurped by the
whites." The editors left no doubt for their readers that Rodríguez
Puebla would somehow promote race war in the congress.[25]

Distance and data provide an opportunity to assess the situation in less vituperative terms. Overall, many dedicated but inexperienced radicals joined the ranks of the new congress in 1833.
The identities of primary electors and deputies from the Federal
District reveal a variation on this theme. Rather than the inexperienced ideologues denounced by some and perhaps evident in provincial positions, the capital's radicals posed a threat precisely
because of their exhilarating, ultimately bitter, experience in the
1820s. Men such as Manuel Reyes Veramendi, Juan Rodríguez
Puebla, Mariano Riva Palacio, and Juan Pablo Anaya had cut their
political teeth in municipal and state politics in and around the
capital in the mid-1820s. They had rallied to the popular radicalism of the York Rite lodges and mobilized the masses for the infamous urban elections of 1826 and 1827. They fretted in 1828 that, if
Guerrero were to lose the presidency, "What hope should we have
that the children of the Mexican nation will prosper?" They were
alleged to have played key roles in the tense moments of the
Acordada Revolt and the Parián riot, and they saw to it that some
of the most important brokers between the masses and the radical
leadership were appointed again to public positions in 1833. One
of the political brokers who returned to the spotlight was Lucas
Balderas, ubiquitous figure in the capital's radical political circles
from Independence through the war with the United States.
Balderas, a tailor by profession and a militia captain, served as a
primary elector in the quintessential Yorkino landslide of 1826, rose
up in the Acordada Revolt, and was named by the Bustamante press
as a key "disciple" in the cult that wanted to "destroy the nation."
In 1833, in acknowledgment of his efforts for the radical cause, he
received a crucial appointment as inspector of the capital's civic
militia.[26]

The correspondence between General José Antonio Mejía and
Lorenzo de Zavala provides additional insight into the electoral
process of 1833. Mejía confessed to Zavala that, out of "fear, ego,
and patriotism," he decided to lay low during the Bustamante administration, but in early 1832 he joined the Liberating Army. By
November, Mejía was convinced that victory was near and that "we
will achieve nothing if we leave the seeds of continued reaction"
planted in Mexican soil. He wrote of the need to construct quickly

"a new edifice that corresponds to the type of government under which we should live" and expressed his discomfort with the idea of compromise. The federalists could now "finish off [our enemies] with cudgel blows." Mejía made a rapid transition from the battlefield to the congressional chambers. He became deeply involved in the electioneering of early 1833, solicited advice from Zavala on loyal and appropriate candidates to promote for local, state, and national office, and then won a place among the triumphant radical electors in Mexico City's congressional elections, which permitted him to act on this advice. Mejía himself received an appointment to the Senate. After the military resolution of December 1832, radicals felt that their opportunity to seize control of Mexico's political destiny rested to a large degree on their skills in electoral organization and occasional intimidation. They grabbed this opportunity, convinced, as one friend of Reyes Veramendi wrote years later, that "elections are the first thing about which we should take care, because losing these we lose everything."[27]

The installation of the congress marked the return of radical popular politics to public rituals as well, with an emphasis on the central role of the legislature. In April, the new regime called for festivities on the days when the congress was to open and the new president and vice president were to take office. The rituals' designers wanted to distinguish republican energy from aristocratic torpor and to emphasize that "the essence of the system of popular representative government that fortunately governs us consists of the periodic renovation of the nation's representatives and high functionaries." According to Guillermo Prieto, all of Mexico "went crazy" over the announcement that international showman Adolfo Theodore would present a balloon ascension in the Plaza de Toros as part of the ongoing festivities. Theodore would rise to the heavens, unfurl the Mexican flag from his gondola, and lead cheers for the congress and the heroic Mexican people. The event never took place, causing political embarrassment and a financial scandal that took years to dissipate. A more successful event occurred on another day, as a circus troupe presented an equestrian extravaganza, "dedicated to the sovereign congress," entitled "America in Triumph." Admission fees started at one-quarter peso.[28]

Once installed, the congress chose an equally aggressive approach to its presumptive role as catalyst for Mexico's radical federalist renaissance. The newly elected congress received a boost in its confidence by President Santa Anna's hide-and-seek antics, since Valentín Gómez Farías seemed "much more appropriate [as an ally] for what has to be done during these first two months." These radicals developed a broader legislative agenda than their predecessors in the 1820s. The legislature trained its sights now primarily on the army and the ecclesiastical hierarchy, whose privileges represented an obstacle to Mexico's political, social, and economic development. Its members acted in a scattershot manner, debating countless proposals and passing legislation on a wide variety of issues with no clear assessment of the balance of political forces. During the course of 1833 incendiary cries for reforms in the relationships among the state, the church, and the military reverberated in the congressional chambers. The legislators debated numerous proposals to curtail military and ecclesiastical special privileges, to strengthen the civic militias, to subordinate regional military commanders to state political authorities, and even to reclaim the Patronato Real, the state's right to appoint the ecclesiastical hierarchy, conceded to the Spanish King by papal edict during the colonial era. This activist legislature also introduced reforms in education and criminal and civil law.[29]

The first major test of wills among the new congress, the absent executive, and the regular army occurred almost immediately. On April 6, Deputy José Fernando Ramírez of Durango introduced a proposal to reduce the federal army's role and increase that of the civic militias. Just a few weeks later the congress declared the state's right to control ecclesiastical appointments. Within six weeks of opening the radical congress managed through these actions to generate hostility from both the Church and the regular army. The growing tension compelled Santa Anna to come to Mexico City and assume the presidency in an attempt to assuage the generals and clerics. Lavish ceremonies to welcome the president drained the public coffers of 4,000 pesos, but neither the pomp nor the caudillo's words of moderation—delivered as a clear rebuke to the congress in their own chambers—stilled the restless generals.[30]

The first army unit to rise up, the Morelia garrison, announced in late May its intention to protect the privileges of the Church and the military and balanced its condemnation of the state and national governments with words of support for Santa Anna. General Mariano Arista, an aide to Santa Anna who joined the rebellion, later described the movement as "conforming to the vote of the people." Arista and other military officers, having been "provoked by the misconduct and excesses of the administration," wanted to "liberate [Mexico] from the horrific chaos that the mood of immorality and anarchy had accelerated." They accused the radicals of

being sansculottes poised on the brink of a reign of terror to be unleashed on clerics, property owners, the military, and all men who,
"having distinguished themselves only through their integrity or
other extraordinary quality, became the target of persecution."[31]

Santa Anna rushed into the breach, only to be "kidnapped" by
the rebels. Rumors soon circulated that Santa Anna had in fact
planned to join the rebellion against the sitting government, of
which he was the elected president. The definitive explanation for
Santa Anna's actions still eludes historians, although it appears most
likely that Santa Anna was weighing the balance of power between
the government and the rebels, and then determined that it still
favored the sitting government. The dalliance between Santa Anna
and the rebels quickly broke down; the hero of Tampico "escaped"
from his captors and rushed to the capital, where three days of celebration, complete with public concerts and a Te Deum, marked
his release.[32] The radical press offered their assessment of the scene
upon his arrival: "Through all the streets of the city ran groups of
people with hatchets in their hands, manifesting their hearts' de-
light and repeating the following: Long live General Santa Anna;
long live the congress; long live the state legislatures; long live the
defenders of the people; death to the *Gachupines*; death to Arista;
death to the false defenders of religion; death to the traitorous
priests."[33]

At this time, Santa Anna reiterated his opposition to the rebellion and his support for Gómez Farías and the congress. These
strange bedfellows then launched a direct attack on their enemies,
implementing a new form of expulsion law, the *ley del caso*, an anti-
subversion bill that forced into exile a heterogeneous universe of
individuals that included Spanish clergy, personal rivals of Santa
Anna, and key figures from the Bustamante regime. The congress
also created a Special Commission on Public Security, further convincing the opposition that Mexico would soon see the triumph of
the sansculottes and a Jacobin reign of terror. Hard-core radicals
tried to shore up the courage of fence-sitters by insisting that any
vacillation at this time would be perceived as weakness and could
only discredit the government. Nonetheless, Santa Anna suspended
the enforcement of existing anticlerical and antimilitary laws while
the rebels remained in arms.[34]

Amid this crisis the radicals turned their attentions to a sim-
mering conflict in the capital's municipal politics and committed a
perverse affront to their own federalist principles. Back in December of 1832, Manuel Gómez Pedraza received a letter from a group

of Mexico City federalists who claimed that the recent municipal council elections had been bogus due to the manipulations of the Decent Men. As a result, the newly elected council members did "not merit the confidence of the people." The petition to annul the elections reached the interim president through Andrés Quintana Roo, and its signatories included Lucas Balderas, as well as a number of other radical activists who would later control the spring's congressional primaries. During his brief caretaker government, Gómez Pedraza did nothing, but the events of early June precipitated decisive action by Valentín Gómez Farías.[35]

As the fate of Santa Anna's expedition to the north remained a mystery, the capital grew restless. Radical newspapers accused the church of stirring up "rebellion and disobedience," and indeed a small troop of approximately forty soldiers stationed in the city proclaimed against Gómez Farías on the night of June 7. Gómez Farías, aided by the capital's militia, described by British Minister Richard Pakenham as "the very dregs of the people, without discipline or subordination," stood firm and the rebellion fizzled. After the incident, the radical press lambasted the municipal council members for remaining "spectators, if not accomplices" in the uprising. At this time, Gómez Farías summoned members of the 1829 municipal council, elected under the radical juggernaut of 1828, to replace those elected during the reign of the Decent Men in 1832.[36]

Upon taking office, the interim council issued a highly inflammatory poster stating that they had been called back to office to help protect Mexico from "the insolent aristocracy in combination with the Spaniards," who wished to overturn the constitution, rape the wives of federalists, and enslave Mexico again. In private correspondence with Gómez Farías, they offered all the resources at their disposal to suffocate the revolution percolating all around. These men soon passed the torch of radicalism, as a result of special legislation, which stipulated that, on July 7, Mexico City's radical congressional electors would choose the municipal council that would serve out the term of those ousted the previous month. *El Fénix de la Libertad* proudly reported that the new council members were all committed federalists. True to this assessment, in secret session shortly after taking office, the new council noted the imminent threat posed by the city's Spaniards and decided that they should be prohibited from owning firearms and meeting in groups. The decision allegedly came as a response to rumors that the "Picaluganos" planned to rise up in the city.[37]

To complicate matters, a devastating outbreak of cholera struck the capital in June, lasting through the summer. While some clergy played an active role in the armed uprising that dragged on, it was more usual for priests to struggle on the rhetorical battlefield, calling the cholera outbreak a punishment from God in response to the government's errant ways. In one pastoral letter, the dean and clerical council of the Metropolitan Cathedral did precisely that, simultaneously feigning ignorance of the legislators' anticlerical motives, asking, "What dementia fills them? What fury agitates them, maddens them?" A new periodical, *La Antorcha*, provided a daily counterattack on the radicals, with "a religious perspective on political themes." Begun in April, and forced to close in June, the paper regularly criticized the radicals, not only for their anticlericalism, but also because their misguided definition of democracy as "government of the plebs" violated natural law. In response, radical supporters intensified their attacks on the Church, reporting everything from the cruelty of individual priests to reprinting with denunciatory commentary the Inquisition's 1810 excommunication order against Independence War hero Miguel Hidalgo.[38]

The relationship between Independence and anticlericalism emerged as the theme of the patriotic celebrations that fall. Radicals Juan Rodríguez Puebla and Mariano Riva Palacio dominated the executive board of the planning commission. With several dozen other ardent patriots in attendance at the first preparatory meeting, the festivities promised to be even more inflammatory than in past years. The cholera infestation forced the commission to postpone the public celebrations until October 4, the day that the 1824 Constitution had been signed. On that day, the selected orator, José de Jesús Huerta, emphasized the ongoing struggle to "throw out tyrants" that had united the movement led by Hidalgo in 1810, the Revolt of the Acordada in 1828, and the uprising that brought the radicals to power at the end of 1832. Lest there be any mistake about the tyrants' identity, the speaker denounced the Catholic Church, which worked hand in hand with Spaniards and aristocrats to oppress the majority of Mexicans.[39]

The month of October brought an end to the uprising of Mariano Arista, whose troops surrendered to Santa Anna. The president returned briefly to the capital, only to claim health problems and, again, he retired to Veracruz. The radical congress, apparently unconcerned with Santa Anna's increasing discomfort with its actions, returned to its hyperactive legislative agenda, while the Ministry of Justice and Ecclesiastical Relations blamed the recent uprising on Church machinations and reiterated a ban on discussion of politics from the pulpit. The reformist furor of the fall and winter of 1833–34 included proposals to wrest the educational system from the Church and to use confiscated ecclesiastical holdings to amortize the public debt. Other legislative items planned to reduce the influence of the army in Mexican affairs.[40]

This ongoing radical campaign allegedly conducted on behalf of the Mexican people could not mask a downward spiral of political participation that manifested itself in two ways. The first was a general decline in the number of votes cast and the number of wards participating in both congressional and municipal elections. Secondly, not only did electoral absenteeism climb, but more and more citizens refused to accept elective offices, and those who did accept often resigned shortly after beginning their tenure. For the crucial congressional elections of January 1833, the number of wards that failed to hold elections reached 12 percent. By the fall's municipal elections, a few short months after the radical purge of the incumbent municipal council, the number more than doubled to 26 percent, leading the new Federal District governor and Santa Anna supporter José María Tornel to report in shocked tones to the Secretary of Interior and External Relations that this unprecedented number of wards (sixty-four) held no elections due to a "lack of citizens who would use their rights." Tornel blamed the low voter turnout on the complicated format resulting from the 1830 electoral reform, which Tornel noted was designed "to concentrate power in certain hands."[41]

Tornel's explanation failed to acknowledge the complexity of the political landscape at this time. No elite faction trusted its future to the electoral arena. The city's population had seen both national and local elections overturned repeatedly by both radicals and their opponents, which had discredited the electoral process. On another level, the current government had assumed power amid cries in the streets denouncing an insolent aristocracy that had murdered Guerrero and conspired with the Spanish, yet the congressional agenda in 1833 operated at a different ideological level from the popular radical program under Guerrero. The Guerrero beloved by the masses had had generally neutral relations with the Catholic Church. The tension between the new radical government and the Church, manifested in the virulent war of words emanating from the legislative chambers and the pulpit, was un-precedented. The impact of this transformation was not unidirec-tional, but it was noticeable in fragmenting popular sentiment. Though not the only important political brokers during Mexico's electoral apprenticeship, parish priests had played a key role in mobilizing voters during the past twenty years. Many were now aligned with the ecclesiastical hierarchy in opposition to the radi-cal federalists. Finally, Santa Anna's fundamentally befuddling politics still rested on a carefully cultivated image as a popular hero, avenger of Guerrero's death, and defender of national sovereignty. Any decision by the general to change alliances would surely draw some ardent followers from the popular classes. This combination rendered popular sentiment toward any political faction a greater unknown than it had been in the 1820s and made coalitions highly mutable.[42]

The key factional mutation erupted in the spring of 1834. In rapid succession, the radicals orchestrated the indictment of five Supreme Court justices, engineered an effort to deport the Bishop of Puebla, and pursued harsh retribution against military officers allegedly responsible for the conspiracy against Guerrero. Santa Anna hurried back to the capital to reclaim the presidency in April and immediately issued a statement saying that he would correct congressional errors while upholding the 1824 Constitution. An increasingly confident and vocal opposition called upon Santa Anna to intervene even more aggressively in politics. Principal among the periodicals that attacked the radicals were *El Mosquito Mexicano* and *La Lima de Vulcano*. *El Mosquito Mexicano* lambasted the con-gress, informing its readers that the Senate had the character of a poor man's tavern and "the chamber of deputies is a school for ill-mannered boys who do not respect their teacher because he is dod-dering and timid. They have no shame." About the same time, a letter to the editors of *La Lima de Vulcano* explained "why the Yorkinos are called Jacobins." It contained a long explication of the French Revolution and compared Gómez Farías to Robespierre. Less sophisticated, more frightening material appeared on posters and hand-lettered flyers splattered around the city. "He who kills a Congressman does not commit a sin," read one. The increasingly besieged congress passed legislation to prohibit the posting of materials that "air political, religious, or ecclesiastical issues" or "attack the reputation of the authorities," but the tide had already turned against the radicals.[43]

Vice President Gómez Farías resigned in April and asked for passage out of Mexico in May. He would spend much of the next decade in exile. That same month coordinated provincial rebellions issued a proclamation calling upon Santa Anna to assume extraordinary powers to overturn much of the last year's legislation, which allegedly exceeded the will of the people. This six-point program, which came to be known as the Cuernavaca Plan, also demanded that all public officials responsible for the radical laws be replaced. Santa Anna accepted leadership of the movement, closed the congress on June 1, and began to place his supporters in key positions around the country. The mouthpiece of radicalism, *El Fénix de la Libertad*, ceased publication only days after Santa Anna closed the congress. The last issue carried the headline, "Caesar has crossed the Rubicon."[44]

As the tide turned against the radicals, Santa Anna supporters devised a strategy to bring Mexico City into the fold. On June 12, 1834, pro–Santa Anna demonstrations occurred in Mexico City. The capital's troops remained in their barracks during these demonstrations so that the movement in favor of the general would appear to be popular and not military in nature. The following day, Santa Anna brought back the municipal council members who had been ousted by fiat in 1833, justifying the procedure with the argument that the people of Mexico City had not had a legitimate municipal government during the last year. The restored council immediately published a decree announcing to the public that the rule of law and the rights of the people had been restored by this act. The decree closed with a series of vivas for religion, federation, Santa Anna, and the Mexican people. Not to be outdone, the Church hierarchy published its own paean to Santa Anna for his brilliant response to the "saddest, most bitter days" that the Mexican Church had ever experienced. July 6 was set aside as a special religious feast day to commemorate this triumph.[45]

Santa Anna soon received a bundle of petitions from the new municipal council. Drawn up primarily in parish houses and monasteries throughout the city on July 15, the documents are similar in language, identical in demands. Most of the documents contain a preamble asserting the right of free and peaceful assembly to consider the common good and then proceed with a supplication to Santa Anna to remedy the evils of the present day by implementing fully all of the features of the Cuernavaca Plan. The petitions ended with a list of signatories and addenda noting that large groups of illiterates seconded the resolution. In San Miguel parish alone, almost 650 people, the vast majority of them illiterate, met to rally around the proposal.[46] Provincial federalists resisted this change of course during the spring of 1834. Almost half of Mexico's states experienced protest movements against the dissolution of the congress. However, divisions within the federalist camp between moderates and radicals again prevented the formation of a unified front against an emerging movement that saw in recent events an opportunity to alter more fundamentally Mexico's political formulas, upon which they acted in the next year.[47]

Notes

1. Anthony Butler to Martin Van Buren, December 31, 1829; Butler to Andrew Jackson, April 15, 1830; Butler to J. Wallace, U.S. Consul, San Antonio, June 1, 1830, copies, in Anthony Butler Papers, Center for American History, University of Texas at Austin (hereafter cited as CHA-UTA).

2. See *Verdadera causa de la revolución del sur, justificándose el que la suscribe con documentos que ecsisten en la Secretaría del Supremo Gobierno del Estado de México, que los certifica, añadidas algunas ocurencias que ha habido después del primer papel que se imprimió con este mismo* (Toluca, Mexico: Imp. del Gobierno del Estado, 1831); Francisco Ibar, *Nuevo clamor de venganza o muerte, contra el intruso gobierno que tantos malos ha producido* (Mexico City: Imp. Martín Rivero, 1831); Josefina Z. Vázquez, "Iglesia, ejército y centralismo," *Historia Mexicana* 39, no. 1 (1989): 214; Guardino, *Peasants, Politics,* 135–36.

3. *Registro Oficial,* October 19, 1830, quoted in Costeloe, *Primera República,* 274.

4. El Loco de Jerusalem, *Oiga el vice presidente la sentencia de su muerte* (Mexico City: Imp. Juan Bautista Gamboa, 1832); Jaime E. Rodríguez O., "Oposición a Bustamante," *Historia Mexicana* 20, no. 2 (October–December 1970): 200–201.

5. Rodrigúez, "Oposición a Bustamante," 226; *El Gladiador* 1:1, March 27, 1830; Arrangoiz, *México desde 1808,* 354; Lucas Alamán, *Un regalo del año nuevo al señor Rocafuerte: O sea consideraciones sobre sus consideraciones escritas por uno que le conoce* (Mexico City, 1832), quoted in Rodríguez O., "Oposición a Bustamante," 215; *Invasión de México por D. Antonio López de Santa Anna, primera parte* (Mexico City: Imp. Alejandro Valdes, 1832); Police Report, March 31, 1830, AGN, Gobernación, Sin Sección, leg. 99, exp. 6.

6. Alamán to M. Michelena, January 19, 1830, BLAC-UTA, HyD, 20-3.4752; Rodríguez O., "Oposición a Bustamante," 200–201; Costeloe, *Primera República,* 295; Tenenbaum, *Politics of Penury,* 35–37; Potash, *Mexican Government,* 39–51.

7. *El Sol,* January 11, 1830; José María Luis Mora, "Discurso sobre la necesidad de fijar el derecho de ciudadanía en la República y hacerlo afecto a la propiedad," *El Observador,* Mexico City, April 14, 1830, in *Obras sueltas de José María Luis Mora, ciudadano mexicano* (Paris: Librería Rosa, 1837),

2:289–305; *Registro Oficial,* May 17, 1830; *El Sol,* May 24, 1830; Anna, *Forging Mexico,* 239; *Voz de la Patria,* March 15, 1830.

8. "Reglas para las elecciones de diputados y de ayuntamientos del distrito y territorios de la República (July 12, 1830)," in *Legislación electoral mexicana,* ed. García Orozco, 46–52; Costeloe, *Primera República,* 281–83; Stanley C. Green, *The Mexican Republic: The First Decade, 1823–1832* (Pittsburgh, Pa.: University of Pittsburgh Press, 1987), 193.

9. *Registro Oficial,* September 20, October 1, 2, and 21, 1830; *El Sol,* December 13, 1830; Governor of Federal District to Municipal Council, October 18, 1830, AACM, vol. 862, exp. 13; Anna, *Forging Mexico,* 240; Costeloe, *Primera República,* 293; Calcott, *Santa Anna,* 86.

10. *Registro Oficial,* September 20, October 1, 2, and 21, December 6, 1830; Election Returns, AACM, vol. 862, exp. 12, 14, and 15.

11. Federal District Governor report, AGN, Ayuntamientos, vol. 14, 265; Municipal Council Report on Electoral Commissioners, AACM, vol. 862, exp. 15; Arrangoiz, *México desde 1808,* 362; Federal District Governor report, November 24, 1836, AGN, Ayuntamientos, vol. 20, 76; Costeloe, *Primera República,* 283.

12. *Memoria del Ministro de Estado y del Despacho de Relaciones Interiores y Exteriores* (Mexico City, 1831); Serrano, "Levas," 148–49; Municipal Council Secret Sessions, April 20, 1830, and January 7, 1831, AACM, vol. 292a, 293a; Municipal Council Minutes, March 2, 1830, AACM, vol. 150a.

13. *Registro Oficial,* September 16 and 18, 1830; Reynaldo Sordo Cedeño, *El Congreso en la primera República centralista* (Mexico City: El Colegio de México–Instituto Tecnológico Autónoma de México, 1993), 115; Francisco Manuel Sánchez de Tagle, "Arenga Cívica que pronunció el 16 de septiembre de 1830," in *La conciencia nacional,* ed. Torre Villar, 75–88.

14. Michael P. Costeloe, "The Junta Patriótica and the Celebration of Independence in Mexico City, 1825–1855," *Mexican Studies/Estudios Mexicanos* 13, no. 1 (Winter 1997): 28; Riva Palacio et al., *Mexico a través,* 4:287–88, quoted in Plasencia, *Independencia,* 39, n. 39; Di Tella, *National Popular Politics,* 220–23; José Domínguez Manso, "Discurso . . . 16 de septiembre de 1832," in *La conciencia nacional,* ed. Torre Villar, 89–94.

15. Anna, *Forging Mexico,* 242–43; Guardino, *Peasants, Politics,* 130–35.

16. Rodríguez O., "Oposición a Bustamante," 201, 212; Anna, *Forging Mexico,* 230–33; Michael P. Costeloe, *The Central Republic in Mexico, 1835–1846: Hombres de Bien in the Age of Santa Anna* (Cambridge, England: Cambridge University Press, 1993), 32.

17. Anna, *Forging Mexico,* 247; Josefina Z. Vázquez, "Political Plans and Collaboration between Civilians and the Military, 1821–1846," *Bulletin of Latin American Research* 15, no. 1 (1996): 27; Santa Anna to Bustamante, January 25, 1832, BLAC-UTA, Mariano Riva Palacio Papers, doc. 206 (hereafter cited as MRP); Di Tella, *National Popular Politics,* 226–27.

18. Rodríguez O., "Oposición a Bustamante," 230–31; Anna, *Forging Mexico,* 249; *El Fénix de la Libertad,* October 13 and 17, 1832.

19. Vázquez, "Political Plans," 28; Anna, *Forging Mexico,* 255; Sordo, *El Congreso,* 19–21; Mora, *Obras sueltas,* 1:57–76; Josefina Z. Vázquez, "La crisis y los partidos políticos, 1833–1846," in *America Latina: Dallo stato coloniale allo stato nazione,* ed. Antonio Annino (Milan: Franco Angeli, 1987), 2:557–58; Rodríguez O., "Oposición a Bustamante," 233–34; Frank N. Samponaro, "Santa Anna and the Abortive Anti-Federalist Revolt of 1833 in Mexico," *The Americas* 40, no. 1 (July 1983): 96.

20. Calcott, *Santa Anna*, 95.

21. *A medio las enchiladas, del barrio de Santa Anita: Y nueva canción a los españoles* (Puebla, Mexico: Imp. Nacional, 1833).

22. Costeloe, *Primera República*, 368.

23. Vázquez, "La crisis y los partidos políticos," 558; *El Fénix de la Libertad*, January 7, 9, 14, 23, 24, 26, and 29, 1833.

24. José María Luis Mora, "Revista política," in *Obras sueltas* (1837; reprint ed., Mexico City, 1963), 45; and Miguel Santa Maria, *Exposición y protexta de MSM ciudadano mexicano* (Mexico City, 1834), 3; both quoted in Sordo, *El Congreso*, 21.

25. *La Verdad Desnuda*, 2 and 5 (March 1833), quoted in Sordo, *El Congreso*, 23.

26. Sordo, *El Congreso*, 23; J. A. Mejía to M. Reyes Veramendi, BNAH, Bustamante Collection, vol. 21, doc. 54; *Un aguinaldo excelente para toda buena gente. Manifiesto que se presenta a la nación de los individuos dignos de toda consideración y premio por su siempre memorable grito de la Acordada, y otros grandes servicios* (Mexico City: Imp. Alejandro Valdes, 1829); Balderas to Manuel Reyes Veramendi, BNAH, Bustamante Collection, vol. 27, doc. 69; Rodríguez O., "Oposición a Bustamante," 223; List of Electors, AACM, vol. 873, exp. 3.

27. J. A. Mejía to L. Zavala, June 15, 1831, November 11 and December 18, 1832, January 4, 16, 17, 22, and 24, 1833, Lorenzo de Zavala Papers, CAH-UTA; *El Telégrafo*, January 31, 1833; Victoriano Morelos y Flores to Manuel Reyes Veramendi, August 29, 1846, BNAH, Bustamante Collection, vol. 41, doc. 25.

28. Proclamation, March 18, 1833, Archivo Histórico de la Secretaría de Salud, Fondo Salubridad Pública, Sección Presidencia, Serie Secretaría, caja 1; Prieto, *Memorias*, 52; Municipal Council Correspondence, AACM, vol. 797, exp. 56; *El Telégrafo*, March 24, 1833.

29. J. A. Mejía to Lorenzo de Zavala, March 22, 1833, Lorenzo de Zavala Papers, CAH-UTA; Sordo, *El Congreso*, 25–28; Costeloe, *Primera República*, 373–75; Di Tella, *National Popular Politics*, 230–33; Anna, *Forging Mexico*, 258; Samponaro, "Santa Anna," 97–98.

30. Samponaro, "Santa Anna," 99; Sordo, *El Congreso*, 29.

31. Costeloe, *Primera República*, 385; Mariano Arista, *Reseña histórica de la revolución* (Mexico City: Imp. Mariano Arévalo, 1835).

32. Samponaro, "Santa Anna," 101–3; Costeloe, *Primera República*, 386; Di Tella, *National Popular Politics*, 232; Sordo, *El Congreso*, 33; Proclamation of Festivities, AACM, vol. 2257, exp. 193.

33. *El Fénix de la Libertad*, June 17, 1833.

34. Sordo, *El Congreso*, 32–36; Lucas Balderas to Manuel Reyes Veramendi, June 26, 1833, BNAH, Bustamante Collection, vol. 27, doc. 69; Samponaro, "Santa Anna," 105.

35. Petition, December 30, 1832, AGN, Ayuntamientos, vol. 16, 121.

36. *El Fénix de la Libertad*, June 6, 1833; Costeloe, *Primera República*, 388; British Consul Richard Pakenham to Lord Palmerston, June 11, 1833, quoted in Di Tella, *National Popular Politics*, 232; *El Fénix de la Libertad*, June 12, 1833; Proclamation, June 13, 1833, AACM, vol. 862, exp. 21.

37. Council to Gómez Farías, June 16, 1833, AACM, vol. 862, exp. 21; Manuel Dublán and José María Lozano, eds., *Legislación mexicana: O colección completa de las disposiciones legislativas expedidas desde la Independencia de la República* (Mexico City: Imp. del Comercio, 1876–1914),

2:536–73; *El Telégrafo,* July 5, 1833; *El Fénix de la Libertad,* July 8 and 13, 1833; Municipal Council Secret Session, July 11, 1833, AACM, vol. 293a.

38. Costeloe, *Primera República,* 394; "Carta pastoral del Dean y Cabildo gobernador de la Santa Iglesia Metropolitana," BNAH, Fondo Especial, 2d series, leg. 9, doc. 26; *La Antorcha,* April 4, 1833; *El Fénix de la Libertad,* July 15 and August 18, 1833.

39. *El Fénix de la Libertad,* July 27, 1833; Costeloe, "Junta Patriótica," 33; José de Jesús Huerta, "Discurso patriótico . . . 4 de octubre," in *La conciencia nacional,* ed. Torre Villar, 95–108.

40. Samponaro, "Santa Anna," 105; Di Tella, *National Popular Politics,* 233; Costeloe, *Primera República,* 407; Proclamation, October 31, 1833, AACM, vol. 2257, exp. 190; Sordo, *El Congreso,* 39–54; Costeloe, *Primera República,* 396.

41. *El Telégrafo,* January 31, 1833; Election Report, AGN, Ayuntamientos, vol. 14, 259; Federal District Governor to Secretary of State, December 3, 1833, AGN, Ayuntamientos, vol. 16, 105.

42. Di Tella, *National Popular Politics,* 230.

43. Sordo, *El Congreso,* 52, 54; Costeloe, *Primera República,* 416–17, 425; *El Fénix de la Libertad,* May 4, 1833, quoted in Sordo, *El Congreso,* 55; *El Mosquito Mexicano,* May 16, 1833; *La Lima de Vulcano,* May 28, 1834; Tornel to Minister of Interior and External Relations, April 30, 1834, AGN Gobernación, Sin Sección, leg. 147, exp. 6.

44. *El Fénix de la Libertad,* June 4, 1834, quoted in Costeloe, *Primera República,* 430.

45. Proclamation, AACM, vol. 862, exp. 24; Riva Palacio et al., *México a través,* 7:344.

46. Petitions, AACM, vol. 862, exp. 24.

47. Sordo, *El Congreso,* 83.

6

The Transition to Centralism, 1834–1837

The events of 1833 and 1834 steeled the resolve of conservatives and convinced others with more moderate views that a stronger national government, guided by men of property and distinction, held perhaps the only promise for Mexico's future. Early efforts to drive the radicals from office, undo the reforms of the previous two years, dismantle the civic militias, and intervene in provincial political affairs met with resistance, particularly in the north, and provided the spark that ignited the tinderbox in Texas. Fear that the country was on the verge of disintegration precipitated a push for further centralist reforms. In 1835 and 1836 a newly elected congress drafted a series of laws that dramatically altered the relationship between the states and national government, and between individuals and the state.

In the capital, the transition to centralism precipitated a series of confrontations that pitted the municipal council against the governor. Familiar issues of jurisdiction and authority took on a new urgency when the centralist legislature promulgated a significant change in the capital's status. As part of the broader overhaul in national structures, the legislature dissolved the Federal District and incorporated Mexico City into the newly formed Department of Mexico, which consisted of the former State of Mexico and the Federal District. A departmental governor selected by the executive branch held responsibility for the new entity. Mexico City became the department's capital. Although disputes between the municipal government and the Federal District governor had been common, this new political geography precipitated further confrontation and a loss of power and prestige for the municipal council.[1]

Centralist reformers also sought to limit the influence of the masses in the political process by reducing the number of elective offices and changing the suffrage requirements. In 1836, for the first time, the legislature passed a national law with a minimum income threshold for the right to vote. This legislation mattered mostly as symbolism, since enthusiasm for elections had dwindled already among all sectors of Mexico City's population. Election-day malaise continued to mount during the centralist transition, although popular political action burst onto the scene repeatedly in other ways. Public protests, riots, and fear of a mass popular uprising provided the bookends for the last years of the first federal republic. Support for a government guided by Decent Men with proper respect for the Church and the military proved thin in the face of the unrest caused by increasing economic hardship, tensions resulting from the demand for canon fodder forcibly recruited on the streets of Mexico City, and the Texas debacle. Under these circumstances, even those who supported change in 1834 found it difficult to cheer during the early days of the new constitutional regime in 1837.

Centralist Housecleaning, 1834

During the summer and fall of 1834, General Santa Anna dismantled the reforms of 1833 and the institutions that formed the backbone of radical federalism. In addition to closing the congress and sacking the capital's municipal council, he formed a new cabinet, reopened the university, overturned the *ley del caso*, disbanded militia units, and halted the confiscation of Church property. The antiradical press lauded a return to the politics of Decent Men, noting the vast improvements that lay on the horizon now that both the "pernicious municipal council" and the "leeches" and "charlatans" in the congress had been deposed. The new editors of *El Telégrafo*, the official government newspaper, quickly laid the foundation for a broader reaction against popular radicalism. They argued that men of property must remain in control of politics, since they were "the only barrier capable of containing the force of excessive desires, of dangerous innovations, of the ardent enthusiasm of extremism." To coincide with this campaign of property versus anarchy, the Santa Anna regime tried to increase surveillance over the city's population and to gain additional recruits for the army. In August 1834 a new executive order required domestic servants at all times to carry identification cards listing their names, their employers, and their salaries. These credentials would be surrendered to public officials on demand, so that the gainfully employed could be distinguished from vagrants who often claimed to be domestic servants when confronted by the authorities. The government contemplated a similar identification-card system for municipal employees as well, suggesting that only fine—and sometimes indistinguishable—outward appearances separated the employed from the vagrant. Soon thereafter, another presidential directive lamented the infestation of the capital by vagrants and urged electoral commissioners to be especially vigilant when distributing ballots for upcoming elections, so that the city's vagrant population, the "fecund seed" of crime and corrupters of the honest working classes, could be denied access to the polls.[2]

Santa Anna's decision to call for new congressional elections in the autumn elicited criticism, both from those who argued that it contravened the 1824 Constitution and from those who insisted it would be a step backward toward factional strife rather than toward consolidation of the new order. Despite the complications and thorny legal issues that emerged, the September elections appeared to bear out the assessment of the Decent Men that the tide had turned in their favor. Opponents of the radicals praised the municipal council's good judgment in its selection of precinct commissioners, the first step in cleansing the electoral rolls. The elections themselves appeared to be a major success for the Decent Men, although some noted that a few radical demagogues still worked the polls and tried to deny their opponents access to the ballot box.[3]

The accelerating absenteeism rate among voters elicited no comment. Even though over one-third of the precincts in Mexico City had no elections, supporters of the new regime claimed a mandate for change, confirmed by the secondary election results. On October 16, *La Lima de Vulcano* printed a letter from "Pepe," who rejoiced that the sansculottes would no longer dominate political debates, now that "the rostrum will be occupied by speakers who merit the attention of a sophisticated public, and the 'coachmen's tutors,' as they are called vulgarly, will not return" to the congress. Almost one-half of the regular participants in the new congress were men who had served in the original congress of Decent Men under President Anastasio Bustamante (1830–1832). Over 63 percent of the new legislators had previous political experience of some weight, a sharp contrast to the inexperienced radical congress of 1833–1834. Some of the most influential representatives included members of the upper clergy and those who could be cast by now as professional politicians.[4]

The conservative press resumed the culture wars of the post-Guerrero era, promoting the theme of renascent civilization versus vanquished anarchy in repeated—and sometimes bizarre— attacks on the radical legacy. The editors of *La Lima de Vulcano* pleaded with the municipal council to remove from the gates of Alameda Park at last the awful free verse scribbled there during the past few years, not only because it was offensive and lacked artistic merit, but because the orthography lacked sophistication. The same newspaper warned that the new government needed to remain ever vigilant lest the radicals, the "insolent, immoral, criminal, and stupid" element of Mexican society, organize a repeat of the Parián riot in a desperate attempt to regain power. In contrast, faced with the annual Independence Day appearance before the masses, the Decent Men selected an orator who chose a discreet tack that emphasized unity and reconciliation in rewriting the history of the last two decades. José María Castañeda y Escalada pronounced that "all good Mexicans, thinking Spaniards of both worlds, educated men from every nation, repeated" Hidalgo's cry for Independence, and that it was "rejected only by the [royal] cabinet in Madrid." He might have added that the Spanish royal court had still not recognized Mexico's Independence at the time of his speech, though this would certainly have exercised the crowd. He was interested more in emphasizing Mexican unity than Spanish recalcitrance. In the current iteration of the myth of Mexico's origin, Agustín de Iturbide emerged once more as a true and useful hero, able to form one Mexican family by reconciling Creoles, Spaniards, and the "Aztec Indian." The speaker also lavished praise on Santa Anna as the "companion of the heroes of Independence," and the "appropriate instrument to establish and consolidate peace." The speech ended by resurrecting a call for the Three Guarantees: Long live our majestic religion, Independence, and union! Some months later the congress passed legislation to inscribe the Hero of Iguala's name in the legislative chambers as a tribute to his memory.[5]

In 1834, Santa Anna supporters added a new day to the patriotic festivities, spending a scandalously large sum of money on celebrations of September 11 to commemorate the day on which Santa Anna defeated the Spanish invasion force at Tampico. Over the next two decades, whenever Santa Anna occupied the executive office, the effort to link him more closely to the September patriotic festivities became a standard feature of the regime. This construction made Santa Anna an indispensable figure in the master fiction of Mexican history. Hidalgo came to be portrayed as the impulsive priest who first raised the cry for Independence. Iturbide became the brilliant designer of the Three Guarantees who succumbed to his own inflated ambitions. It fell upon Santa Anna, then, to consummate Independence finally in 1829.[6]

The last months of 1834 were comparatively tranquil, considering the upheaval that inaugurated the year and that which was to come. As the year came to a close, December's municipal council elections posed one last procedural and political dilemma. The arbitrary nonelectoral appointments of the last two years had damaged the local government's credibility. Most of the sitting members of the council had been selected three years ago, and several vacancies over the summer of 1834 had been filled with men selected by primary electors who themselves had been chosen back in 1832. In order to begin with a clean slate for the New Year, the executive branch ordered that the entire municipal council be replaced, even though the law stipulated that only one-half of the council should be selected each year.[7]

Despite their increasing confidence, centralists still feared the radical electoral machine. In the weeks before the next municipal council election, allegations emerged that radical organizers attempted to gain votes through bribery, intimidation, and secret conferences designed to fix the elections. In response, the conservative press published lists of their approved candidates for the new city council. Although only three candidates endorsed by *La Lima de Vulcano* made the final cut, this procentralist newspaper reported that the secondary elections went smoothly enough to yield the selection of men from whom much could be expected. A report in *El Mosquito Mexicano* concurred. Its readers received the happy news that the Yorkinos could no longer control elections using their old tactics. The paper's editors noted a "general contentedness in the public due to the sensible election of the new council members," enlightened men who could well serve a dejected populace. Fully cognizant of the awful state of municipal affairs, the paper implored the newly elected men to accept their appointments willingly. In the end, however, no smooth transition in municipal authority occurred. A combination of anomie and legal maneuvers torpedoed the council even before it met for the first time. Some newly elected councilors displayed neither public spirit nor fear of prosecution and simply rejected the call to take their posts. Confusion over the thorny legal question of whether or not some sitting members of the council could be reelected turned the entire process into a political morass that paralyzed the municipal government through much of 1835.[8]

Centralist Consolidation, 1835

In November 1834 a pamphlet titled "Cuestión de día" (The Issue of the Day) opened with William Shakespeare's "To be or not to be?" The author referred in this case to the principal issue—federalism or centralism—that hung in the balance as a new congress sat in January 1835. The question could have applied equally to President Santa Anna. Critics of the capital's city council members who refused to take office did not find an exemplar in Santa Anna, who dodged for the time being the pressing issues of the day and again requested a medical leave of absence. In theory the president's feigned illness left the exiled Vice President Valentín Gómez Farías in control of the executive branch again. Quick action on the part of the congress resolved the potential crisis, as the members proclaimed Santa Anna physically impaired, Gómez Farías morally impaired, and former Minister of War Miguel Barragán interim executive.[9]

The new congress began to dismantle the radical reforms step by step, generally cleaving to the Cuernavaca Plan. In the early sessions, deputies recalibrated church-state relations, hearing little opposition either within or without the legislative chambers. In contrast, as spring approached and initiatives were passed to alter relations between the national and state governments, such as the order to reduce the state militias drastically, provincial unrest broke out. In the south, popular Independence War hero Juan Alvarez rebelled briefly in March, but soon retired to his hacienda, where he kept his distance from national politics for the next five years. In the north, larger problems emerged, as federalist stalwarts in Zacatecas rose up. Santa Anna shook off his malaise to lead the national army into battle. With no armed challenges in other regions, Santa Anna's troops proved capable of subduing that revolt. The victory convinced Santa Anna's personal supporters, as well as ideological centralists wary of the president's early intentions, that a corner had been turned. It proved to be a blind corner with unexpected obstacles just around it.[10]

The movement to consolidate centralist gains accelerated in May 1835. By the end of the congressional sessions late in the month, in Veracruz State, the municipal council of Orizaba announced its support for a formal transition to centralism with the backing of a large number of the city's residents. Other town councils and state governments followed in the subsequent weeks. On June 12 the capital's municipal council received a note from the Federal District governor informing it that he had received twenty-four petitions drawn up by the "immense majority" of the city's population, manifesting its desire that the political system be changed from federalism to centralism, that the congress become a unicameral constitutional convention, that the present municipal authorities remain for the time being, and that Santa Anna preside over the transition as supreme chief. The following day, the feast of Santa Anna's saintly namesake, crowds gathered in the streets of the capital, waving flags emblazoned with slogans such as "In Revolt for Popular Government." In this case, "popular government" meant the form supported by the petitions delivered to the Federal District governor: centralism.[11]

These events set off a great debate in the municipal council. Juan Flores, its highest-ranking member, argued that he had sworn to uphold the 1824 Constitution and must continue to do so. Other council members responded that they were in a very weak position and did not have the luxury of resisting the movement. José María Rodríguez suggested a bureaucratic solution—to buy some time by forming a commission to study the matter—but the forces of pragmatism won the day. The council seconded the popular movement and passed the petitions on to the national government as evidence of the general sentiment in the capital. If the council members needed further evidence of the weakness of their position in the current political climate, they got it shortly thereafter. On June 16 the Minister of External and Interior Relations required the municipal council to meet with the French delegation, which had decided to offer a bust of Napoleon as a gift to the city in honor of Santa Anna. Shortly thereafter, Flores resigned. Three other council members joined him some days later.[12]

Mexico's Napoleon entered the capital again on June 17. Nothing in the fanfare and triumphal rhetoric about his unique role in unifying the nation hinted at Santa Anna's looming Waterloo in the north, although tensions had been percolating there for years. After Mexico gained its Independence from Spain, liberal land and migration policies in the far north began the transformation of Texas. Its population grew by a factor of ten over little more than a decade. Anglos composed a majority of Texas migrants, and a significant number of them arrived with slaves, despite Mexico's abolition of the practice of slaveholding soon after Independence. Conflict escalated in the 1830s between some residents of Texas and the national government, first as immigration laws changed and then as the new centralist government moved toward consolidation and a lasting resolution of the ongoing problems in the north. Texans pushing for dramatic change in the relationship between the province and the Mexican national government forced the issue, rising up in arms in mid-June of 1835. Anticipating a military occupation and harsh retribution, others joined the effort to defend Texas against the approach of centralist troops in the fall. Delegates from around the province issued an unequivocal Declaration of Independence in March of 1836. Months before that declaration, Santa Anna assumed command of the Mexican forces. Although his supporters took pains to deny that Santa Anna fancied himself a second Napoleon, the warrior president bragged that he would march across the continent to Washington, D.C., and plant the Mexican flag on the United States Capitol if necessary.[13]

Although the most dramatic events of 1835 occurred in the far north, the move to centralize government authority had consequences for the capital as well. Symbolic struggles between the central government and Mexico City's municipal council accelerated in June, when a new marching order for public processions and seating at ceremonies relegated the councilors to a much less prominent position than in the past. The council members complained bitterly that the new order placed many other officials in more prestigious positions than theirs, even though the others "are not named popularly, nor as individuals can they merit a place like that of a corporation that represents all of the citizens of the capital of Mexico." Interim President Barragán replied that he did not intend to insult the municipal council members, but that the order emerged from his desire to represent symbolically, in the "most appropriate and natural manner, true hierarchy." The president insisted that the municipal council had to understand that the seating provided to national-level officials reflected the superior position that they occupied in the new political landscape. Both sides agreed that they did not want a public confrontation, but one proved unavoidable, as the council vowed to absent themselves from all public events, after the June celebrations of Santa Anna ended, until the issue achieved satisfactory resolution.[14]

The subordination of municipal authority had concrete as well as symbolic manifestations. In July the Federal District governor established a new position of police assistant, whose primary responsibility consisted of rounding up vagrants to fill the growing demands of the army. The following year this decision and the actions of the post's incumbent became the focal points of tension between the municipal council and the governor. Other events also contributed to the council's growing unease about its place in the new system. On the evening of August 10, a commotion on the streets drew a member of the municipal council's auxiliary forces from his home to witness a military patrol arrest an irate coachbuilder's apprentice on the pretense that he was a vagrant. Confirming that he knew the man and endorsing him as a respectable citizen, the official asked for his neighbor's release. The military patrol's leader denied that municipal authorities had any jurisdiction in the matter. When the official returned with a city council member, the army patrol ran them off with shots, threatening to kill both men. The next day, the municipal council demanded that the national government order the capital's military detachments to recognize the local political authorities' jurisdiction.[15]

The council later appealed to the congress, meeting in special summer session, for redress on all issues of rights, privileges, and responsibilities. Few in the congress had the time or inclination to champion the municipal council, since the legislators were at the moment immersed in some of the most crucial debates about the nature of their mandate. The municipal council raised the issue of seating arrangements again as the Independence Day celebrations approached. The Minister of External and Interior Relations rebuffed their protests, responding that the precedents on which they based their institutional claims "had fallen into disuse." He refused to pass their petition on to the congress and warned that President Barragán would take it as a personal insult if the council failed to show up for the festivities. At this point, the council members were again split in their responses. Some argued that circumstances had changed since these symbolic conflicts first emerged in June and that the time had come for the council to make a strategic retreat, because their position in future battles would be harmed if they took a hard line and refused to attend the Independence Day celebrations. This particular holiday, they argued, was too important to the people for the council to turn it into a public rebuke of the national government. Others responded that the event's importance provided a unique opportunity to take a stand for their institution. This view became the majority position, and soon the council sent letters to the president, the Federal District governor, and the civic organizing committee to explain the absence of council members.[16]

The council missed a good show. Senator Antonio Pacheco Leal, a leader of the anti-Bustamante forces from 1830 to 1832, recounted his increasing disillusion with radicalism and his increasing admiration for Santa Anna. He spoke of Independence as a process begun in 1810, but only "consummated by Iturbide in September of 1821 and by Santa Anna in the same month of 1829." He justified the current state of affairs by recounting the frightening radical detour of 1833 as an "uninterrupted series of calamities" that brought "disease, war, [and] persecution," frightened all property owners and forced the clergy to "abandon their flocks."[17]

To give the seasonal celebrations additional cachet that year, renowned French hot-air balloonist Eugene Robertson performed a number of times. The crowds cheered as Robertson rose high above the city, accompanied by the Mexican flag, a sign proclaiming "Mexican Liberty," a portrait of Santa Anna, and even a young Mexican woman selected from the crowd, an unprecedented act. At the pinnacle of his ascent, Robertson tossed out copies of these verses:

> Free the balloonist roams the air
> Just as a great people enjoys its freedom
> Yet, as the balloon pays heed to nature
> And recognizes the pull of gravity
> The sovereign, independent nation
> Kneels before the law.[18]

Few failed to recognize that the balloon served as a metaphor for the rise of centralism. In case anyone missed the message, the government canceled the annual commemorations of the signing of the 1824 Constitution scheduled for early October, for good measure.[19]

Amid the flurry of patriotic festivities, the two legislative chambers merged to form one constitutional congress. In early October, the congress dissolved the state legislatures and placed all governors under the control of the executive branch. Federalism officially ended on October 23, 1835, with the publication of a new set of governing principles, the *Siete Leyes* (Seven Laws). These laws laid out the new responsibilities of the executive, legislative, and judicial branches of the national government, established the parameters of citizenship, demarcated new territorial divisions, and created an additional branch of government, the Supreme Conservative Power. In theory this oversight committee served to assure that none of the other branches of government overstepped its bounds, but the law defined its mandate in the vaguest terms. The congress also announced its intention to enact a uniform code of criminal, civil, and fiscal laws for the entire nation. These steps theoretically rewired the circuitry of political and economic power back through a small, national elite based in the capital. Over the course of the next year, legislators turned their attention to elaborating a new constitution to solidify this transformation.[20]

Reflecting on the changes over the last year, the centralist newspaper *El Mosquito Mexicano* gloated that the "mob no longer rules." Yet a conundrum remained. The engineers of reform always declared that they had followed the will of the people in their abandonment of the 1824 Constitution, but no changes had been made in the procedures for the transfer of elected office, one of the ways in which the sovereign people were supposed periodically to express their will. As the fall elections approached, the municipal council inquired if it should proceed as usual with elections based on the July 1830 law and received a positive reply. Federalists still believed that elections presented them with some opportunity to retrench, although there was little optimism for the short term. On the eve of the vote, the desperate editors of *El Cosmopólita* pushed for the inclusion of some federalists in government when they expressed the hope that the new municipal council would be composed of the best men for the job, regardless of their political affiliation. They also criticized the ongoing campaign against the municipal council's authority and blamed that for the miserable state of affairs in the capital. Of the Federal District governor's continued attack on municipal council prerogatives, they wrote, "When one authority invades [the realm] of others, the necessary result is unease and public disorder."[21]

The 1835 Municipal Elections

On the morning of December 6, 1835, Electoral Commissioner José Ugalde, like many of his counterparts across the city, set up a polling station for electoral Ward 54 in San Pablo parish. In conformity with the extant electoral law, the citizens gathered at the polls selected Alejandro Villaseñor, a university graduate, to preside over the vote and four secretaries to assist him. Voting commenced immediately thereafter. As the day passed, artisans, professionals, retired military officers, clerics, manual laborers, merchants, and business owners approached the table to submit numbered ballots on which they had written the name of their preferred candidate. At 2 P.M. the polls closed and the junta counted votes. Sixty-one of the ward's 161 eligible voters exercised the suffrage. Artisans and manual laborers voted in numbers just about equal to those of professionals, merchants, and business owners. Twelve different candidates received at least one vote, including a master carpenter, two merchants, a tailor, a cleric, a master blacksmith, and a commander of the customs house guard. The winner, Juan Acosta, a merchant and municipal council member, received twenty-three votes. Alejandro Villaseñor then posted the results for public perusal at the corner where the Aduana Bridge met San Gerónimo Street.

Through fortuitous circumstances, more rich evidence like this has survived for the 1835 municipal council elections than for any other election in the city between 1812 and 1837. At least some documentation exists for sixty electoral wards in five different parishes, or more than 20 percent of all wards. The documents came primarily from the center and south of the city. Sagrario, San Miguel, and Salto del Agua parishes had almost the same number of wards, San Pablo had two, and Santa Veracruz only one. The electoral details vary for each ward. Some reports only noted whether or not elections occurred, while many others contained electoral censuses and ballots. This information enables a more detailed analysis of voting patterns here than for any other elections discussed in this study. Although the census contained no data on socioeconomic status other than occupation, a sample of rent-paying adults from the nearest available general census of the population (1848) can provide additional data to suggest some conclusions about the population of voters and voting behavior.[22]

Not every ward conformed to the model behavior of the citizens and functionaries of Ward 54. Elections occurred in only thirty-two of the sixty wards in the sample, a continuation of the pattern of absenteeism that first emerged dramatically in the data from 1833. According to electoral commissioners, voter apathy pervaded most of the wards that did not have elections. Election day came, but the voters did not. Overall voter turnout for the thirty-two wards holding elections reached 32.6 percent (955 votes cast out of 2,932 eligible voters). The participation rate varied widely by ward, with a turnout as high as 90 percent in one small ward with fewer than twenty eligible voters and as low as 17.5 percent in a ward with more than two hundred eligible voters. Comparing these elections to the first carried out under the extant law, turnout in 1835 increased over 1830 in two wards, but declined significantly in all the other wards in the sample.

People at all levels of the socioeconomic scale received ballots in 1835, including domestic servants, manual laborers, and artisans of all skill levels, though not necessarily in numbers representative of their presence in the general population. Electoral commissioners played the decisive role in determining who received ballots in each ward, as well as the general conduct of the electoral process, and the variations are significant. The breakdown of votes cast by employment category shows that, in general, artisans and manual laborers were at least as likely to vote as the general population of those who received ballots. Shoemakers and carpenters, the artisans most often associated with chronic unemployment and vagrancy, were well represented in the voting sample. Over 37 percent of carpenters and almost 32 percent of shoemakers cast their votes in wards where elections took place. Bricklayers and porters, commonly dismissed as *léperos* by contemporary observers, also performed their civic duties at rates higher than the average during a time when their alleged radical Svengalis were in retreat. Together, these four groups of workers, those most commonly accused of vagrancy and troublemaking, comprised about 14.5 percent of those casting votes, just shy of their total of 15.6 percent of the city's general population of adult men in 1848. Overall, in those wards in which occupation was listed, almost 44 percent of those casting votes fell into employment categories with median rents below the overall median rent for the entire 1848 census sample. These data demonstrate that economic status alone did not determine voter participation. Across the socioeconomic spectrum, about one-third of Mexico City's eligible voters exercised the franchise in wards with elections. Of these, the city's poorer classes participated as actively as any other class, which also means that they were by now as alienated from the election process as any other citizens (see Tables 2 and 3).

A comprehensive explanation of voting patterns is impossible, although some clues exist. Some workers relied on a close connection to the municipal political structure for their livelihood. Water carriers, for example, depended on a complex patronage system to maintain access to the city's public fountains. This system brought them into contact with municipal officials on a regular basis, which may explain why water carriers emerged as one of the most active categories among voters. Almost half of the water carriers in the city who received ballots showed up to vote.[23]

Table 2. Voters by Selected Occupations, 1835 Municipal Council Elections
(For Wards with Elections)

	Number of Voters	Number of Nonvoters	% of Occupation Voting
Charcoal maker	0	6	0.0
Lawyer	2	9	18.2
Printer	4	14	22.2
Clerk (*empleado*)	28	75	27.2
Merchant	116	294	28.3
Shop assistant (*dependiente*)	23	55	29.5
Shoemaker	59	127	31.7
Porter	17	32	34.7
Bricklayer	29	48	37.7
Carpenter	34	56	37.8
Water carrier	18	20	47.4
Voter turnout for all wards	955	1,977	32.6

Note: Electoral returns were drawn from the following wards: 43, 44, 45, 51, 54, 55, 56, 57, 59, 60, 63, 64, 66, 68, 75, 79, 80, 81, 82, 83, 84, 90, 91, 92, 93, 94, 95, 96, and 99. AGN, Gobernación (Casa Amarilla), leg. 1616, exp. 1–5.
Source: Richard Warren, "Elections and Popular Political Participation in Mexico, 1808–1836," in *Liberals, Politics, and Power: State Formation in Nineteenth-Century Latin America*, ed. Vincent C. Peloso and Barbara A. Tenenbaum (Athens: University of Georgia Press, 1996), 48.

Commissioners and other electoral officials emerge as keys to different outcomes. In Ward 54, master blacksmith and Commissioner Juan Ugalde's enthusiastic distribution of 161 ballots outpaced every other commissioner in the sample except one. His ward's voter turnout of 38 percent also outpaced the sample's average. The number of ballots distributed in wards varied widely, from as few as 7 to as many as 229. Although no distinct occupational or residential pattern distinguished wards where elections occurred from those where they did not happen, a significant difference emerges when comparing the total number of ballots distributed. For wards with elections, commissioners distributed an average of almost 95 ballots. The average fell to 60 for wards without elections. Given that the vast majority of wards in the sample were in the same densely populated neighborhoods and that the wards' populations were supposed to be roughly equal, the contrast is significant. Unfortunately, little documentation is available to identify commissioners other than by their professions. Of those identified for 39 wards, merchants were by far the most common (18). No other categories had more than 2 commissioners apiece, which yielded a diverse group of volunteers, including porters, butchers, printers, and blacksmiths. Only 8 commissioners became electors for their own wards, which represents a decline in proportion from previous elections for which similar data are available. When the electors met to select a new city council, however, those in attendance reflected a long-standing pattern. The evidence supports data from earlier elections that demonstrate that ecclesiastics, military officers, merchants, and members of the liberal professions still filled the majority of electors' seats.

Table 3. Median Monthly Rents for Selected Occupations (1848 Census Sample)

	Median Monthly Rent (in Pesos)	Sample Size	% of All Workers
Bricklayer	1.12	117	4.7
Charcoal maker	1.13	26	1.0
Porter	1.25	38	1.5
Water carrier	1.50	35	1.4
Shoemaker	1.75	154	6.1
Carpenter	2.00	82	3.3
Printer	6.00	17	0.7
Shop assistant (*dependiente*)	6.00	29	1.2
Merchant	8.00	335	13.3
Clerk (*empleado*)	12.00	62	2.5
Lawyer	35.00	12	0.5
For all occupations	3.00	2,512	100.0

Note: Data were drawn from a full sample of adult males in twenty-four wards (approximately one in ten wards). Wards were chosen to reflect available electoral census data from other years. The following wards were included: 33, 35, 36, 37, 38, 39, 40, 43, 54, 57, 62, 67, 74, 80, 82, 93, 94, 95, 98, 136, 152, 153, 222, 243. AACM, vol. 3408–3409.
Source: Warren, "Elections and Popular Participation," 50.

El Diario del Gobierno, the national government's mouthpiece, expressed cautious optimism about the incoming municipal council, lauding the newly elected members as men of "probity and knowledge," who might substitute a concern for the common good for the factionalism of the past. Shortly thereafter, the same newspaper reported that the government rejected the appeals of a number of those elected who wished to renounce their positions before taking office. The outgoing municipal council, beleaguered and short-handed, endured the scorn of the national government through their last days in office. In a long editorial that expounded on the obligations of the municipal council to keep the city clean and free of vagrants, *El Diario del Gobierno* excoriated the council members of 1835 for their lack of dedication and failure to understand the nature of their work. To defend themselves, the council members agreed that they should publish a review of the events of 1835 so that the public could understand matters from their perspective. The manifesto focused on the paralysis in municipal government created by the chronic jurisdictional disputes that absorbed so much of the council's time and also noted that up to six positions in the municipal government went unfilled at any given time during the year.[24]

A Turn for the Worse, 1836

The editors of *El Diario del Gobierno* would soon wish to retract their praise for the newly elected councilors, who almost immediately moved to preserve their institutional power and resumed the struggle with the governor over Mariano Dosamantes, the aggressive police assistant. In one of its very first sessions, the new council questioned both the legal basis for the position and the personal qualifications of the man who filled it. The council placed its protest in the context of its own role as elected protector of the public trust and the city's tranquility. It also noted on a practical level that complaints against Dosamantes mounted on a regular basis. The federalist press obliged gladly with its own reports about the police officer's excesses.[25]

At first, the governor tried a solicitous strategy with the new council members, suggesting that they think of Dosamantes as their servant, although he continued to insist that Dosamantes worked under the direct authority of the governor alone. The council replied that this contravened the law and usurped its role as guardian of public order. From this point on, the relationship between the municipal council and the governor deteriorated rapidly. The official press stepped up its attacks, mocking the councilors' pretensions and performance. The municipal council accused Dosamantes of pocketing fines that he collected around the city. The governor and the council traded mutual accusations. Some increasingly frustrated council members abandoned their offices. By mid-March five council seats were empty, and a number of potential replacements had flatly refused to serve.[26]

That same month the remaining councilors decided to appeal directly to the new interim President José Justo Corro, who had replaced an ailing Miguel Barragán in February. The council declined to share copies of their petition with the governor, who retaliated by suspending three councilors. They in turn vowed to fight this action in the courts. By the end of May, the council published another account of the confrontation, appealing to the public for support of its rights and privileges. Governor Gómez de la Cortina was not intimidated by this act, since much of this dirty laundry had already been aired in the press, and the governor understood that he had the support of the congress and the executive. This pattern held into the summer. *El Cosmopólita* continued its attack on the conduct of both Dosamantes and Gómez de la Cortina, and the governor retaliated by ordering the arrest of another council member in July. In August city attorney Gabriel Sagaceta on behalf of the council wrote to the congress that Dosamantes had conducted a persecution campaign against an innocent population by arresting people on false accusations of vagrancy and sending them into the military without trials. The appeal concluded that the governor and his assistant had gone far beyond the bounds of their authority, taking on police and judicial duties that belonged only to the popularly elected municipal council.[27]

The general state of municipal and national affairs during the spring and summer of 1836 exacerbated tensions and brought a sense of the absurd to the rancorous debates over local political protocol. News from the Texas front trumpeted Santa Anna's exploits and special public celebrations commemorated his victories. Official sources continued to deny rumors of his reversal of fortune until Santa Anna's defeat at San Jacinto in April could no longer be hidden from the public. When the extent of the travesty began to sink in, the political factions blamed each other. Epidemic disease arrived in June, along with a growing currency crisis. The war in Texas weighed heavily on the public coffers, aggravating the chronic shortage of government revenue. Monetary policy encouraged the production of counterfeit copper coin, which debased the currency and led to huge discounts in the marketplace. Overnight, the street value of copper coin fell 15 percent, even though it already traded at steep discounts. Some merchants would not accept copper coin under any circumstances. The constituent congress spent hours debating the revenue crisis, but took no decisive action until the following year. In the meantime, the city's principal factions hurled accusations of arrogance, lack of patriotism, opportunism, and plain stupidity at each other.[28]

The yearly political celebrations that September loomed as a significant moment in this struggle. A military parade on September 11 provided die-hard Santa Anna supporters the opportunity to remind the public that the discredited general had once been a hero. Days later, a full-blown scandal erupted from resurgent federalists' attempts to use Independence Day to rally the public against the centralist consolidation. The federalist press complained that few public funds were forthcoming for the holiday, because the present government could not bear to expose its failure to live up to the promise of Independence. In their efforts to create an appropriate ambience, on the morning of September 16 federalists plastered flyers around town conveying insults against the national government. In his public oration, José María Aguilar y Bustamante responded to the attack on federalism made in the previous year's speech and in the revisionist press accounts of the last decade's events. Aguilar openly attacked the Seven Laws, which trampled the 1824 Constitution. One source present at the speech claimed that this bold statement brought the crowd to its feet in spontaneous applause. Even though he did not actually attend the day's events, Carlos María de Bustamante countered in his diary, "The speech displeased the audience and turned it against the speaker." After transcribing the gist of Aguilar's diatribe, Bustamante concluded that he did not "know how the President could suffer through it without making [the speaker] shut up." Congress demanded an investigation into the events, accusing Aguilar of sedition. With rumors flying that all existing copies of the speech had been collected and burned, *El Cosmopólita* drew an analogy to broader national events. It suggested that an innocent population had been sent to burn in Texas, just as the truth of Aguilar's words went up in smoke in the capital. Aguilar defended himself in the press and in court, where he was exonerated.[29]

In this autumnal tumult, the controversy between the municipal council and the Federal District governor ended in an ugly fashion for all the protagonists. The national government dismissed both Dosamantes and Governor Gómez de la Cortina. From the moment the new Federal District Governor Francisco García Conde took office, critics excoriated him as an administrative novice, a professional soldier whose inadequacies were clear, since he had not been fighting at a crucial military juncture in Mexican history. The ignominious departure of their rivals provided only a small victory for the municipal councilors in a larger war that they were losing. The principles upon which they had raised their protests went unacknowledged. National authorities continued to intervene in municipal affairs. In November 1836 additional municipal council members resigned. Even the editors of *El Mosquito Mexicano*, no friends of the federalists, acknowledged that the resignations made sense for men who refused to play "indolent fools or suffer constant martyrdom." In contrast, *El Diario del Gobierno* crowed that these latest resignations gave further indication that the municipal council ultimately would yield to the centralist juggernaut.[30]

As the 1836 elections approached, the conflict between the municipal government and the executive branch simmered, even though the personnel had changed. On October 4 the governor admonished the council to select electoral commissioners carefully.[31] Days later, alarmed by the choices the council had made, García Conde wrote to his superiors that the councilors intended to use the elections to agitate against the national government. He noted that "there are among these [commissioners] not a small number of persons notoriously disaffected from the present administration." The report also highlighted ongoing class antagonisms, as the governor continued: "So that you know the negligence with which [things] have proceeded, you should know that in an electoral precinct in Mexico City's center, inhabited by a multitude of decent people, a servant has been named, perhaps he is a citizen, but without a doubt he is not the most useful for this job, and it is enough that he is the commissioner that the residents will resist coming to the election."[32]

The following day, *El Diario del Gobierno* noted that these would surely be the last elections carried out under the 1830 legislation, the many flaws of which would be rectified by a new electoral law that had just passed through congress by an overwhelming majority of votes. By the end of the month, congress suspended the electoral process until the new legislation could be implemented. The decision outraged the federalist press, while centralists applauded. When the new legislation was published, *La Lima de Vulcano* called it "a mortal blow" to the radical federalists, who were again compared to those who precipitated the French Revolution's "Reign of Terror."[33]

The commission charged with drafting the new law provided a detailed explanation of its objectives, couching them in a review of Mexico's electoral history. They blamed many of Mexico's problems on the fact that it was still a young nation whose citizens remained unaccustomed to freedom. As a result, "parties and class or individual intrigues" distorted the national interest. Any new law had to guarantee that the voice of the true majority would emerge in elections, which could only come about if the law delivered good order in the electoral process, secured freedom of choice

at the polls, and provided stopgap measures against fraud. All legislative precedent came under scrutiny in this effort to develop a
national standard to replace the myriad state procedures. The commissioners heaped praise on the Federal District's July 1830 electoral law, with its precincts and commissioners, preelectoral census
and ballot distribution. It became the model for electoral organization under the new law.[34]

The conservative press gloated that the 1836 reform would once
and for all rob the radicals of the strategies that had delivered victory at the polls and unrest in the streets. Their assessment grew
from two key alterations of the July 1830 Federal District law. The
innovations that so animated conservatives focused on excluding
certain classes from the polls and holding office. The minimum
annual income for the suffrage rose to one hundred pesos, while
the rules returned to a colonial precedent once again by explicitly
barring domestic servants from voting regardless of their income.
The income threshold for holding national office reached fifteen
hundred pesos per annum for both the Senate and Chamber of
Deputies. There was no indication in the proposal as to how legislators arrived at the figure of one hundred pesos as the appropriate minimum income for voting. Members of this congress had been
heard to say that any resident of Mexico with an income of less
than forty pesos per month was a ne'er-do-well, and critics of the
previous election laws had called for a much higher limit. Most
scholars agree, however, that the one-hundred-peso requirement
disenfranchised the vast majority of the rural peasantry. Others
contend that up to 80 percent of the urban population would also
have been excluded from the polls. The scant evidence available
for the first elections under the new law, discussed below, suggests
that the income threshold may have had little practical impact on
who voted in the capital, since the franchise had lost its legitimacy
long before the law changed. Symbolically, however, the law had
great significance as representative of the socioeconomic biases of
the new regime's architects.[35]

The Decent Men remained haunted by the specter of class warfare. Shortly after the elections were suspended and the new law
announced, *El Diario del Gobierno* began a series of reports warning
the public that the "heroes of December 4, 1828, want their anniversary of pillage." The editors blamed their rivals at *El Cosmopólita*,
who "enliven the passions of the multitude," and they warned that
those who play with fire might get burnt by a general assault on
property. Over the course of the following days, *El Diario del*

Gobierno reported that the conspiracy had been nipped in the bud. The newspaper ended the year promoting the new constitution, which the editors hoped would finally sever completely the relationship between the course of recent Mexican history and that of France during the dark days of Revolution.[36]

The Fitful Start of a New Regime, 1837

In many ways, the year just ended had proved depressing. The party that had promised to bring national order lost Texas and failed to resolve the fiscal crisis. Improved relations with Spain and the Vatican provided scant compensation. The new constitution's promoters hoped that some ritual flash might start the New Year off on the right foot. Elaborate ceremonies took place in the congressional chambers and other public buildings, as elected and appointed officials in turn swore to uphold the new order. A choir sang the Te Deum in the Metropolitan Cathedral on New Year's Day. On January 4 a mixed procession of civil, military, and clerical authorities marched through the streets, carrying a copy of the constitution. But, in 1837, no one recruited people of all classes and ages to pledge allegiance. No priests delivered homilies about the rights of individuals. No one announced to Mexico City's masses, as in previous celebrations, the dawn of an age of equality. Was it any surprise that these ceremonies, inaugurating the third constitution in as many decades, generated little excitement?[37]

Instead, popular concern focused on the grave fiscal crisis that gripped Mexico. The centralist government had inherited a deficit from the federalists, while the demands of war in Texas further strained public resources. Readily available counterfeit specie fueled a downward spiral of confidence in copper coin. Legislators could delay the difficult choices no longer. In January, the congress ordered a freeze on the production of copper currency and agreed to amortize at its face value the specie already in circulation. Unpersuaded by these measures, merchants throughout the country continued to discount the currency. Speculators began flooding Mexico City with both legitimate and counterfeit coin, in the expectation that it would hold more of its value in the capital. This influx of coin set off a round of severe inflation in the city, as consumers panicked and merchants began to levy even greater discounts on copper coin, and then more refused to accept it at all.[38]

For those intrepid council members who still hoped to redeem the reputation of the municipal council and shore up its place in the institutional hierarchies of power and privilege, the growing copper currency crisis provided one potential means to those ends. When rumors of a devaluation circulated in mid-January and mills and slaughterhouses began to accept only gold or silver in payment for their services, the municipal council considered posting a public appeal to the national government for redress on behalf of its constituency. Since the congress appeared on the verge of issuing new legislation on the matter, the council agreed for the time being to publish only its exchange of letters with the governor to acknowledge that both parties were aware of the currency difficulties and were waiting to see how the congress would respond.[39]

The municipal council was not well positioned to fight the institutional battles ahead. Local government functioned under a huge cloud of public suspicions of embezzlement, sweetheart contracts, and general malfeasance. The council had not handed its accounts records over to higher authorities since 1828, and in the year past, several municipal employees and councilors had been accused of crimes ranging from diverting public resources for private ends to rape. The council had ongoing difficulties in achieving a quorum to conduct business and could not fill its vacancies. The remaining members spent most of their time in early 1837 distracted by the national government's decision to place the newly formed departmental governor's offices in the municipal council building, a literal and metaphorical displacement of the municipal council that enraged them. They also faced the first elections to be conducted under the new national legislation.[40]

The major Mexico City and U.S. archives yielded little documentation on these congressional elections conducted in early February. Electoral records for only seven wards remain in the municipal archives, a sample too small to reveal broad trends, but sufficient to suggest lines of inquiry. Aggregate voter turnout in these wards was almost exactly the same in 1837 as it was for the 1830 congressional elections, the first elections conducted under the July 1830 reforms of the Decent Men. A difference of two votes separated the outcomes. The proportion of manual laborers, such as porters and masons, among eligible voters is much lower in 1837 than in 1835, although one must consider that these groups of workers tended to live in higher concentrations in certain neighborhoods, and therefore the phenomenon may be a result of the small number of extant censuses. In contrast, carpenters and shoemakers were represented in similar proportions among eligible voters for both years. Domestic servants, over 3 percent of those receiving ballots in 1835, had been wiped from the voter rolls by the electoral commissioners of these words.[41]

For election day, the city's 245 wards were consolidated into only 81 polling sections. Elections took place in 80 of them. In Section Four, Colonel José Ignacio Ormaechéa conducted the preelectoral census and emerged as the winner, a repeat of his victory in the 1830 congressional elections. Pedro Escobedo, who received the most votes in Section 11, also joined the numerous electoral delegates who repeated their victories from the Age of Decent Men in 1830 and 1831. Partisan observers offered alternative interpretations of this process. One federalist wrote of the "determined actions taken by the aristocratic party to dominate the people, who viewed with the greatest contempt" these first national elections under the new regime. In contrast, *El Diario del Gobierno* suggested that the outcome legitimized the transition to centralism and made more difficult any "foolhardy attempts" of the federalists to retake power. Having found a formula that promised to deliver votes to the cause of the centralists and Decent Men, the paper's editors now warned that "excesses [are] brought not by electoral power but by intrigue and force."[42]

This hypothesis would be tested shortly. Unnerved by public response to its January currency legislation, the congress reversed its decision and passed new guidelines on March 8 for the amortization of copper currency at its accepted market value, which at the time was about half its nominal value. Rumors of such a move had been reported in the press for days, leading one newspaper to report that the capital teetered on the lip of a volcano, about to succumb to riots reminiscent of the bloodiest scenes of the French Revolution.[43]

A generous deployment of troops and cannon at the entrances to the National Palace maintained the peace on the day congress issued its decree. Tensions grew the following day, as some stores closed their doors early, while others ran out of staple goods, refused to accept copper currency, or demanded significant premiums for accepting payment in copper. A dramatic confrontation ensued on March 11. That morning, large crowds took to the streets of the capital. One group descended on the main plaza, gathered outside the congressional chambers, and demanded entry. Others ran through the streets, shouted slogans, traded insults with the military, threw rocks, and threatened local businesses. Popular disturbances also occurred in the towns of Orizaba, Acámbaro, Querétaro, and Morelia.[44]

Carlos María de Bustamante described the Mexico City riot as the wild actions of a mob of *léperos* under the sway of radical federalists. He recorded in his diary a conversation with a military officer at the National Palace, who told him, "Here we have a planned undertaking, the pretext is copper, but the objectives are different." *El Diario del Gobierno* concurred that "the infamous machinations of anarchists" caused the unrest. A very different picture emerged from the observations of an anonymous writer, whose federalist sympathies are evident in passages of his diary. He wrote that, although "the poorest folk" formed a majority of participants, "many persons of distinct opinions" joined this unpremeditated uprising. Despite differing interpretations of the motivations of the participants and the larger meaning of these events, the sources do concur on a number of details of the crowd's actions.[45]

The crowd emerges as a heterogeneous group of actors, whose status cannot be reduced to a vague socioeconomic category, such as "the poor," and whose motivations cannot be reduced to hunger, the search for booty, or manipulation from above. From a number of sources, we know that some groups attacked commercial establishments, which one would expect given the context of rising prices and food shortages. Others gathered to force their way into the National Palace to confront the congress, some stoned the home of interim President José Justo Corro, and still others engaged in altercations with military detachments. Although both political and material desire and frustration mixed in the day's events, no general, random attacks on property occurred.

Another striking feature of the copper currency riot was the hostility manifested between the crowds and the military. Antagonisms ranged from the exchange of insults to physical altercations resulting in injuries and several deaths. This violence raises interesting questions about the fluid nature of civil-military relations in the capital after Independence. The mid-1830s apparently was a time of rising tensions between soldiers and civilians, due to the increased use of the levy for troops of the line during the Texas war and resentment of and disillusionment with the army's poor performance in the north. The national government had long been disappointed by municipal council efforts to enlist sufficient troops through the Vagrancy Tribunal and suspended that court's functions in August 1836. In turn, the army stepped up its efforts to round up recruits directly. These actions increased both the friction between the council and the central government and the street confrontations over the levy.[46]

Not only was this a battle of stones, flesh, and coin, it was a discursive battle as well. Protesters tore down posters produced by the departmental governor to announce measures designed to restore order and plastered the city with their own flyers. As one might expect, hostility towards the current government and the desire for a viable and stable currency emerged as major themes. A poem, reproduced on flyers hung around the city, captured the anger of the protesters. Loosely translated, it read:

> Jesus Christ in his Passion
> Gave the criminal relief
> The Congress for its pleasure
> Makes the honest man a thief.[47]

Much of the rhetoric shouted by the protesters appears prefabricated, perhaps garnered in the last few days from the "seditious posters and public allocutions of some well-known apostles of disorder."[48] People in the crowd chanted, "Death to the congress," "Long live federalism," and "Give us back our currency." These well-worn formulas mixed with visceral exclamations that revealed a popular sentiment beyond the control of elites. In the height of the excitement, rioters referred to the heady days of popular radicalism, denouncing merchants and shouting a chorus of "Death to foreigners." The strong popular resentment of merchants and foreigners frightened even opposition leaders, many of whom were involved in commerce and most of whom had spent plenty of time dealing with foreigners in their own intermittent exiles, family affairs, and business dealings. Even critics of foreign moneylenders denounced, and attempted to downplay, this facet of crowd sentiment, labeling it the work of a few perverse elements. Finally, one person added the anomalous lament, "We do not want treaties with the pope!" This iconoclast reaped nothing but ridicule in the press. Yet one might also think of him as an individual offering up an inspired, improvisational addendum to the day's goals, perhaps a call to revive the radical anticlericalism of 1833 and 1834. He certainly demonstrated an awareness that Mexico's long rift with the Vatican was healing, as well as suspicion of the implications of that rapprochement. After all, only a few short weeks before the riot, public celebrations trumpeted the recent papal recognition of Mexico's Independence.[49]

The enthusiasms on the day of the riot quickly gave way to a universally noted quiescence the following morning. Here, the actions of the city's civil and military authorities had played the key role. A new departmental governor had been appointed in February. Both he and the municipal council members saw the currency crisis as another battleground in their institutional struggle. When unrest broke out on March 11, a small number of councilors came together to discuss a course of action. They agreed that the council's first act should be to make its analysis of the situation known to the congress and ostensibly to calm the city's residents. The council members issued a poster to alert the public that they would send representatives to the congress that very day. The appeal to congress, the essence of which was stated in the poster, suggested that the redemption of copper coin for a limited time at its predèvaluation level should be guaranteed, and then be followed by a reduction to its current market value. The message to congress also warned that the people of Mexico City had suffered more than any other population in the country, that the crisis affected not only the poorest classes, but also public employees and the military who were paid in copper. If actions were not taken soon, the council warned, violence might escalate and perhaps destabilize the national government. The councilors also sent notices to the farmers on the outskirts of the city asking them to bring staples to market. They offered to waive the traditional gratuity charged on incoming goods by the city's market administrators in exchange for the farmers' patriotism during the capital's food shortage. Governor Vieyra, like the municipal council members, employed a public relations strategy as his earliest response to the devaluation. On March 9 his office produced a poster that thanked Mexico City's residents for their calm response to the copper crisis. At the same time, he ordered all shops in the city to remain open during their regular business hours.[50]

These were not novel acts for either the councilors or the governor, but within the broader context of the centralist transition and the crisis of 1837, council members made several fundamental miscalculations. Most important among them, they entertained the misguided belief that their suggested solution would have a tranquilizing effect in the marketplace. The implication that copper currency would be subjected to further government manipulation of unclear duration provided scant comfort to anyone. There is little indication that the proprietors of the farms on the city's outskirts responded with any more enthusiasm to the council's appeals than merchants or consumers did. The councilors' belief that, under the pressing circumstances of the day, they could eschew protocol and address the congress directly on any issue without first receiving the approval of the departmental governor—let alone advocate changes in national policy—proved to be another grave political mistake. Governor Vieyra responded quickly and dramatically.[51]

When unrest broke out on March 11, the governor left his desk and took to the streets to lead the efforts to preserve order. He instituted several emergency measures over the next few days. Civilians were forbidden to ride horses, all public entertainment was postponed, and gatherings of more than five persons were banned. He also prohibited the posting of flyers or other information in public places by anyone, whether public functionaries or private citizens, without his prior consent. The governor's concerns extended beyond the immediate restoration of public order. He emphasized in his irate communications with the municipal council that it now operated in a "reduced orbit," subordinate to the governor himself. From Vieyra's perspective, the municipal council's actions on March 11 were doubly subversive. On one level, the council had flouted the governor's authority by corresponding directly with the congress—indeed, by taking any action without first consulting with, and receiving approval from, his office. The governor explained that, as far as he was concerned, the capital's municipal government had no more authority to act independently than any of the other 217 municipalities in the Department of Mexico. By writing to the congress and publicizing this action the councilors had clearly breached the lines of institutional authority. On another level, while pursuing this power play, the municipal council had failed, in the governor's eyes, to carry out its fundamental duty to preserve public order in the capital.[52]

The council responded that necessity in the middle of a crisis, and not insubordination with delusions of a federalist renaissance, had motivated them, but they failed to convince the governor, who called the council into permanent session in the evening of March 11. Comments about the council's mix of arrogance and incompetence peppered the governor's correspondence. He wrote angrily that he had been out on the streets risking his life while the council had remained ensconced in its offices composing subversive correspondence. Such actions suggested to Vieyra that the councilors felt their primary function was to spend other people's money rather than to preserve public order. In retaliation, the governor levied a fine of fifty pesos against each of the individuals who had signed the letter to congress. By the end of the month he had implemented an audit of the municipal council's financial dealings and revoked the council's ability to spend money without the auditor's approval.[53]

These restrictions persisted for months, during which time the municipal council virtually disbanded. Between April 4 and June 12, the council members met only once, shortly before the newly elected members were supposed to assume local power, although little incentive remained for anyone else to fill these positions. Debate over the municipal council's performance during the crisis of 1837, and the broader questions about the nature of political authority under the centralist regime, continued through early 1838. Many individuals tapped for service in the municipal government during the next year refused to take office, frightened away from public service by the ongoing dispute. If further discouragement were needed, it came from the poor state of the city's fiscal resources and infrastructure.[54]

A final key to understanding the importance of the 1837 riot lay in the behavior of the city's military regiments. Despite the fact that most of the troops were paid in the same depreciating copper currency as the rebellious groups in the streets, they remained loyal to the government. This stands in sharp contrast to the events of December 1828, when the capital's regiments joined the Rebellion of the Acordada to bring Vicente Guerrero to power and then joined in the looting of the Parián market.[55] In 1837, when at least one military unit was accused of aiding a crowd intent on sacking a business, the timely arrival of other troops thwarted even that much collaboration.

The soldiers who held firm in March received a reward for their loyalty. Their commander general published a note of appreciation to his troops. The national government soon granted a special bonus to the capital's regiments for their performance during the crisis.[56] For all the recent debates over civilian political processes, the congress recognized the obvious: the military held the key to the new regime's survival. In March, the city's troops sided with the sitting government. A healthy bonus might provide some insurance for the future.

Notes

1. Sordo, *El Congreso*, 233; *Legislación Mexicana*, ed. Dublán and Lozano, 3:295–96.

2. Di Tella, *National Popular Politics*, 236; Sordo, *El Congreso*, 84; Costeloe, *Central Republic*, 37–38; *El Mosquito Mexicano*, June 17 and July 4,

1834; *El Telégrafo,* June 23, 1834, quoted in Costeloe, *Central Republic,* 42; Proclamation, August 8, 1834, in *Legislación electoral mexicana,* ed. García Orozco, 55; Notice to Municipal Council, August 11, 1834, AACM, vol. 4151, exp. 6.

3. Sordo, *El Congreso,* 84–106.

4. *El Mosquito Mexicano,* September 23 and 26, 1834; *La Lima de Vulcano,* October 16, 1834; *El Telégrafo,* September 25, 1834; Sordo, *El Congreso,* 105, 110–11; 122–26; Costeloe, *Central Republic,* 43–44.

5. *La Lima de Vulcano,* October 16 and 23, 1834; José María Castañeda y Escalada, "Oración Cívica . . . 16 de septiembre de 1834," in *La conciencia nacional,* ed. Torre Villar, 109–15; Legislation, May 20, 1835, *Legislación mexicana,* ed. Dublán y Lozano, 3:48.

6. Letter to the Editor, *El Mosquito Mexicano,* September 23, 1834; Costeloe, "Junta Patriótica," 36–37; Richard Warren, "The Construction of Independence Day in Mexico, 1821–1864," paper presented at "Culture, Power, and Politics in Nineteenth Century Mexico: A Conference in Memory of Dr. Nettie Lee Benson," University of Texas, Austin, April 1994, 11–12.

7. *El Telégrafo,* August 16, 1834; Superior Order, October 28, 1834, AGN, Ayuntamientos, vol. 16, 235.

8. *El Mosquito Mexicano,* December 6, 12, 16, 17, and 19, 1834; *La Lima de Vulcano,* December 16, 1834; *El Telégrafo,* December 8 and 22, 1834; Municipal Council Correspondence, AGN, Ayuntamientos, vol. 16, 236–64.

9. *Cuestión del día, o nuestros males y sus remedios* (Morelia, Mexico: Imp. Juan Evaristo de Oñate, 1834); Sordo, *El Congreso,* 147–53.

10. Guardino, *Peasants, Politics,* 139; Sordo, *El Congreso,* 157–60.

11. Sordo, *El Congreso,* 174–78; Municipal Council Minutes, June 12, 1835, AACM, vol. 155a; Costeloe, *Central Republic,* 62.

12. Municipal Council Minutes, June 13–16, 1835, AACM, vol. 155a; Municipal Council Correspondence, AGN, Ayuntamientos, vol. 19, 2–6, 140.

13. David J. Weber, *The Mexican Frontier, 1821–1846: The American Southwest under Mexico* (Albuquerque: University of New Mexico Press, 1982), 242–51; Sordo, *El Congreso,* 239; *Diario del Gobierno,* November 7, 1835, quoted in Costeloe, *Central Republic,* 52; Calcott, *Santa Anna,* 126.

14. Municipal Council Minutes, June 20 and 23, 1835, AACM, vol. 294a; Gortari, "Política y administración," 172–75.

15. Serrano Ortega, "Levas," 152; Municipal Council Minutes, August 11, 1835, AACM, vol. 294a.

16. Municipal Council Minutes, September 14 and 15, 1835, AACM, vol 294a; *Representación que el Ayuntamiento de México elevó a las augustas cámaras en defensa de los derechos y prerogativas de la Capital de la República* (Mexico City: Imp. Ignacio Cumplido, 1836).

17. *Discurso pronunciado por el ciudadano Antonio Pacheco Leal . . .* (Mexico City: Imp. Ignacio Cumplido, 1835); Sordo, *El Congreso,* 196; Vázquez, "La crisis," 560.

18. *El Diario del Gobierno,* September 19 and 30, 1835.

19. Proclamation, September 22, 1835, in *Legislación mexicana,* eds. Dublán y Lozano, 3:74.

20. Costeloe, *Central Republic,* 99–103; Sordo, *El Congreso,* 203–5; Guardino, *Peasants, Politics,* 140–41; Tenenbaum, *Politics of Penury,* 42.

21. *El Mosquito Mexicano*, September 22, 1835; Municipal Council Minutes, October 27 and November 3, 1835, AACM, vol. 155a; *El Cosmopólita*, December 19, 1835.

22. 1835 Election Documents, AGN, Gobernación, Casa Amarilla, leg. 1616, exp. 1–5; 1848 Census Documents, AACM, vol. 3408–3409.

23. The patronage system for water carriers is described in Alejandra Moreno Toscano, "Los trabajadores y el proyecto de industrialización, 1810–1867," in *La clase obrera en la historia de México*, vol. 1, *De la colonia al imperio*, ed. Enrique Florescano, 5th ed. (Mexico City: Siglo XXI, 1986), 329.

24. *Diario del Gobierno*, December 20 and 22, 1835, January 7, 1836; Municipal Council Secret Session, December 23, 1835, AACM, vol. 294a; *Manifiesto del ayuntamiento de 1835 al público mexicano* (Mexico City: Imp. Tomás Uribe y Alcalde, 1836).

25. Municipal Council Secret Sessions, January 13 and 21, 1836, AACM, vol. 295a; *El Cosmopólita*, January 13, 1836.

26. Municipal Council Secret Sessions, January 21, 1836, AACM, vol. 295a; *Diario del Gobierno*, February 18 and March 23, 1836; Municipal Council Correspondence, March 21, 1836, AGN, Ayuntamientos, vol. 19, 157; Municipal Council Correspondence, January through March 1836, AACM, vol. 862, exp. 26.

27. Municipal Council Minutes, March 22, April 19, May 27 and 28, 1836, AACM, vol. 156a; *Acta del cabildo celebrado por el exmo Ayuntamiento de México el 30 de mayo de 1836, mandada imprimir por el mismo con los documentos a que se refiere* (Mexico City: Imp. Jose Mariano F. de Lara, 1836); *El Cosmopólita*, June 4 and July 20, 1836; Municipal Council Secret Sessions, July 12, 1836, AACM, vol. 295a; *Acusación que el Licenciado Gabriel Sagazeta, Síndico Segundo del exmo. Ayuntamiento de esta capital, eleva, como Procurador del Común, al Soberano Congreso Nacional contra el Señor Gobernador del Distrito don José Gómez de la Cortina* (Mexico City: Imp. de Galván, 1836).

28. *Diario del Gobierno*, April 18, May 14, June 25, July 13 and 16, August 6, 8, and 9, 1836; *El Cosmopólita*, June 25, 1836; Costeloe, *Central Republic*, 80; Sordo, *El Congreso*, 249; *Proceso del General Santa Anna* (Mexico City: Imp. Francisco Torres, 1836).

29. *Diario del Gobierno*, September 11, 12, and 22, 1836, February 4, 1837; *El Cosmopólita*, September 24 and October 1, 1836; Bustamante, "Diario histórico," entry of September 16, 1836, BNAH, microfilm, roll 13; Plasencia, *Independencia y nacionalismo*, 47.

30. *La Lima de Vulcano*, November 3, 1836; *El Mosquito Mexicano*, November 8, 1836; *Diario del Gobierno*, November 3, 1836.

31. Governor to Municipal Council, AACM, vol. 862, exp. 27.

32. Governor to Minister of Interior and External Relations, November 24, 1836, AGN, Ayuntamientos, vol. 20, 76.

33. Sordo, *El Congreso*, 232; Municipal Council Correspondence, November 29, 1836, AACM, vol. 862, exp. 27; *Diario del Gobierno*, December 6, 1836.

34 . Juan Gómez de Navarrete, *Proyecto de ley para el establecimiento de Colegios Electorales en la República mexicana* (Mexico City: Imp. del Aguila, 1834).

35. Anna, *Forging Mexico*, 261; Guardino, *Peasants, Politics*, 100; Costeloe, *Central Republic*, 107–9.

36. *Diario del Gobierno*, December 9, 11, 12, and 28, 1836.

37. Proclamation, AACM, vol. 2253, exp. 23.

38. *El Cosmopólita*, June 25, 1836, February 18, 1837; *Diario del Gobierno*, July 13, 1836; Costeloe, *Central Republic*, 80; Sordo, *El Congreso*, 249–51; Municipal Council Correspondence, AACM, vol. 3284, exp. 10, doc. 1.

39. Municipal Council Minutes, January 16, 1837, AACM, vol. 157a; *Diario del Gobierno*, January 22, 1837.

40. *El Mosquito Mexicano*, February 3 and August 16, 1837; Municipal Council Minutes, 1867 and 1837, AACM, vol. 156a, 157a; Municipal Council Secret Sessions, 1836 and 1837, AACM, vol. 268a, 269a; Municipal Council Correspondence, AGN, Ayuntamientos, vol. 20; *El Mosquito Mexicano*, February 3, 1837; *Diario del Gobierno*, February 11, 1837.

41. 1830 Election Results, *Registro Oficial*, October 2, 1830; 1835 Electoral Census, AGN, Gobernación, Casa Amarilla, leg. 1616, exp. 1–5; 1837 Electoral Census and Results, AACM, vol. 4155, exp. 226, 227.

42. Number of Sections Voting, Costeloe, *Central Republic*, 119; Election Results, AACM, vol. 4155, exp. 226, 227; federalist comment, "Diario político y militar, 1836–1837," entry of February 5, 1837, BLAC-UTA, GG, doc. G441; *Diario del Gobierno*, February 14 and March 8, 1837.

43. *Diario del Gobierno*, March 9, 1837; *La Lima de Vulcano*, March 4, 1837.

44. *La Lima de Vulcano*, March 9, 1837; *El Mosquito Mexicano*, March 14, 1837.

45. Bustamante, "Diario histórico," entry of March 11, 1837, BNAH, microfilm, roll 14; *Diario del Gobierno*, March 14, 1837; "Diario político y militar," entries of March 11 and 14, 1837, BLAC-UTA, GG, doc. G441.

46. Serrano Ortega, "Levas," 144; Richard Warren, "Desafío y trastorno en el gobierno municipal: El Ayuntamiento de México y la dinámica política nacional, 1821–1855," in *Ciudad de México: Instituciones, actores sociales, y conflicto político, 1774–1932*, ed. Carlos Illades and Ariel Rodríguez Kuri (Mexico City: El Colegio de Michoacán and Universidad Autónoma Metropolitana, 1996), 127.

47. José Ramón Malo, *Diario de sucesos notables* (Mexico City: Editorial Patria, 1948), quoted in Sordo, *El Congreso*, 251.

48. *Diario del Gobierno*, March 14, 1837.

49. Sordo, *El Congreso*, 251; "Diario político y militar," entry of March 11, 1837, BLAC-UTA, GG, doc. G441; *El Mosquito Mexicano*, March 17, 1837; *El Cosmopólita*, February 25, 1837.

50. Municipal Council Proclamation and Correspondence, AACM, vol. 3284, exp. 10, doc. 7, 9, 12, 13; Governor's Proclamations, *Diario del Gobierno*, March 10, 1837.

51. Municipal Council Correspondence, AACM, vol. 3284, exp. 10, doc. 7–10, 13–14; Municipal Council Minutes, March 11, 1837, AACM, vol. 157a.

52. Proclamations of March 11 and 12, 1837, *Diario del Gobierno*, March 12 and 13, 1837; Governor to Municipal Council, in *Manifestación que hace el ayuntamiento de esta capital sobre las contestaciones originadas por la exposición que elevó al Soberano Congreso Nacional el día 11 del presente* (Mexico City: Oficina de Luis Abadiano, 1837); Rodríguez Kuri, "Política e institu-cionalidad," 2:82.

53. Municipal Council Correspondence, AACM, vol. 3284, exp. 10, doc. 17–18; Municipal Council Minutes, March 29, 1837, AACM, vol. 157a.

54. Municipal Council Minutes, June 23, 1837, AACM, vol. 157a; *Diario del Gobierno*, January 27, 1838; Municipal Council Correspondence, AACM, vol. 862, exp. 28, 29.

55. Arrom, "Popular Politics," 245–68.

56. *Diario del Gobierno*, March 12, 1837; *El Mosquito Mexicano*, March 17, 1837.

Conclusion

As a youth during the Independence War, Lucas Alamán lived through the traumatic attack by Miguel Hidalgo's mass army on his hometown of Guanajuato. Four decades later, in 1849, Alamán served on Mexico City's municipal council during the partisan strife that followed the devastating war with the United States. In early December, an irate group took to the streets, shouting insults, breaking windows, and physically threatening the council members. In a letter to the governor, the councilors noted that these actions spoke "in a language all too clear and very well understood." They all resigned. Events such as these provided the fodder for Alamán's most famous work, the multivolume *History of Mexico*. Alamán modeled his book on the work of English conservative Edmund Burke, hoping that his review of Mexican history since Independence would do for the understanding of Mexico what Burke's *Reflections on the Revolution in France* had done for shaping many perceptions of the quintessential revolution.[1]

Alamán was not alone in this kind of enterprise. Observers and activists across the political spectrum turned to Europe, especially France, as their reference point when searching for appropriate comparisons and insights in their attempts to comprehend the political dilemmas of their new nation-state. Recent scholarship has revived the trans-Atlantic comparative method in the search for a better understanding of what Latin America shared with other nation-states during the Age of Revolution, as well as of what may have been unusual or unique about the region.[2] Turning this method to the rituals and mechanisms of popular political participation provides both a useful antidote to the still-common interpretation of a geographically proscribed progressive democratic teleology and highlights the relevance of the Mexican experience for understanding better the relationship among popular sovereignty, mass politics, and nation-state formation.

Elections and Popular Political Participation

Mexico's roller-coaster ride of electoral politics mirrors that of other nations during this era. For generations in Europe and the Americas, debates raged over the nature of citizenship and the necessary qualities of citizens. State builders tinkered with suffrage requirements and electoral mechanisms to manage the way people inserted themselves into the political process as voters, officeholders, and in others ways as claimants to their rights as citizens. Because Alamán and his contemporaries most often used the French Revolution as their touchstone, it may be worth following their lead. In revolutionary France, the "electoral system was the weakest spot in a precarious constitutional structure."[3] Suffrage criteria were modified on four occasions and voting mechanisms changed almost annually, as French state builders, like their Mexican counterparts, searched for ways to mesh a more democratic suffrage and an antiquated electoral process in which the concept of voting itself was still ambiguously defined and organizers were uncertain about the appropriate mechanisms for the summation of individual choice rather than the corporate consensus traditionally associated with political decisions.[4]

Early distinctions between the broader universe of those with civil rights (passive citizens) and the smaller universe of eligible voters (active citizens), selected not only because of their control of property but also their length of tenure in one place, reflected the limited nature of popular participation envisioned during the early phases of the French Revolution. Those eligible to serve as electors and hold office occupied the smallest of political worlds. All in all, about two-thirds of the adult male population had the right to vote in 1791, while there were probably no more than fifty thousand men in all of France who met the requirements to be electors. When the revolution accelerated, the distinction between active and passive citizens disappeared and the franchise was greatly expanded, but the most radical reforms did not survive the end of the decade.[5]

As the interplay between political theory and electoral mechanics evolved, ambitious politicians gained their apprenticeship, patrolling the taverns, mobilizing through the Masonic lodges, and distributing prefabricated lists of their associates for use on election day. A new political activism, which included artisans and small shopkeepers, began to develop in the cities of France, leading conservative critics to lament the loss of politics to the "dregs of society." Ultimately, however, the republican leadership that emerged in urban France was decidedly bourgeois in class origin and outlook. Its thinking about the suffrage reflected a strong belief in the relationship between property, place, and political rights. While electoral procedures and suffrage laws changed constantly in the Age of Revolution, in all but five of the fifty-seven years between 1791 and 1848, "holders of property had greater political rights than their propertyless fellow citizens." The electoral law of 1831, for example, based the suffrage on tax status and enfranchised only 20 to 25 percent of all males over twenty-one for municipal elections. The cutoff for national elections was much stricter. During the revolutionary upheavals of 1848, the provisional government again announced universal adult male suffrage, but this expansion did not last long. The conservative reaction in 1850 cut the size of the electorate by almost 30 percent. It would take several more generations for French elites to become reconciled to the fact that universal male suffrage was not by definition a threat to the social order.[6]

The French pattern also resonates with the Mexican in terms of the trajectories of voter participation. Trends in voter turnout during the revolutionary decade in France reflect a concern with effective suffrage similar to that found in Mexico during the 1830s. Available figures suggest a dramatic variation in voting by place, with turnout conspicuously low in Paris, where it rarely exceeded 15 percent of the eligible population, and at times, fell under 10 percent. Voters abandoned the polls early in the revolutionary decade out of frustration, not because of any particular outcome, but because of the lack of any demonstrable results from participation.[7] As one prescient assembly deputy observed, "Repeated governmental interference with the electoral process" caused "disaffection and depoliticization."[8] In both Mexico and France, a distinct failure to countenance parties or accept the peaceful disputation of interests contributed to disaffection. A paradoxical situation resulted in both countries. Intense factional competition mobilized the masses through legitimate channels such as elections and public rallies, yet this behavior frightened elites of all persuasions, who often condemned the activities of their rivals. Voices of moderation in France, like their Mexican counterparts, urged voters to avoid factionalism in political life and to look for leaders lacking personal ambition, who would therefore legislate for the good of the entire nation, rather than any particular interest. Yet a common accusation against those who did not share one's own view of the national interest was that they had ceased to be legitimate actors in the public realm. The rejection of pluralism drove down electoral participation, but it did not reduce the odds of the kind of popular unrest most feared by elites. In fact, the early development of competition through a party system proved in other societies to be one of the principal means of reconciling popular participation with political stability in the presence of pronounced material inequalities.[9]

In this respect the English pattern presents some fascinating comparative opportunities that look beyond franchise legislation as the sole gauge of popular political participation. A long history of public competition for office, coupled with regional and temporal oscillations in the franchise and the frequency of elections, created a rich and complex tradition. Although only a strictly limited number of men held the vote in comparison to the total population, by the seventeenth century the absolute number of voters in county constituencies and large boroughs had become so large that political factions had to develop techniques of political persuasion, which created a large public sphere for the discussion of partisan politics. As an ever increasing number of electoral pamphlets found their way into print, most villages and towns began to display internal party divisions. All manner of rituals associated with the election season proliferated as well. These rituals appealed to voters and nonvoters alike, and gave even the disenfranchised a role to play in elections. Campaign practices, such as processions, canvassing, and passionate stump speeches, all linked with music and fireworks, broke the routines of daily life for the cyclical conduct of competitive politics. The postelection tradition of "chairing" gave the masses a role in metaphorically carrying candidates to victory, even when they could not actually cast a ballot. These activities were widespread, expected, and to a great extent, coordinated by the competing factions who worked equally hard at campaigning and maintaining peace and order during the election season. Candidates invoked images of how good citizens mixed enthusiasm with restraint, and postelection accounts almost always emphasized in equal measure the extent of participation and the good order that prevailed. Nonetheless, between 1689 and 1715, partisan politics grew particularly contentious, forcing twelve general elections, only one less than occurred in the rest of the eighteenth century. The intensity, expense, and unpredictability of this competition exhausted and frightened members of all political factions, who began to manipulate the mechanisms at hand to whittle away at popular participation, so that by the middle of the eighteenth century much of the tradition described above had been lost.[10]

The fitful history of subsequent reform in England is beyond the reach of this brief review. However, a number of key points of comparison stand out amid the slow accretion of new categories of voters: the synchronization of municipal and national suffrage regulations, the adoption of the secret ballot, and the full expansion of the suffrage to adult men and women in the twentieth century. Most important would be the endurance of a greatly restricted universe of eligible voters by law, compared to that of Mexico and the rest of Latin America. The Great Reform Act of 1832 increased the proportion of enfranchised adult men to one in five in England and Wales, one in eight men in Scotland, and one in twenty in Ireland. The Municipal Reform Act of 1835, which enfranchised voters for borough council elections, placed even greater restrictions on the suffrage than those established in 1832 for parliamentary elections. All told, perhaps 4.2 percent of the adult population could vote in 1833, a lower percentage of the population than in Queen Anne's time in the early eighteenth century.[11] In contrast, in Mexico City, while data on the number of eligible voters is difficult to estimate, undisputed turnout for municipal elections in the period from 1829 to 1831 hovered around 27 percent of the city's estimated total male population. Turnout in contests for national and local office over the three decades discussed in this study renders it difficult to regard such data as unimportant or anomalous.[12]

Historians have uncovered similarly provocative data all over Latin America, which has triggered an ongoing challenge to traditional thinking about political culture and the role of elections.[13] The study of elections in Latin America must begin with the most fundamental surprise of all: that, "with a few exceptions, in most Latin American countries the idea of an extended suffrage gained ground during the first half of the nineteenth century to an extent which has few parallels in the western world."[14] This precocious rise of a broad franchise can be traced to the imperial crisis of the early nineteenth century, not only because of events in Spain, but also because of the actions of both elites and masses in the Americas. Among others, Mexican delegates to the Cortes argued that they came to Spain to forge a constitution that erased the colonial distinctions of caste. Against conservative proposals that attempted to restrict political rights, they noted that popular upheaval was already at hand and that Mexico's masses expected equality to be guaranteed in any documents that emerged from the Cortes. As a consequence, the 1812 Constitution reflected not only a prevailing political philosophy, but also contained some concessions to the reality of popular upheaval as well as the hope that these concessions would preclude further distress.

Important and lasting results followed in the places where the 1812 Constitution was implemented. The experiences in Mexico City are only one example. The proliferation of newly competitive municipal offices throughout New Spain is another well-documented instance. This change in political and administrative structure reverberated in struggles over the control of resources throughout Mexico in the post-Independence era. The 1812 Constitution left a practical and philosophical legacy to the next generation, which had to contend with the notion that, if the new nations of the Americas formed constitutions that were less liberal than the 1812 Constitution by which they had been ruled and which denied to their citizens certain rights that they already thought they had, the new order would contain "the seed of its own destruction."[15]

Despite a common heritage, crucial differences in political culture emerged among the new nations of Latin America. A growing number of authors have attempted to discern the extent of popular participation, the frequency, organization, and conduct of elections, and the place of electoral rituals in the broader political life of the nascent states. Within the context of a generally broad suffrage, investigators have discovered great variation in both law and practice on the national, regional, and local levels. Before the middle of the nineteenth century, most Latin American states had some restrictions on the suffrage in the form of property ownership, income, occupation, or a literacy requirement. Like Mexico, the threshold for participation was often simply that an adult male be gainfully employed. Those states, like Chile after 1833, that imposed a minimum income also provided numerous loopholes, such as exemptions for veterans of the Independence War. Others placed the barrier to entry so low that most artisans, salaried workers, small-scale merchants, and mine workers qualified. The 1821 Constitution of Buenos Aires Province contained a simple and precocious provision for universal adult male suffrage, which set the standard for at least three other provinces in Argentina. Later, minimal professional or educational restrictions placed only token barriers to suffrage on the population.[16]

Although the extent of the franchise is one important indication of any national political project, this study finds its place among those that have demonstrated that this is only one facet of the complex mechanisms of representative government. Eligibility to hold office, the frequency of elections, the number of elected offices at the local, regional, and national levels, even the voter registration and election procedures themselves must all be analyzed as both law and practice in order to capture more fully the nature of political participation and its variation across time and place. Each of the new Latin American nations manifested unique combinations of the above factors that yielded divergent outcomes. In Chile, for example, with few exceptions throughout most of the nineteenth century, congressional and municipal elections were held consistently every three years, and contests for the presidency occurred every five years. The voter registration process proved to be an important facet of the Chilean system, as citizens had to reconfirm their eligibility before each electoral contest, and in doing so, received voter registration cards. Elections often became contests among factions, which organized public rallies, carried on debates in partisan publications, distributed candidate lists, and also purchased voter registration cards and fought to control the qualifying committees. Although national actors often manipulated local processes from above, and scandal was common, the urban popular sectors participated in large numbers. These experiences made important contributions to the evolution of twentieth-century Chilean politics.[17]

In the nineteenth century Colombia developed a tradition of rival parties that gained supporters from all social classes. Although voter turnout in Bogotá in the 1820s (under 15 percent of the adult male population) might be considered low by Mexican standards for the same decade, Colombia developed a more stable party system than Mexico. By the middle of the nineteenth century, two political factions had emerged that would survive into the twentieth century. In their pursuit of political power, these factions negotiated with urban nonelites, such as artisans, and provided a stage on which the popular classes joined in shaping political alliances and outcomes.[18]

While these early practices provided an important avenue to the construction of an active citizenry and the foundations for a competitive electoral politics in Chile and Colombia, other South American states had different outcomes. A central historical issue for Argentina was the contrast between the broadest suffrage in the Americas and low turnout throughout the nineteenth century. An oft-cited report of Argentine indifference to elections noted that, in the 1821 Buenos Aires elections, 328 men showed up to vote, out of a population of sixty thousand. At its height after the fall of Juan Manuel de Rosas, voter turnout may have reached 25 percent of the population of adult males, but more often attendance was on the order of 10 percent, even though elections were direct, which in theory offered the masses a greater incentive to participate. Although members of the popular classes were represented among the small number of voters organized and deployed by well-oiled political machines, voting "did not seem to lead anywhere," so few "thought of voting as a privilege or as a means of exerting direct influence on the authorities." Other practices of more effective representation of demands developed alongside the political machines as the mediation space between civil society and political power.[19]

In Peru, elections played a small role in raising the "political consciousness" of the urban masses, but electoral culture was much less effervescent than in Chile, Colombia, or Mexico during the first half of the nineteenth century. Offices were attained indirectly, through highly complex procedures that helped to render electoral politics a relatively private affair devoid of competition or party organization. Congressional elections often involved the local elite's selection of one reluctant candidate, with little campaigning and hardly any challenge from or appeal to the voting constituency. Electoral reform in the mid-1850s briefly changed this pattern, but in general, Peru's tightly managed elections failed to engage the popular classes or contribute to the development of a party system.[20]

This review helps to clarify the role of the urban masses in Mexico City's electoral politics during the first decades of the nineteenth century. The data suggest that electoral participation rates in Mexico City were comparatively high, which may come as a surprise even to readers familiar with Mexican history. Voter turnout for municipal elections of the late 1820s and early 1830s fluctuated in the range of 25 to 70 percent. For the highly controversial congressional elections in 1826 and 1828, turnout may have been as high as 75 percent of the adult male population. Even if we were to discount several thousand ballots as fraudulent, that would still leave many thousands of artisans and manual laborers as an important and consistent part of the voting population in both municipal and national elections throughout the period under study. The decline in voter turnout in the 1830s resulted from a combination of forces that reflected the broader legitimacy crisis of the Mexican state, but also contributed to it.

The comparative perspective also calls into question a simple definition of effective suffrage. At least sporadically through the first half of the nineteenth century, both municipal and congressional elections were contested, and offices changed hands between representatives of one faction and another as a result. The presence of these highly polarized elite factions contributed to skyrocketing electoral participation, pushed even higher by other factors. The flexible definition of eligibility for the franchise and vague electoral mechanisms provided opportunities for electoral participation and strategies that were absent in other contexts. Attempts to refine those mechanisms to purify the political process became tied up with larger factional conflicts that rendered moot the call for electoral reform. In the 1830s the urban masses in Mexico learned, like their counterparts in Argentina and France, that the franchise alone is no gauge of a political system's responsiveness or health. Among all the transactions that define the relationship between citizens and the state, suffrage lost its currency. Ultimately, Mexico City's masses walked away from the polls as much as they were driven from them, although they did not simply disappear.

The Masses and Political Ritual

In 1833, Federal District Governor José María Tornel called the elections that he helped to organize the only political ritual in which the Mexican people "exercise directly" their sovereignty.[21] In his long career, this ardent Santa Anna supporter also played a key role in organizing dozens of other political rituals designed to condition how the people understood their sovereignty. During the first decades of the nineteenth century, Mexicans witnessed and participated in a wide array of ceremonies that influenced their perceptions of the "principles, formulae, and ground rules of political interaction," and their actions.[22] One can gain insight into elite perspectives on the changing political culture by analyzing the rituals they organized, which expose "the ideological lineaments of authority and consent in a particular historical context."[23] It is important to remember, however, that elites constructed these rituals for a broad audience, invited its participation, and therefore encouraged its reflection on the role of the public in politics.[24] The successful transfer of any lessons encoded in these rituals depended on a string of unpredictable variables, including the response of those in attendance. Crowds were a necessary component of most public political rituals, but the individuals who made up a crowd proved unruly and dangerous. Efforts to transform completely active participants into passive spectators often failed, as factions used these opportunities to make "contentious claims in public arenas."[25] The individuals in the crowd brought expectations. They also brought the potential to alter the nature of any lesson about politics contained in the ritual. Indeed, the importance of political ritual did not end with its design or even its completion. Debates about the meaning of events continued for years afterward in the press and lingered in popular memory, forming a key component of competing narratives about the new nation.[26]

The essential foundation rituals that emerged in the first half of the nineteenth century, the implementation of new constitutions and Independence Days, well illustrate these phenomena. Each of these rituals was related in very complex ways to others, and it would have been impossible to view them without placing each within a broader context formed by a great variety of civic and religious celebrations. Some aspects of the colonial vocabulary of celebration were incorporated into new rituals, while those rejected were often dropped consciously, with the decisions publicly explained and justified. The celebrations surrounding the introduction of constitutions in 1812, 1820, 1824, and 1836 provide fascinating examples of the ways in which tensions between tradition and innovation, precedent and expectation, played out.

Celebrations to introduce the 1812 Constitution were designed in general to resemble those that commemorated royal succession while simultaneously incorporating innovations, the combination of which sent a terribly mixed message to the inhabitants of Mexico City. Traditional demonstrations of hierarchy and royal beneficence merged with a more egalitarian impulse.[27] What exactly could the poor inhabitants of Mexico City have been thinking as royal officials tossed coins to them and moments later announced the arrival of liberty? How would a multiethnic audience raised in a caste system, watching processions composed of representatives of the colonial Church, state, and indigenous corporate groups, understand and respond to the message that "whoever is equal to you has arrived at the highest state"?

A difficult lesson learned by the holders of power was that rituals take place in space and time, which allowed history and memory to disrupt the utopian symbolism of their festivals. The constitutional celebrations of 1812 set precedents by which others were judged in 1820, 1824, and 1836. The return of the Spanish Constitution in 1820 was greeted with the same formalities as in the year 1812, yet popular enthusiasm was greatly curtailed. Its framers introduced the federalist 1824 Constitution with some of the same rituals, including parish masses and public readings of the constitution, but the elimination of corporate representation of the indigenous community signaled one clear change under the new regime. The absence of extensive public readings of the centralist 1836 Constitution spoke volumes about the concerns of those in power at the time. Finally, the very repetition of celebrations introducing new constitutions altered the way they were interpreted by their audience. Rituals honoring three different constitutions in three decades communicated a message of instability and provided dissidents the opportunity to develop a vocabulary of contention, to incorporate cries of "Restore the true constitution" into their repertoire.

Other celebrations were designed for repetition across time. The commemoration of Independence became the most enduring political celebration to emerge from this period, but few national celebrations in any country ever emerge with unanimous consent and remain beyond dispute.[28] Mexico's Independence Day proved to be no exception, in large part because of growing fears among Mexico's elite about the message that September 16 celebrations of Father Hidalgo's uprising conveyed about the relationship between the masses and political power. After the abdication of Agustín de Iturbide in 1823, September 16 emerged as the most important holiday commemorating the Independence War. Its transformation into a raucous and potentially dangerous celebration of popular sovereignty can be directly attributed to the partisan politics of the mid-1820s. As York Rite Masonic lodges promoted popular mobilization around their efforts to secure political power, they focused among other things on tapping into popular anti-Spanish sentiment, using the Independence Day celebration as one venue. September 16 thus became the anchor of the national political calendar.

Struggles over the appropriate messages and manifestations of Independence Day remained part and parcel of partisan conflicts through the liberal reform era in the mid-nineteenth century. Just as radical federalists pushed their popular appeals through the iconography of Hidalgo's message to the masses, moderates and conservatives increasingly promoted the image and message of Iturbide's movement (mature, creole, savvy) in contrast to that of

Hidalgo (immature, *casta*, naive) and moved to add an appropriate coda to the patriotic festival calendar. Beginning in the 1830s, conservative and moderate governments remolded the festivities, adding September 27 to the political calendar and conjuring up the imagery of the Army of the Three Guarantees and the creole ingenuity of Iturbide as the necessary ingredients for consummating Independence, after the raw urges of the peasants of 1810 failed to achieve that goal. The first indisputable evidence of the new official public celebration of September 27 in Mexico City came in 1837, the year the centralist constitution was introduced. That fall the patriotic organizing committee held matching events on September 16 and 27. The following year, Iturbide's remains were transferred to Mexico City and reinterred in a lavish ceremony organized by President Anastasio Bustamante.[29]

The revived Iturbide became an icon of stability, religion, and national unity. In 1844 the patriotic organizing committee arranged identical public diversions for both September 16 and 27: fireworks, hot-air balloons, and music. They also organized a procession to retrace the path taken by the Army of the Three Guarantees in 1821. The editors of the moderate newspaper *El Siglo XIX* hailed this as the only appropriate construction of the national-origin myth for the times. In the context of violent peasant uprisings during the 1840s and the near disintegration of the nation during and after the war with the United States, the idea of constructing a national-origin myth based on unity, one that downplayed the role of peasants and mass mobilization, only grew in appeal. This construction of two Independence Days lasted, with few exceptions, into the early 1860s.[30]

Struggles over the meaning of Independence were not simply a matter of changing symbols. They also could be moments of upheaval and danger, because they were explicitly public lessons about political power that required the presence of crowds to affirm their efficacy. September 16 became, in fact, one of the days on which this tension between state needs for popular rituals to affirm authority and the dangers inherent in the gathering of crowds was most obvious, particularly at times when elite politics was at its most fragmented. Each year the local authorities spent hours organizing security for the Independence Day festivities. Rumors that political dissidents would disrupt the peace during these celebrations spread in 1823, 1828, 1829, 1836, and 1837. Urban political violence turned from rumor to fact with distressing frequency.

The Legacy of Urban Upheaval

Lucas Alamán's ignominious fate as a municipal council member in 1849, physically and verbally harassed into resignation, offers a small example of the ongoing political turmoil that extends well beyond the chronological scope of this study. Between 1837 and 1841 alone there were eighty-four *pronunciamientos*. From 1833 to 1855, Mexico had more than thirty presidents, who lasted an average of seven and one-half months in office. Santa Anna alone served nine times, completing his political career as the ostentatious and dictatorial Supreme Highness from 1853 to 1855, before he was hounded from Mexican politics once and for all during the Revolution of Ayutla. At the local level, as the inefficacy of the ballot box endured, the capital's residents voiced their political opinions through other actions. Riots gripped the city in 1838, 1841, 1844, and 1847, as well as in 1849. Protesters filled the Chamber of Deputies in 1838, demanding a return to the 1824 Constitution. Copper currency devaluations brought irate crowds into the streets again in 1841. Three years later Santa Anna's increasingly autocratic rule drove a raucous group into the city's streets to join the uprising that would drive him from power again. In 1847, a popular resistance defied its own government and continued to harass the occupation forces of the U.S. Army from the rooftops of the capital.[31]

Over the decades the relationship between the predominant elite factions and the urban masses changed. The triumphant national political leaders who emerged after the war with the United States to lead the liberal reforms of the mid-century disarticulated their movement from popular radical federalism, although they still claimed the legacy of Hidalgo and Guerrero, the 1824 Constitution, and the popular support that these icons generated. Events in the early 1840s provide a fine example both of the process of disarticulation in its early stages and of the way the history of the republic was rewritten to accommodate this realignment.[32]

In 1841 a heterogeneous coalition of disgruntled army officers and businessmen ousted President Anastasio Bustamante. In an effort to gain national legitimacy for the new regime, the triumphant coalition called for elections of a constituent congress based on a new electoral law. A resurgent and increasingly conservative Santa Anna designated 67 of the 125 delegates selected to draft the legislation, while others in the victorious coalition promoted the fortunes of men associated with more liberal political ideas. The

committee's proposal for the new electoral law contained an intro-
ductory retrospective on legislation since Independence. The authors suggested that the 1823 electoral law had enjoyed "greater
acceptance" among the people than any other. The more restrictive
laws of 1830 and 1836 were reviewed, the motivations of their per-
petrators questioned, and their results condemned. The committee
denounced as "pretexts of deception" the efforts to blame instability on the "natural character" of a new nation. The laws of 1830
and 1836 were described as a desperate effort to control electoral
outcomes and deny the popular will. Santa Anna tinkered with
details, but the resulting legislation still removed for the time being the income restrictions on the suffrage imposed in 1836 and
paid·lip service to the "popular acclaim" enjoyed by the tenets of
1823. On the other hand, minimum property requirements for
officeholding remained. In many other ways the legislation closely
resembled the July 1830 Federal District electoral law.[33]

In Mexico City's ensuing elections for the constituent assembly, moderate federalists with liberal social leanings dominated,
prompting the conservative press to revive references to the upheavals of the late 1820s. They lamented that the "rogues of the
Acordada" would soon return to establish a government of *léperos*.
The predominant newspaper of nascent liberalism, *El Siglo XIX*,
responded to these accusations in revealing fashion. In their rebuke of the conservative hysteria, the paper's editors distanced
themselves from the radical traditions of the 1820s and denied the
connection between the moderates entering the constituent congress and the radical federalists of the earlier era. They pointed out
with pride that Manuel Gómez Pedraza was the only liberal in the
new constituent congress who had been involved in the popular
upheavals of 1828, but that he had been a victim of the radicals,
neither a fellow traveler nor the instigator of popular agitation. In
contrast to the 1820s federalists, these men did not embrace "even
the most wretched citizen," but instead distanced themselves from
popular radicalism.[34]

A convergence of economic, political, and social circumstances
brought the urban masses to center stage in early nineteenth-
century Mexico. Popular grievances and aspirations converged with
intense elite factionalism to generate new opportunities and structures for political participation. Some aspirants to power attempted
to gain office or defend themselves and their programs by recruiting mass support at the polls and in the streets. In the 1820s radical
federalists in Mexico City parlayed this strategy not only into con-

trol of Mexico City's municipal council and congressional seats, but they also tapped into a potent force for exerting pressure on the state through direct action. Their success galvanized much of the moderate and conservative elite, who saw this invocation of popular sovereignty as a threat to the entire social order. When moderates and conservatives joined to enact reforms in the 1830s, they hoped to develop a system that meshed with their vision of Mexico's future. When they focused on the nature of political contention and the way actors should make claims on the system, that vision was of a well-ordered Mexico operating according to clearly defined rules, just as the rules of the natural world raised Eugene Robertson's hot-air balloon in 1835. This reverie of a passive nation "kneeling before the law" responded directly to more apocalyptic images of Mexican politics, first conjured up by outraged royalists in 1812 and revived during the partisan struggles of the mid-1820s. The alternative image was of poor folk, dressed in rags, storming the citadel of power, and in giddy triumph shouting, "Now we rule!"

Notes

1. Municipal Council Correspondence, AACM, vol. 863, exp. 44; Alamán, *Historia de Méjico*.
2. Jaime E. Rodríguez O., "Two Revolutions: France 1789 and Mexico 1810," *The Americas* 47, no. 2 (October 1990): 161–76; François-Xavier Guerra, "The Spanish-American Tradition of Representation and Its European Roots," *Journal of Latin American Studies* 26, no. 1 (February 1994): 1–35; Alan Knight, "The Peculiarities of Mexican History: Mexico Compared to Latin America, 1821–1992," ibid., 24, Quincentenary Supplement (1992): 99–144; idem, "Viewpoint: Revisionism and Revolution: Mexico Compared to England and France," *Past and Present* 134 (February 1992): 159–99; Jaime E. Rodríguez O., "The Emancipation of America," *American Historical Review* 105, no. 1 (February 2000): 131–52.
3. Hunt, *Politics, Culture*, 126.
4. Malcolm Crook, *Elections in the French Revolution: An Apprenticeship in Democracy, 1789–1799* (Cambridge, England: Cambridge University Press, 1996), 5, 15.
5. William Sewell Jr., *Work and Revolution in France: The Language of Labor from the Old Regime to 1848* (Cambridge, England: Cambridge University Press, 1987), 104, 137.
6. Crook, *Elections*, 27–28, 173; Hunt, *Politics, Culture*, 155–59, 167; Ronald Aminzade, *Ballots and Barricades: Class Formation and Republican Politics in France, 1830–1871* (Princeton, N.J.: Princeton University Press, 1993), 36–41, 54; Sewell, *Work and Revolution*, 138, 245.
7. Crook, *Elections*, 15–17, 54; Hunt, *Politics, Culture*, 127.
8. Crook, *Elections*, 156.

9. Hunt, *Politics, Culture*, 229; C. B. Macpherson, *The Life and Times of Liberal Democracy* (Oxford: Oxford University Press, 1977), 69.

10. J. H. Plumb, *The Origins of Political Stability, England, 1675–1725* (Boston: Houghton Mifflin, 1967), 43, 66–98; idem, "The Growth of the Electorate in England from 1600 to 1715," *Past and Present* 45 (November 1969): 92; Frank O'Gorman, "Campaign Rituals and Ceremonies: The Social Meaning of Elections in England, 1780–1860," *Past and Present* 135 (May 1992): 92–93, 103.

11. Phillip Corrigan and Derek Sayer, *The Great Arch: English State Formation as Cultural Revolution* (Oxford: Basil Blackwell, 1985), 148; Plumb, "The Growth," 111.

12. Electoral data, *Registro Oficial*, September 20, October 1, 2, and 21, December 6, 1830; AACM, vol. 862, exp. 12, 14, and 15; 1842 census data, AACM, vol. 3406–3407, in Pérez Toledo, *Los hijos del trabajo*, 44, table 2.

13. See Antonio Annino, ed., *Historia de las elecciones en Iberoamérica: Siglo. XIX* (Mexico City: Fondo de Cultura Económica, 1995); Eduardo Posada-Carbó, ed., *Elections before Democracy: The History of Elections in Europe and Latin America* (New York: St. Martin's, 1996); Vincent C. Peloso and Barbara A. Tenenbaum, eds., *Liberals, Politics, and Power: State Formation in Nineteenth-Century Latin America* (Athens: University of Georgia Press, 1996).

14. Eduardo Posada-Carbó, "Elections before Democracy: Some Considerations on Electoral History from a Comparative Approach," in *Elections before Democracy*, ed. Posada-Carbó, 6.

15. Alicia Hernández Chávez, *La tradición repúblicana del buen gobierno* (Mexico City: El Colegio de México–Fondo de Cultura Económica, 1993), 26–27; Michael T. Ducey, "Village Organization under Siege: The *Repúblicas de Indios* in Independent Mexico, *Sujeto* Villages, and Caste War," paper presented at the Latin American Studies Association 21st International Congress, Chicago, September 1998; *Gaceta Imperial de México*, March 23, 1822.

16. David Bushnell, "La evolución del principio representativo, de liberal a democrático, en Latinoamérica independiente," in *America Latina: Dallo stato coloniale allo stato nazione*, ed. Antonio Annino (Milan: Franco Angeli, 1987), 2:618; James A. Wood, "The Chilean Elections of 1850–1851: A Key Moment in the History of Cross-Class Political Mobilization in Nineteenth-Century Santiago," paper presented at the Latin American Studies Association 21st International Congress, Chicago, September 1998, 5; J. Samuel Valenzuela, "Building Aspects of Democracy before Democracy: Electoral Practices in Nineteenth-Century Chile," in *Elections before Democracy*, ed. Posada-Carbó, 224; Paula Alonso, "Voting in Buenos Aires, Argentina, before 1912," in *Elections before Democracy*, ed. Posada-Carbó, 182.

17. Valenzuela, "Building," 223–25, 248.

18. Bushnell, "La evolución," 616; Malcolm Deas, "The Role of the Church, the Army and the Police in Colombian Elections, c. 1850–1930," in *Elections before Democracy*, ed. Posada-Carbó, 163; David Sowell, *The Early Colombian Labor Movement: Artisans and Politics in Bogotá, 1832–1919* (Philadelphia, Pa.: Temple University Press, 1992).

19. Hilda Sábato, "Citizenship, Political Participation and the Formation of the Public Sphere in Buenos Aires, 1850s–1880s," *Past and Present*

136 (1992): 143, 149–51; Alonso, "Voting," 183; Bushnell, "La evolución," 625.

20. Vincent C. Peloso, "Liberals, Electoral Reform, and the Popular Vote in Mid-Nineteenth-Century Peru," in *Liberals, Politics, and Power*, ed. Peloso and Tenenbaum, 187, 189, 191, 204.

21. Tornel to Minister of State, December 3, 1833, AGN, Ayuntamientos, vol. 16, 105.

22. Hunt, *Politics, Culture*, 13.

23. Sean Wilentz, "Introduction: Teufelsdröckh's Dilemma: On Symbolism, Politics, and History," in *Rites of Power: Symbolism, Ritual, and Politics since the Middle Ages*, ed. Sean Wilentz (Philadelphia: University of Pennsylvania Press, 1985), 4.

24. Arlette Farge, *Subversive Words: Public Opinion in Eighteenth-Century France*, trans. Rosemary Morris (University Park: Pennsylvania State University Press, 1995), 35.

25. Tilly, "Conclusion," 228.

26. Waldstreicher, *In the Midst*, 142.

27. Antonio Annino, "The Ballot, Land and Sovereignty: Cádiz and the Origins of Mexican Local Government, 1812–1820," in *Elections before Democracy*, ed. Posada-Carbó, 61–86.

28. Ozouf, *Festivals*, 174.

29. Iturbide Proclamation, AACM, vol. 1067, exp. 13.

30. *El Siglo XIX*, September 27, 1844; Warren, "The Construction."

31. Jan Bazant, "Mexico from Independence to 1867," in *The Cambridge History of Latin America*, ed. Leslie Bethell (Cambridge, England: Cambridge University Press, 1985), 3:435–53; Cecilia Noriega Elío, *El constituyente de 1842* (Mexico City: Universidad Nacional Autónoma de México, 1986), 18; Arrom, "Introduction," 7; Shaw, "Poverty and Politics," 323, 331–33; Stevens, *Origins of Instability*, 37; *Diario de Gobierno*, February 23, 1841; Luis Fernando Granados, "Piedras y pobres: Notas para explicar el alzamiento de la Ciudad de México," paper presented at the Colloquium, "La guerra entre México y Estados Unidos: Representación y participantes," Biblioteca Nacional de México, September 23, 1997, http://sunsite.unam. mx/revistas/1847/Piedras-1.html.

32. Guardino, *Peasants, Politics*; Mallon, *Peasant and Nation*.

33. *Dictamen del Consejo de Gobierno sobre convocatoria* (Mexico City: Imp. del Aguila, 1841); *Manifiesto y convocatoria del Poder Ejecutivo Provisional de la República Mexicana, 10 de diciembre de 1841* (Mexico City: Imp. del Aguila, 1841). For a detailed analysis of these events, see Noriega, *El constituyente*, and Michael P. Costeloe, "Generals versus Politicians: Santa Anna and the 1842 Congressional Elections in Mexico," *Bulletin of Latin American Research* 8, no. 2 (1989): 257–74.

34. *El Siglo XIX*, April 18, 1842, quoted in Noriega, *El constituyente*, 71.

Selected Bibliography

Archives and Special Collections

Mexico

Archivo Histórico del Antiguo Ayuntamiento de la Ciudad de
México, Mexico City
Archivo General de la Nación, Mexico City
Archivo Histórico del Tribunal de Justicia del Distrito Federal,
Mexico City
Archivo Histórico de la Secretaría de Salud, Mexico City
Biblioteca Nacional de Antropología e Historia, Mexico City
Biblioteca Nacional de México, Mexico City
Hemeroteca Nacional de México, Mexico City

United States

National Archives, Washington, D.C.
Benson Latin American Collection, General Libraries, University
of Texas, Austin
Center for American History, General Libraries, University of
Texas, Austin
Library of Congress, Washington, D.C.

Nineteenth-Century Mexico City Periodicals

El Aguila Mexicana
El Amigo del Pueblo
La Antorcha
El Correo de la Federación Mexicana
El Cosmopólita
El Diario de México
El Fénix de la Libertad
Gaceta de México
Gaceta Imperial de México
El Gladiador
La Lima de Vulcano

El Mosquito Mexicano
Registro Oficial
El Sol
El Telégrafo
La Verdad Desnuda
La Voz de la Patria

Other Publications

Abusos de las elecciones populares. Mexico City: Imprenta Alejandro Valdes, 1820.
Acábense los yorkinos y salvemos a la patria. Mexico City: Imprenta Mariano Ontiveros, 1827.
Acta del cabildo celebrado por el exmo. Ayuntamiento de México el 30 de mayo de 1836, mandada imprimir por el mismo con los documentos a que se refiere. Mexico City: Imprenta José Mariano F. de Lara, 1836.
Actas constitucionales mexicanas (1821–1824). 10 vols. 1821–1824. Reprint ed., Mexico City: Universidad Nacional Autónoma de México, 1980.
Acusación que el Licenciado Gabriel Sagazeta, Síndico Segundo del exmo. Ayuntamiento de esta capital, eleva, como Procurador del Común, al Soberano Congreso Nacional contra el Señor Gobernador del Distrito don José Gómez de la Cortina. Mexico City: Imprenta de Galván, 1836.
Un aguinaldo excelente para toda buena gente. Manifiesto que se presenta a la nación de los individuos dignos de toda consideración y premio por su siempre memorable grito de la Acordada, y otros grandes servicios. Mexico City: Imprenta Alejandro Valdes, 1829.
Alamán, Lucas. *Historia de Méjico desde los primeros movimientos que prepararon su Independencia en el año de 1808 hasta la época presente.* 5 vols. Mexico City: Imprenta J. M. Lara, 1849.
Alba, Rafael de, ed. *La constitución de 1812 en la Nueva España.* 2 vols. Mexico City: Secretaría de Relaciones Exteriores, Imprenta Guerrero Hermanos, 1912–1913.
Alonso, Paula. "Voting in Buenos Aires, Argentina, before 1912." In *Elections before Democracy: The History of Elections in Europe and Latin America*, edited by Eduardo Posada-Carbó, 181–200. New York: St. Martin's, 1996.
Aminzade, Ronald. *Ballots and Barricades: Class Formation and Republican Politics in France, 1830–1871.* Princeton, N.J.: Princeton University Press, 1993.
Anderson, Rodney. "Race and Social Stratification: A Comparison of Working-Class Spaniards, Indians and *Castas* in Guadalajara, Mexico in 1821." *Hispanic American Historical Review* 68, no. 2 (1988): 209–43.
Anderson, W. Woodrow. "Reform as a Means to Quell Revolution." In *Mexico and the Spanish Cortes, 1810–1822*, edited by Nettie Lee Benson, 185–207. Austin: University of Texas Press, 1966.

Anna, Timothy E. *The Fall of the Royal Government in Mexico City*. Lincoln: University of Nebraska Press, 1978.

————. *Forging Mexico, 1821–1835*. Lincoln: University of Nebraska Press, 1998.

————. "Francisco Novella and the Last Stand of the Royal Army in New Spain." *Hispanic American Historical Review* 51, no. 1 (1971): 92–111.

————. "The Independence of Mexico and Central America." In *The Cambridge History of Latin America*, edited by Leslie Bethell, 3:51–94. Cambridge, England: Cambridge University Press, 1985.

————. *The Mexican Empire of Iturbide*. Lincoln: University of Nebraska Press, 1990.

Annino, Antonio. "The Ballot, Land and Sovereignty: Cádiz and the Origins of Mexican Local Government, 1812–1820." In *Elections before Democracy: The History of Elections in Europe and Latin America*, edited by Eduardo Posada-Carbó, 61–86. New York: St. Martin's, 1996.

————. "El pacto y la norma: Los orígenes de la legalidad oligárquica en México." *Historias* 5 (1984): 3–31.

————. "Prácticas criollas y liberalismo en la crisis del espacio urbano colonial: El 29 de noviembre de 1812 en la Ciudad de México." *Secuencia* 24 (September–December 1992): 121–58.

————, ed. *America Latina: Dallo stato coloniale allo stato nazione*. 2 vols. Milan: Franco Angeli, 1987.

————, ed. *Historia de las elecciones en Iberoamérica: Siglo xix*. Mexico City: Fondo de Cultura Económica, 1995.

Arista, Mariano. *Reseña histórica de la revolución que desde 6 de junio hasta 8 de octubre tuvo lugar en la República el año de 1833 a favor del sistema central. La publica en vindicación de su honor injustamente vulnerado Mariano Artista*. Mexico City: Imprenta Mariano Arévalo, 1835.

Arrangoiz, Francisco de Paula de. *México desde 1808 hasta 1867*. 1871–72. Reprint ed., Mexico City: Porrúa, 1968.

Arrom, Silvia M. "Documentos para el estudio del Tribunal de Vagos, 1828–1848: Respuesta a una problemática sin solución." *Anuario Mexicano de Historia del Derecho* 1 (1989): 215–35.

————. "Introduction: Rethinking Urban Politics in Latin America before the Populist Era." In *Riots in the Cities: Popular Politics and the Urban Poor in Latin America, 1765–1910*, edited by Silvia M. Arrom and Servando Ortoll, 1–16. Wilmington, Del.: Scholarly Resources, 1996.

————. "Popular Politics in Mexico City: The Parián Riot, 1828." *Hispanic American Historical Review* 68, no. 2 (May 1988): 245–68.

————. "Vagos y méndigos en la legislación mexicana, 1745–1845." In *Memoria del IV Congreso de Historia del Derecho Mexicano*, 1:71–87. Mexico City: Universidad Nacional Autónoma de México, 1988.

Arrom, Silvia M., and Servando Ortoll, eds. *Riots in the Cities: Popular Politics and the Urban Poor in Latin America, 1765–1910.* Wilmington, Del.: Scholarly Resources, 1996.

Ataque a los hipócritas que seducen el pueblo. Mexico City: Imprenta Alejandro Valdes, 1820.

Bazant, Jan. "Mexico from Independence to 1867." In *The Cambridge History of Latin America,* edited by Leslie Bethell, 3:423–70. Cambridge, England: Cambridge University Press, 1985.

Beaufoy, Mark. *Mexican Illustrations, Founded upon Facts, Indicative of the Present Condition of Society, Manners, Religion, and Morals among the Inhabitants of Mexico, With Observations upon the Government and Resources of the Republic of Mexico as They Appeared during Part of the Years 1825, 1826 and 1827, Interspersed with Occasional Remarks upon the Climate, Produce and Antiquities of the Country, Mode of Working the Mines, Etc.* London: Carpenter and Son, 1828.

Benson, Nettie Lee. "The Contested Mexican Election of 1812." *Hispanic American Historical Review* 26, no. 3 (1946): 336–50.

_____, ed. *Mexico and the Spanish Cortes, 1810–1822.* Austin: University of Texas Press, 1966.

Berruezo León, María Teresa. "La presencia americana en las Cortes de Cádiz." In *Materiales para el estudio de la constitución de 1812,* 53–74. Madrid: Editorial Tecnos, 1989.

Berry, Charles R. "The Election of the Mexican Deputies to the Spanish Cortes, 1810–1822." In *Mexico and the Spanish Cortes, 1810–1822,* edited by Nettie Lee Benson, 10–42. Austin: University of Texas Press, 1966.

Bethell, Leslie, ed. *The Cambridge History of Latin America.* Vol. 3, *From Independence to c. 1870.* Cambridge, England: Cambridge University Press, 1985.

Brading, David A. *The First America: The Spanish Monarchy, Creole Patriots, and the Liberal State, 1492–1867.* Cambridge, England: Cambridge University Press, 1991.

_____. "Government and Elite in Late Colonial Mexico." *Hispanic American Historical Review* 53, no. 3 (1973): 389–414.

Burkholder, Mark A., and D. S. Chandler. *From Impotence to Authority: The Spanish Crown and the American Audiencias, 1687–1808.* Columbia: University of Missouri Press, 1977.

Bushnell, David. "La evolución del principio representativo, de liberal a democrático, en latinoamérica independiente." In *America Latina: Dallo stato coloniale allo stato nazione,* edited by Antonio Annino, 2:615–32. Milan: Franco Angeli, 1987.

Bustamante, Carlos María de. *Cuadro histórico de la revolución mexicana.* 8 vols. 1844. Reprint ed., Mexico City: Fondo de Cultura Económica, 1985.

Cada cual piensa en su cabeza. Mexico City: Imprenta D.J.M. Betancourt, 1821.

Calcott, Wilfrid Hardy. *Santa Anna: The Story of an Enigma Who Once Was Mexico*. Norman: University of Oklahoma Press, 1936.

Cardoso, Ciro F. S. *La industria en México antes del porfiriato*. Mexico City: Dirección de Investigaciones Históricas, Instituto Nacional de Antropología e Historia, 1978.

Chowning, Margaret. "The Contours of the Post-1810 Depression in Mexico: A Reappraisal from a Regional Perspective." *Latin American Research Review* 27, no. 2 (1992): 119–50.

Christiansen, E. *The Origins of Military Power in Spain, 1800–54*. London: Oxford University Press, 1967.

Coatsworth, John H. "Obstacles to Economic Growth in Nineteenth-Century Mexico." *American Historical Review* 83, no. 1 (1978): 80–100.

Colección de artículos selectos sobre política, sacados del Aguila Mexicana del año de 1828. Mexico City: Imprenta de Galván, 1828.

Consejos y bigotes ya no se usan, pero si advertencias. Mexico City: Imprenta Doña Herculana del Villar, 1822.

Conversación del barbero y su marchante. Mexico City: Imprenta Alejandro Valdes, 1820.

Cooper, Donald B. *Epidemic Disease in Mexico City, 1761–1813: An Administrative, Social, and Medical Study*. Austin: University of Texas Press, 1965.

Cope, R. Douglas. *The Limits of Racial Domination: Plebeian Society in Colonial Mexico City, 1660–1720*. Madison: University of Wisconsin Press, 1994.

Corrigan, Phillip, and Derek Sayer. *The Great Arch: English State Formation as Cultural Revolution*. Oxford: Basil Blackwell, 1985.

Costeloe, Michael P. *The Central Republic in Mexico City, 1835–1846: Hombres de Bien in the Age of Santa Anna*. Cambridge, England: Cambridge University Press, 1993.

———. *Church Wealth in Mexico: A Study of the "Juzgado de Capellanías" in the Archbishopric of Mexico, 1800–1856*. Cambridge, England: Cambridge University Press, 1967.

———. "Generals versus Politicians: Santa Anna and the 1842 Congressional Elections in Mexico City." *Bulletin of Latin American Research* 8, no. 2 (October 1989): 257–74.

———. "The Junta Patriótica and the Celebration of Independence in Mexico City, 1825–1855." *Mexican Studies/Estudios Mexicanos* 13, no. 1 (Winter 1997): 21–53.

———. *La primera República federal de México (1824–1835): Un estudio de los partidos políticos en el México independiente*. Mexico City: Fondo de Cultura Económica, 1975.

El Coyote Manso. *Manuel Gómez Pedraza, segundo Emperador de los mexicanos*. Mexico City: Imprenta de las Escalerillas, 1828.

Crook, Malcolm. *Elections in the French Revolution: An Apprenticeship in Democracy, 1789–1799*. Cambridge, England: Cambridge University Press, 1996.

Cuestión del día, o nuestros males y sus remedies. Morelia, Mexico: Imprenta Juan Evaristo de Oñate, 1834.

Davis, Thomas B., and Amado Ricon Virulegio, eds. The Political Plans of Mexico. Lanham, Md.: University Press of America, 1987.

Deans-Smith, Susan. Bureaucrats, Planters, and Workers: the Making of the Tobacco Monopoly in Bourbon Mexico City. Austin: University of Texas Press, 1992.

Deas, Malcolm. "The Role of the Church, the Army and the Police in Colombian Elections, c. 1850–1930." In Elections before Democracy: The History of Elections in Europe and Latin America, edited by Eduardo Posada-Carbó, 163–80. New York: St. Martin's, 1996.

de la Garza, Luis Alberto. "Hombres de bien, demagogos y revolución social en la primera República." Historias 15 (October–December 1986): 43–54.

de la Maza, Francisco. "Los restos de Hernán Cortés." Cuadernos Americanos 32 (1947): 153–74.

Demélas-Bohy, M.D., and F.-X. Guerra, "The Hispanic Revolutions: The Adoption of Modern Forms of Representation in Spain and America, 1808–1810." In Elections before Democracy: The History of Elections in Europe and Latin America, edited by Eduardo Posada-Carbó, 33–60. New York: St. Martin's, 1996.

Derechos convincentes para elegir Emperador Americano. Mexico City: Imprenta Don Alejandro Valdes, 1821.

Description of the Panorama of the Superb City of Mexico and the Surrounding Scenery, Painted on 2700 Square Feet of Canvas, by Robert Buford, Esq., from Drawings Made on the Spot, at the Request of the Mexican Government by Mr. William Bullock, Jr., Now Open for Inspection at the Rotunda, New-York. New York: E. Conrad, 1828.

Dictamen del Consejo de Gobierno sobre convocatoria. Mexico City: Imprenta del Aguila, 1841.

Discurso pronunciado en el Senado por el ciudadano Cañedo, en la sesión del 24 de abril, contra el proyecto de ley que presentó el ciudadano Cevallos para la estinción de las juntas secretas. Mexico City: Imprenta del Aguila, 1826.

Di Tella, Torcuato S. Iturbide y el cesarismo popular. Cuadernos Simón Rodríguez. Buenos Aires: Editorial Biblos, n.d.

_____. National Popular Politics in Early Independent Mexico, 1820–1847. Albuquerque: University of New Mexico Press, 1996.

D. J. C. Catecismo político arreglado a la constitución de la monarquía española; Para ilustración del pueblo, instrucción de la juventud, y uso de las escuelas de primeras letras. Puebla, Mexico: Imprenta San Felipe Neri, 1820.

D. J. E. F. Busca-pies al Pensador Mexicano. Mexico City: Imprenta Mariano Ontiveros, 1821.

_____. Proyecto de nuevo reglamento para las elecciones. Mexico City: Imprenta D.J.M. Benavente y Socios, 1821.

Dublán, Manuel, and José María Lozano, eds. Legislación mexicana: O colección completa de las disposiciones legislativas expedidas desde *la Independencia de la República*. 34 vols. Mexico City: Imprenta del Comercio, 1876–1914.

Ducey, Michael T. "From Village Riot to Rural Rebellion: Social Protest in the Huasteca, Mexico, 1760–1870." Doctoral dissertation, University of Chicago, 1992.

———. "Village Organization under Siege: The *Repúblicas de Indios* in Independent Mexico City, *Sujeto* Villages, and Caste War." Paper presented at the Latin American Studies Association 21st International Congress, Chicago, September 1998.

E. A. *Derecho del pueblo mexicano para elegir Emperador*. Mexico City: Imprenta D.J.M. Benavente y Socios, 1821.

Estado político de la República al tiempo de la elección del Presidente. Mexico City: Imprenta de Galván, 1828.

Estevez Ravanillo, Juan Nepomuceno. *Vindicación de Señor Diputado de Cortes don Francisco de Paula Puig, por la parte en que lo injuria el diálogo entre el tejedor y el zapatero*. Puebla, Mexico: Imprenta Don Pedro de la Rosa, 1822.

Extracto del noticioso general de México, del lunes 22 de julio de 1822, segundo de nuestra Independencia. Puebla, Mexico: Imprenta Don Pedro de la Rosa, 1822.

Farge, Arlette. *Subversive Words: Public Opinion in Eighteenth-Century France*. Translated by Rosemary Morris. University Park: Pennsylvania State University Press, 1995.

El Fernandino constitucional a los fidelísimos mexicanos. Mexico City: Imprenta Arizpe, 1820.

El Fernandino constitucional al sr. ex-Diputado de Cortes. Mexico City: Imprenta Mariano Ontiveros, 1820.

Flinchpaugh, Steven. "Economic Aspects of the Viceregal Entrance in Mexico City." *The Americas* 52, no. 3 (January 1996): 345–66.

Flores Caballero, Romeo. *Counterrevolution: The Role of the Spaniards in the Independence of Mexico, 1804–1838*. Translated by Jaime E. Rodríguez O. Lincoln: University of Nebraska Press, 1974.

Florescano, Enrique, ed., *La clase obrera en al história de México*. Volume 1, *De la colonia al imperio*. 5th ed. Mexico City: Siglo xxi, 1986.

Frost, E. C., M. C. Meyer, and J. Z. Vázquez, eds. *El trabajo y los trabajadores en la historia de México*. Mexico City: El Colegio de México, 1979.

García, Genaro, ed. *Documentos históricos mexicanos. Obra conmemorativa del primer centenario de la Independencia de México*. 7 vols. 1910. Reprint ed., Nendeln, Leichtenstein: Kraus-Thomson Publishers, 1971.

García Orozco, Antonio, ed. *Legislación electoral mexicana, 1812–1977*. 2d ed. Mexico City: Comisión Federal Electoral, 1978.

Gilmore, N. Ray. "The Condition of the Poor in Mexico, 1834." *Hispanic American Historical Review* 32, no. 2 (1957): 213–26.

Gómez de Navarrete, Juan. *Proyecto de ley para el establecimiento de Colegios Electorales en la República mexicana*. Mexico City: Imprenta del Águila, 1834.

González Angulo Aguirre, Jorge. *Artesenado y Ciudad a finales del siglo xviii.* Mexico City: Fondo de Cultura Económica, 1983.

González Obregón, Luis. *México viejo.* 1895. Reprint ed., Mexico City: Patria, 1988.

Gortari, Hira de. "Política y administración en la Ciudad de México. Relaciones entre el Ayuntamiento y el gobierno del Distrito Federal, y el Departamental: 1824–1843." In *La Ciudad de México en la primera mitad del siglo xix,* edited by Regina Hernández Franyuti, 2:166–86. Mexico City: Instituto de Investigaciones Dr. José María Luis Mora, 1994.

Granados, Luis Fernando. "Piedras y pobres: Notas para explicar el alzamiento de la Ciudad de México." Paper presented at the Colloquium, "La guerra entre México y Estados Unidos: Representación y participantes," September 23, 1997, Biblioteca Nacional de México. http://sunsite.unam.mx/revistas/1847/Piedras-1.html.

Green, Stanley C. *The Mexican Republic: The First Decade, 1823–1832.* Pittsburgh, Pa.: University of Pittsburgh Press, 1987.

Gualdi, Pedro. *Views of the City of Mexico.* Mexico City: Imprenta J. M. Lara, 1850.

Guardino, Peter F. *Peasants, Politics and the Formation of Mexico's National State: Guerrero 1800–1857.* Stanford, Calif.: Stanford University Press, 1996.

Guedea, Virginia. *En busca de un gobierno alterno: Los Guadalupes de México.* Mexico City: Universidad Nacional Autónoma de México, 1992.

―――. "Las primeras elecciones populares en la Ciudad de México, 1812–1813." *Mexican Studies/Estudios Mexicanos* 7, no. 1 (Winter 1991): 1–28.

―――. "El pueblo de México y la política capitalina: 1808 y 1812." *Mexican Studies/Estudios Mexicanos,* 10, no. 1 (Winter 1994): 27–61.

Guerra, François-Xavier. *Modernidad e independencias: Ensayos sobre las revoluciones hispánicas.* Madrid: Editorial Mapfre, 1992.

―――. "The Spanish-American Tradition of Representation and Its European Roots." *Journal of Latin American Studies* 26, no. 1 (February 1994): 1–35.

Guthrie, Chester L. "Riots in Seventeenth-Century Mexico City: A Study of Social and Economic Conditions." In *Greater America: Essays in Honor of Herbert Eugene Bolton,* edited by Adele Ogden and Engel Sluiter, 243–58. Berkeley: University of California Press, 1945.

Hale, Charles A. *Mexican Liberalism in the Age of Mora, 1821–1853.* New Haven, Conn.: Yale University Press, 1968.

Hamill, Hugh M., Jr. *The Hidalgo Revolt: Prelude to Mexican Independence.* Gainesville: University of Florida Press, 1966.

―――. "Royalist Propaganda and *la porción humilde del pueblo* during Mexican Independence." *The Americas* 36, no. 4 (1980): 423–44.

Hamnett, Brian R. "Mexico's Royalist Coalition: The Response to Revolution, 1808–1821." *Journal of Latin American Studies* 12 (1980): 55–86.

Hernández Chávez, Alicia. *La tradición repúblicana del buen gobierno.* Mexico City: El Colegio de México–Fondo de Cultura Económica, 1993.

Hernández Franyuti, Regina, ed. *La Ciudad de México en la primera mitad del siglo xix.* 2 vols. Mexico City: Instituto de Investigaciones Dr. José María Luis Mora, 1994.

Hernández y Dávalos, Juan E. *Colección de documentos para la historia de la guerra de Independencia de México de 1808 a 1821.* 1877–1882. Reprint ed., Mexico City: Instituto Nacional de Estudios Históricos de la Revolución Mexicana, 1985.

Hunt, Lynn. *Politics, Culture, and Class in the French Revolution.* Berkeley: University of California Press, 1984.

Ibar, Francisco. *Nuevo clamor de venganza o muerte, contra el intruso gobierno que tantos malos ha producido.* Mexico City: Imprenta Martín Rivero, 1831.

Ideas sobre el ciudadano en diálogo. Mexico City: Imprenta Alejandro Valdes, 1820.

Illades, Carlos, and Ariel Rodríguez Kuri, eds. *Ciudad de México: Instituciones, actores sociales, y conflicto político, 1774–1932.* Mexico City: El Colegio de Michoacán–Universidad Autónoma Metropolitana, 1996.

Ilustración sobre la sociedad de francmasones. Mexico City: Imprenta Mariano Ontiveros, 1822.

An Impartial British Observer. *A Letter to a Member of the British Parliament, on Events Civil and Military of the Past and Present Year in Mexico City, to the Period of the Banishment of General Bravo, Ex-Vice President of the Mexican Republic.* N.p.: Imprenta Cornelius C. Sebring, 1828.

El Indio Constitucional. Mexico City: Imprenta Alejandro Valdes, 1820.

Invasión de México por D. Antonio López de Santa Anna, primera parte. Mexico City: Imprenta Alejandro Valdes, 1832.

Iturbide, Agustín de. *Pensamiento que en grande ha propuesto el que subscribe como un particular, para la pronta convocatoria de las próximas Cortes, bajo el concepto de que se podrá aumentar o disminuir el número de representantes de cada clase, conforme acuerde la Junta Soberana con el Congreso de Regencia.* Mexico City: Imprenta Don Alejandro Valdes, 1821.

Jacobsen, Nils, and Hans Jürgen Puhle, eds. *The Economies of Mexico and Peru during the Late Colonial Period.* Berlin: Colloquium Verlag, Bibliotheca Ibero-Americana, 1986.

J. M. R. *Lo que interesa a la patria, por el artesano y su amigo.* Mexico City: Imprenta Americana de José María Betancourt, 1821.

Katz, Friedrich. "Introduction: Rural Revolts in Mexico." In *Riot, Rebellion, and Revolution: Rural Social Conflict in Mexico,* edited by

Friedrich Katz, 3–17. Princeton, N.J.: Princeton University Press, 1988.

_____, ed., *Riot, Rebellion and Revolution: Rural Social Conflict in Mexico*. Princeton, N.J.: Princeton University Press, 1988.

Kicza, John E. *Colonial Entrepreneurs: Families and Business in Bourbon Mexico City*. Albuquerque: University of New Mexico Press, 1983.

_____. "The Great Families of Mexico: Elite Maintenance and Business Practices in Late Colonial Mexico City." *Hispanic American Historical Review* 62, no. 3 (1982): 429–57.

_____. "Life Patterns and Social Differentiation among Common People in Late Colonial Mexico City." *Estudios de Historia Novohispana* 11 (1991): 183–200.

King, James F. "The Colored Castes and the American Representation in the *Cortes* of Cádiz." *Hispanic American Historical Review* 33, no. 1 (February 1953): 33–64.

Klein, Herbert S. "The Demographic Structure of Mexico City in 1811." *Journal of Urban History* 23, no. 1 (November 1996): 66–93.

Knight, Alan. "The Peculiarities of Mexican History: Mexico Compared to Latin America, 1821–1992." *Journal of Latin American Studies* 24, Quincentenary Supplement (1992): 99–144.

_____. "Viewpoint: Revisionism and Revolution: Mexico Compared to England and France." *Past and Present* 134 (February 1992): 159–99.

Ladd, Doris M. *The Mexican Nobility at Independence, 1780–1826.* Austin: University of Texas Press, 1976.

L. C. *Un nuevo plan de revolución: Infamias de los escoseses que conspiran en la patria, o sea, respuesta al impreso titulado infamias de los yorkinos.* Mexico City: Imprenta de la ex-Inquisición, 1827.

Legitimidad de la elección de nuestro Emperador. Mexico City: Imprenta de Doña Herculana del Villar y Socios, 1822.

El Loco de Jerusalem. *Oiga el vice presidente la sentencia de su muerte*. Mexico City: Imprenta Juan Bautista Gamboa, 1832.

López Monjardín, Adriana "El artesano urbano a mediadios del siglo xix." In *Organización de producción y relaciones de trabajo en el siglo xix en México*, edited by Sonia Lombardo. Mexico City: Dirección de Investigaciones Históricas, Instituto Nacional de Antropología e Historia, Cuaderno de Trabajo 29, 1979.

Lovett, Gabriel H. *Napoleon and the Birth of Modern Spain*, 2 vols. New York: New York University Press, 1965.

Macaulay, Neill. "The Army of New Spain and the Mexican Delegation to the Spanish Cortes." In *Mexico and the Spanish Cortes*, edited by Nettie Lee Benson, 134–52. Austin: University of Texas Press, 1966.

MacLachlan, Colin M., and Jaime E. Rodríguez O. *The Forging of the Cosmic Race: A Reinterpretation of Colonial Mexico*. Berkeley: University of California Press, 1980.

Macpherson, C. B. *The Life and Times of Liberal Democracy*. Oxford: Oxford University Press, 1977.

Mallon, Florencia E. *Peasant and Nation: The Making of Postcolonial Mexico and Peru*. Berkeley: University of California Press, 1995.

Manifestación que hace el Ayuntamiento de esta capital sobre las contestaciones originadas por la exposición que elevó al Soberano Congreso Nacional el día 11 del presente. Mexico City: Oficina de Luis Abadiano, 1837.

Manifiesto del ayuntamiento de 1835 al público mexicano. Mexico City: Imprenta Tomás Uribe y Alcalde, 1836.

Manifiesto y convocatoria del Poder Ejecutivo Provisional de la República Mexicana, 10 de diciembre de 1841. Mexico City: Imprenta del Aguila, 1841.

Mateos, Antonio. *Proyecto acerca de elecciones de Diputados . . . al enhornarse tuerce el pan*. Mexico City: Imprenta Alejandro Valdes, 1821.

Mateos, Juan Antonio, ed. *Historia parlamentaria de los congresos mexicanos de 1821 a 1857*. 15 vols. Mexico City: U. S. Reyes, 1877.

Mayer, Brantz. *Mexico as It Was and as It Is*. New York: J. Winchester New World Press, 1844.

A medio las enchiladas, del barrio de Santa Anita: Y nueva canción a los españoles. Puebla, Mexico: Imprenta Nacional, 1833.

Memoria del Ministro de Estado y del Despacho de Relaciones Interiores y Exteriores. Mexico City, 1831.

M. G. de V. *El importante voto de un ciudadano*. Mexico City: Imprenta de José María Benavente y Socios, 1821.

Mora, José María Luis. *Obras sueltas de José María Luis Mora, ciudadano mexicano*. 2 vols. Paris: Librería Rosa, 1837.

Morales, María Dolores. "Cambios en la traza de la estructura vial de la Ciudad de México." In *La Ciudad de México en la primera mitad del siglo xix*, edited by Regina Hernández Franyuti, 1:161–224. Mexico City: Instituto de Investigaciones Dr. José María Luis Mora, 1994.

Moreno Toscano, Alejandra. "Los trabajadores y el proyecto de industrialización, 1810–1867." In *La clase obrera en la historia de México*. Vol. 1, *De la colonia al imperio*, edited by Enrique Florescano, 1:302–50. 5th edition. Mexico City: Siglo xxi, 1986.

Noriega Elío, Cecilia. *El constituyente de 1842*. Mexico City: Universidad Nacional Autónoma de México, 1986.

En nuestras instituciones no caben los francmasones. Mexico City: Imprenta por José Ximeno, 1826.

Nuevos diálogos entre el cohetero y el tamborillero. Mexico City: Imprenta Alejandro Valdes, 1829.

O'Gorman, Frank. "Campaign Rituals and Ceremonies: The Social Meaning of Elections in England, 1780–1860." *Past and Present* 135 (May 1992): 79–115.

Oigan las legislaturas los proyectos de Madrid. Mexico City: Imprenta José Márquez, 1828.

Ozouf, Mona. *Festivals and the French Revolution*. Translated by Alan Sheridan. Cambridge, Mass.: Harvard University Press, 1988.

Pacheco Leal, Antonio. *Discurso pronunciado por el ciudadano Antonio Pacheco Leal*. Mexico City: Imprenta Ignacio Cumplido, 1835.

Parabien al Fernandino arrepentido, por el colegial. Mexico City: Imprenta Alejandro Valdes, 1820.

Para estos lances sirve la imprenta: Diálogo: un zapatero y un tejedor. Puebla, Mexico: Imprenta Liberal de Moreno Hermanos, 1822.

El Payo de Rosario [Pablo Villavicencio]. *Manifiesto del payo de Rosario a sus compatriotas, o sea suplemento a la memoria del Señor Iturbide*. Mexico City: Imprenta de la ex-Inquisición, 1827.

Paz, José Ignacio. *Estupendo grito en la Acordada*. Mexico City: Imprenta del Correo, 1829.

Peloso, Vincent C. "Liberals, Electoral Reform, and the Popular Vote in Mid-Nineteenth-Century Peru." In *Liberals, Politics and Power: State Formation in Nineteenth-Century Latin America*, edited by Vincent C. Peloso and Barbara A. Tenenbaum, 186–211. Athens: University of Georgia Press, 1996.

Peloso, Vincent C., and Barbara A. Tenenbaum, eds. *Liberals, Politics and Power: State Formation in Nineteenth-Century Latin America*. Athens: University of Georgia Press, 1996.

El Pensador Mexicano [José Joaquín Fernández de Lizardi]. *Ideas políticas y liberales*. Mexico City: Imprenta Imperial, 1821.

Pérez Toledo, Sonia. *Los hijos del trabajo: Los artesanos de la Ciudad de México, 1780–1853*. Mexico City: Universidad Autónoma Metropolitana Iztapalapa–El Colegio de México, 1996.

_____. "Los vagos de la Ciudad de México y el Tribunal de Vagos en la primera mitad del siglo xix." *Secuencia* 27 (1993): 27–42.

A perro viejo no hay tus tus: O sea diálogo entre un zapatero y su marchante. Mexico City: Imprenta Mariano Ontiveros, 1821.

Planes en la nación mexicana. 10 vols. Mexico City: Senado de la República, 1987.

Plasencia de la Parra, Enrique. *Independencia y nacionalismo a la luz del discurso conmemorativo (1825–1867)*. Mexico City: Consejo Nacional para la Cultura y las Artes, 1991.

Plumb, J. H. "The Growth of the Electorate in England from 1600 to 1715." *Past and Present* 45 (November 1969): 90–116.

_____. *The Origins of Political Stability, England, 1675–1725*. Boston: Houghton Mifflin, 1967.

Poinsett, Joel R. *Espocisión de la conducta política de los Estados Unidos, para con las nuevas Repúblicas de América*. Mexico City: Imprenta de la ex-Inquisición, 1827.

_____. *Notes on Mexico, Made in the Autumn of 1822*. 1824. Reprint ed., New York: Frederick A. Praeger, 1969.

Posada-Carbó, Eduardo, "Elections before Democracy: Some Considerations on Electoral History from a Comparative Approach." In *Elections before Democracy: The History of Elections in Europe and*

Latin America, edited by Eduardo Posada-Carbó, 1–16. New York: St. Martin's, 1996.

_____, ed. Elections before Democracy: The History of Elections in Europe and Latin America. New York: St. Martin's, 1996.

Potash, Robert A. Mexican Government and Industrial Development in the Early Republic: The Banco de Avío. Amherst: University of Massachusetts Press, 1983.

Prieto, Guillermo. Memorias de mis tiempos. 1906. Reprint ed., Mexico City: Editorial Porrúa, 1985.

Primera representación del comercio solicitando una indemnización de las pérdidas que sufrió en los primeros días de diciembre de 1828, por conducto y con el correspondiente apoyo del exmo. Ayuntamiento, del Gobierno del Distrito y del Supremo Gobierno, al Congreso General de los Estados Unidos Mexicanos. Mexico City: Imprenta Vicente García Torres, 1849.

Proceso del General Santa Anna. Mexico City: Imprenta Francisco Torres, 1836.

Proyecto del ceremonial que para la inauguración, consagración, y coronación de su magestad el Emperador Agustín Primero se presentó por la comisión encargada de formarlo, al Soberano Congreso en 17 de junio de 1822. Mexico City: Imprenta José María Ramos Palomera, 1822.

"Quilibet." El más sublime heroísmo del exmo. Sr. Iturbide y sus dignos compañeros de armas, contra el llamado importante voto de un ciudadano. Mexico City: Imprenta Mariano Ontiveros, 1821.

Reflexiones políticas sobre la elección de emperador. Mexico City: Imprenta Americana de José María Betancourt, 1821.

Reglamentos de la r.l. # 3, titulada la independencia mexicana. Mexico City: n.p., 1826.

Representación del comercio solicitando una indemnización de las pérdidas que sufrió en los primeros días de diciembre de 1828, por conducto y con el correspondiente apoyo del exmo. Ayuntamiento, del Gobierno del Distrito y del Supremo Gobierno, al Congreso General de los Estados Unidos Mexicanos. Mexico City: Imprenta del Correo, 1829.

Representación de varios electores a la Junta General hecha al Congreso del Estado. N.p., [1826].

Representación que el Ayuntamiento de México elevó a las augustas cámaras en defensa de los derechos y prerogativas de la Capital de la República. Mexico City: Imprenta Ignacio Cumplido, 1836.

R. H. Al tejedor y el zapatero. Puebla, Mexico: Imprenta Pedro de la Rosa, 1822.

Riva Palacio, Vicente, et al. México a través de los siglos. 10 vols. 1889. Reprint ed., Mexico City: Editorial Cumbre, 1980.

Rodríguez Kuri, Ariel. La experiencia olvidada: El Ayuntamiento de México, política y gobierno, 1876–1912. Mexico City: El Colegio de México, Centro de Estudios Históricos–Universidad Autónoma Metropolitana Azcapotzalco, 1996.

_____. "Política e institucionalidad: El Ayuntamiento de México y la evolución del conflicto jurisdiccional, 1808–1850." In *La Ciudad de México en la primera mitad del siglo xix*, edited by Regina Hernández Franyuti, 2:51–94. Mexico City: Instituto de Investigaciones Dr. José María Luis Mora, 1994.

Rodríguez O., Jaime E. "The Emancipation of America." *American Historical Review* 105, no. 1 (February 2000): 131–52.

_____. "From Royal Subject to Republican Citizen: The Role of the Autonomists in the Independence of Mexico." In *The Independence of Mexico and the Creation of the New Nation*, edited by Jaime E. Rodríguez O., 19–43. Los Angeles: UCLA Latin American Center Publications, 1989.

_____. *The Independence of Spanish America*. Cambridge, England: Cambridge University Press, 1998.

_____. "La Independencia de la América española: Una reinterpretación." *Historia Mexicana* 42, no. 3 (1993): 571–620.

_____. "Oposición a Bustamante." *Historia Mexicana* 20, no. 2 (1970): 199–234.

_____. "The Struggle for Dominance: The Legislature versus the Executive in Early Mexico City." Paper presented at the conference, "The Mexican Wars of Independence, the Empire, and the Early Republic." University of Calgary, Canada, April 1991.

_____. "The Struggle for the Nation: The First Centralist-Federalist Conflict in Mexico City." *The Americas* 49, no. 1 (July 1992): 1–22.

_____. "The Transition from Colony to Nation: New Spain 1820–21." In *Mexico in the Age of Democratic Revolutions, 1750–1850*, edited by Jaime E. Rodríguez O., 97–132. Boulder, Colo.: Lynne Rienner, 1994.

_____. "Two Revolutions: France 1789 and Mexico City 1810," *The Americas* 47, no. 2 (October 1990): 161–76.

_____, ed. *The Independence of Mexico and the Creation of the New Nation*. Los Angeles: UCLA Latin American Center Publications, 1989.

_____, ed. *Mexico in the Age of Democratic Revolutions, 1750–1850*. Boulder, Colo.: Lynne Rienner, 1994.

Sábato, Hilda. "Citizenship, Political Participation and the Formation of the Public Sphere in Buenos Aires, 1850s–1880s." *Past and Present* 136 (1992): 139–63.

Safford, Frank. "Politics, Ideology and Society." In *The Cambridge History of Latin America*, edited by Leslie Bethell, 3:347–422. Cambridge, England: Cambridge University Press, 1985.

Salvucci, Richard J. *Textiles and Capitalism in Mexico: An Economic History of the Obrajes, 1539–1840*. Princeton, N.J.: Princeton University Press, 1987.

Samponaro, Frank N. "Santa Anna and the Abortive Anti-Federalist Revolt of 1833 in Mexico City." *The Americas* 40, no. 1 (July 1983): 95–107.

San Martín, José de. *Cuestiones importantes sobre las Cortes, número uno*. Mexico City: Imprenta D.J.M. Benavente y Socios, 1822.

Sartorius, Carl Christian. *México hacia 1850*. 1858. Reprint ed., translated and edited by Brígida von Mentz. Mexico City: Consejo Nacional para la Cultura y las Artes, 1990.

Satisfacción que los artesanos de esta Ciudad abajo suscritos dan al señor su Diputado don Francisco de Paula Puig, por las expresiones que vierte el diálogo del tejedor y el zapatero. Puebla, Mexico: Imprenta Don Pedro de la Rosa, 1822.

Scardaville, Michael C. "Crime and the Urban Poor: Mexico City in the Late Colonial Period." Doctoral dissertation, University of Florida, 1977.

Schmitt, Karl. "Church and State in Mexico City: A Corporatist Relationship." *The Americas* 40, no. 3 (January 1984): 349–76

Se denuncian al buen juicio las sociedades secretas y caballeros masones. Mexico City: Imprenta Alejandro Valdes, 1826.

Segunda plática del tejedor y su compadre. Puebla, Mexico: Imprenta Mariano Ontiveros, 1820.

Serrano Ortega, José Antonio, "Levas, Tribunal de Vagos y Ayuntamiento: La Ciudad de México, 1825–1835." In *Ciudad de México: Instituciones, actores sociales, y conflicto político, 1774–1932*, edited by Carlos Illades and Ariel Rodríguez Kuri, 131–54. Mexico City: El Colegio de Michoacán and Universidad Autónoma Metropolitana, 1996.

Sewell, William, Jr. *Work and Revolution in France: The Language of Labor from the Old Regime to 1848*. Cambridge, England: Cambridge University Press, 1987.

Shaw, Frederick J. "The Artisan in Mexico City." In *El trabajo y los trabajadores en la historia de México*, edited by E. C. Frost, M. C. Meyer, and J. Z. Vázquez, 399–418. Mexico City: El Colegio de México, 1979.

_____. "Poverty and Politics in Mexico City, 1824–1854." Doctoral dissertation, University of Florida, 1975.

Sims, Harold Dana. *The Expulsion of Mexico City's Spaniards*. Pittsburgh, Pa.: University of Pittsburgh Press, 1990.

Sordo Cedeño, Reynaldo. *El Congreso en la primera República centralista*. Mexico City: El Colegio de México–Instituto Tecnológico Autónoma de México, 1993.

Sowell, David. *The Early Colombian Labor Movement: Artisans and Politics in Bogotá, 1832–1919*. Philadelphia, Pa.: Temple University Press, 1992.

Sprague, William Forrest. *Vicente Guerrero, Mexican Liberator: A Study in Patriotism*. Chicago: R. R. Donnelly and Sons, 1939.

Stein, Stanley J. "Bureaucracy and Business in the Spanish Empire, 1759–1804: Failure of a Bourbon Reform in Mexico and Peru." *Hispanic American Historical Review*, 61, no. 1 (1981): 2–28.

Stevens, Donald Fithian. *Origins of Instability in Early Republican Mexico*. Durham, N.C.: Duke University Press, 1991.

El tejedor poblano y su compadre: Plática familiar entre éstos y su aprendiz. Puebla, Mexico: Imprenta Mariano Ontiveros, 1820.

Tenenbaum, Barbara A. *The Politics of Penury: Debts and Taxes in Mexico, 1821–1856.* Albuquerque: University of New Mexico Press, 1986.

Tilly, Charles. "Conclusion: Contention and the Urban Poor in Eighteenth- and Nineteenth-Century Latin America." In *Riots in the Cities: Popular Politics and the Urban Poor in Latin America, 1765–1910,* edited by Silvia M. Arrom and Servando Ortoll, 225–42. Wilmington, Del.: Scholarly Resources, 1996.

Timmons, Wilbert. "Los Guadalupes: A Secret Society in the Mexican Revolution for Independence." *Hispanic American Historical Review* 30, no. 4 (1950): 453–99.

Torre, Villar, Ernesto de la, ed. *La conciencia nacional y su formación: Discursos cívicos septembrinos (1825–1871).* Mexico City: Universidad Nacional Autónoma de México, 1988.

El tribuno de la plebe: Diálogo entre el tribuno y el vulgo, número dos. Mexico City: Imprenta D. J. M. Benavente y Socios, 1821.

El tribuno de la plebe, o escritor de los pelados, número uno. Mexico City: Imprenta D. J. M. Benavente y Socios, 1821.

Valenzuela, J. Samuel. "Building Aspects of Democracy before Democracy: Electoral Practices in Nineteenth-Century Chile." In *Elections before Democracy: The History of Elections in Europe and Latin America,* edited by Eduardo Posada-Carbó, 223–58. New York: St. Martin's, 1996.

Van Young, Eric. "The Age of Paradox: Mexican Agriculture at the End of the Colonial Period, 1750–1810." In *The Economies of Mexico and Peru during the Late Colonial Period,* edited by Nils Jacobsen and Hans Jürgen Puhle, 64–90. Berlin: Colloquium Verlag Bibliotheca Ibero-Americana, 1986.

———. "Islands in the Storm: Quiet Cities and Violent Countrysides in the Mexican Independence Era." *Past and Present* 118 (1988): 130–55.

———. "The Rich Get Richer and the Poor Get Skewed: Real Wages and Popular Living Standards in Late Colonial Mexico." Paper presented to the All–University of California Group in Economic History, California Institute of Technology, May 1987.

Vázquez, Josefina Zoraida. "La crisis y los partidos políticos, 1833–1846." In *America Latina: Dallo stato coloniale allo stato nazione,* edited by Antonio Annino, 2:557–72. Milan: Franco Angeli, 1987.

———. "Iglesia, ejército y centralismo." *Historia Mexicana* 39, no. 1 (1989): 205–34.

———. "Political Plans and Collaboration between Civilians and the Military, 1821–1846." *Bulletin of Latin American Research* 15, no. 1 (1996): 19–38.

Vázquez Gómez, Juana. *Prontuario de gobernantes de México, 1325–1989.* Mexico City: Editorial Diana, 1989.

Verdadera causa de la revolución del sur, justificándose el que la suscribe con documentos que ecsisten en la Secretaría del Supremo Gobierno del Estado de México, que los certifica, añadidas algunas ocurencias que ha habido después del primer papel que se imprimió con este mismo rubro. Toluca, Mexico: Imprenta del Gobierno del Estado, 1831.

Villaseñor Cervantes, Juan Ignacio. *Algo de masones, o sea diálogo entre un filósofo y una maestra de amiga.* Mexico City: Imprenta del Aguila, 1826.

_____. *Algo de masones, o sea segunda parte del diálogo entre doña Tecla y don Canuto.* Mexico City: Imprenta del Aguila, 1827.

Villoro, Luis. *El proceso ideológico de la revolución de Independencia.* 2d ed. Mexico City: Universidad Nacional Autónoma de México, 1967.

Viqueira Albán, Juan Pedro. *Relajados o reprimidos: Diversiones públicas y vida social en la Ciudad de México durante el siglo de las luces.* Mexico City: Fondo de Cultura Económica, 1987.

Voekel, Pamela. "Peeing on the Palace: Bodily Resistance to Bourbon Reforms in Mexico City." *Journal of Historical Sociology* 5, no. 2 (June 1992): 183–208.

Waldstreicher, David. *In the Midst of Perpetual Fetes: The Making of American Nationalism, 1776–1820.* Chapel Hill: University of North Carolina Press, 1997.

Warren, Richard. "The Construction of Independence Day in Mexico, 1821–1864." Paper presented at the conference, "Culture, Power, and Politics in Nineteenth-Century Mexico: A Conference in Memory of Dr. Nettie Lee Benson," University of Texas, Austin, April 1994.

_____. "Desafío y trastorno en el gobierno municipal: El Ayuntamiento de México y la dinámica política nacional, 1821–1855." In *Ciudad de México: Instituciones, actores sociales, y conflicto político, 1774–1932,* edited by Carlos Illades and Ariel Rodríguez Kuri, 117–130. Mexico City: El Colegio de Michoacán–Universidad Autónoma Metropolitana, 1996.

_____. "Elections and Popular Participation in Mexico, 1808–1836." In *Liberals, Politics and Power: State Formation in Nineteenth-Century Latin America,* edited by Vincent C. Peloso and Barbara A. Tenenbaum, 30–58. Athens: University of Georgia Press, 1996.

_____. "Entre la participación política y el control social: La vagancia, las clases pobres de la Ciudad de México y la transición desde la colonia hacia el estado nacional." *Historia y Grafía* 6 (1996): 37–54.

Weber, David J. *The Mexican Frontier, 1821–1846: The American Southwest under Mexico.* Albuquerque: University of New Mexico Press, 1982.

Wilentz, Sean. "Introduction: Teufelsdröckh's Dilemma: On Symbolism, Politics, and History." In *Rites of Power: Symbolism, Ritual,* _and Politics since the Middle Ages,_ edited by Sean Wilentz, 1–10. Philadelphia: University of Pennsylvania Press, 1985.

_____, ed. _Rites of Power: Symbolism, Ritual, and Politics since the Middle Ages._ Philadelphia: University of Pennsylvania Press, 1985.

Wood, James A. "The Chilean Elections of 1850–1851: A Key Moment in the History of Cross-Class Political Mobilization in Nineteenth-Century Santiago." Paper presented at the Latin American Studies Association 21st International Congress, Chicago, September 1998.

Ya agoniza el despotismo y otorga su testamento. 1823. Reprint ed., Mexico City: Imprenta Nacional, 1823.

Zavala, Lorenzo de. _Ensayo histórico de las revoluciones de México desde 1808 hasta 1830._ 1831–32. Reprint ed., edited by Manuel González Ramírez. Mexico City: Porrúa, 1969.

_____. _Juicio imparcial sobre los acontecimientos de México en 1828 y 1829._ New York: C. S. Winkle, n.d. Reprint ed., Mexico City: Imprenta de Galván, n.d.

Index

Acordada Revolt, 90, 111, 116, 152, 170
Acosta, Juan, 136
Africans, 32–33
Agriculture, and Bourbon reforms, 4
El Aguila Mexicana: election of 1826 and, 80, 81; election of 1827 and, 85; on Guerrero, 89; on Independence Day, 77, 79; on moderates, 83–84; on municipal elections, 86
Aguilar y Bustamante, José María, 142
Agustín I. *See* Iturbide, Agustín de
Alamán, Lucas: Bustamante regime and, 100; on elections, 53, 59, 68; on Independence Day celebrations, 78; as interim executive, 94; on municipal councils, 104–5; opposition to, 76, 108, 169; Victoria and, 70; writings of, 157
Alameda Park, 128
Alcalá, José María, 37, 40, 41
Alcaldes, 12
Alcoholic beverages, 12, 78
Aldermen, colonial period, 12
Alpuche, José María, 76
Alvarez, Juan, 107, 130
El Amigo del Pueblo, 83, 88
Anarchy, 75, 93, 126
Anaya, Juan Pablo, 111
Andrade, José Antonio de, 66
Anticlericalism, 116, 149
Anti-Spanish movement: Cortés's tomb and, 68; election of 1833 and, 109–10; expulsion decrees and, 91–92, 101, 106, 114; Gómez Pedraza and, 88;

Masonic lodges and, 76, 80; radical federalists and, 52–53; Spanish invasion of 1829 and, 92, 93; York Rite Masonic lodges and, 77, 82–83, 167. *See also* Spaniards
La Antorcha, 116
Apodaca, Juan Ruiz de, 2, 53, 56, 57
Arenas Conspiracy, 82–83
Argentina, suffrage in, 162, 163–64
Arista, Mariano, 113–14, 116–17
Army. *See* Military
Army of the Three Guarantees, 56, 63, 64, 106, 168
Arrangoiz, Francisco de Paula de, 68
Artisans, 10–11, 12; elections and, 135–36, 137, 162, 164–65; in France, 158; Gómez Pedraza and, 88; representation of, 60; as vagrants, 87
Attorneys, 12, 138, 139
Audiencias. *See* Regional courts
Autonomists: Constitution of 1812 and, 42–43; election of 1812 and, 35; election of 1813 and, 40; indigenous people and, 26–27; Iturbide and, 50; overthrow of, 28–39
Autonomy, 55
Avecinado, 33
Ayuntamiento. *See* Municipal council
Ayutla, Revolution of, 169
Azcárate (municipal councilor), 29

Bajío, 30
Balderas, Lucas, 111, 115
Balloons, hot-air, 134, 168, 171

193

LATIN AMERICAN SILHOUETTES

Editors: William H. Beezley and Judith Ewell

The U.S.-Mexican Border in the Twentieth Century
   By David E. Lorey
Addicted to Failure: U.S. Security Policy in Latin America and the Andean Region
   Edited by Brian Loveman
For la Patria: Politics and the Armed Forces in Latin America
   By Brian Loveman
The Politics of Antipolitics: The Military in Latin America, Third Edition
   Edited by Brian Loveman and Thomas M. Davies, Jr.
Argentine Caudillo: Juan Manuel de Rosas
   By John Lynch
The Women's Revolution in Mexico, 1910–1953
   Edited by Stephanie E. Mitchell and Patience A. Schell
Gringolandia: Mexican Identity and Perceptions of the United States
   By Stephen D. Morris
Real Life in Castro's Cuba
   By Catherine Moses
Brazil in the Making: Facets of National Identity
   Edited by Carmen Nava and Ludwig Lauerhass, Jr
Mexico in the 1940s: Modernity, Politics, and Corruption
   By Stephen R Niblo
Feeding Mexico: The Political Uses of Food since 1910
   By Enrique C. Ochoa
Impressions of Cuba in the Nineteenth Century. The Travel Diary of Joseph J. Dimock
   Edited by Louis A. Pérez, Jr
Cantinflas and the Chaos of Mexican Modernity
   By Jeffrey M. Pilcher
The Divine Charter: Constitutionalism and Liberalism in Nineteenth-Century Mexico
   Edited by Jaime E. Rodríguez O
Myths, Misdeeds, and Misunderstandings The Roots of Conflict in U.S.-Mexican Relations
   Edited by Jaime E Rodríguez O and Kathryn Vincent
The Origins of Mexican National Politics, 1808–1847
   Edited by Jaime E Rodríguez O
Integral Outsiders: The American Colony in Mexico City, 1876–1911
   By William Schell, Jr.
The French in Central America: Culture and Commerce
   By Thomas D. Schoonover
The Tale of Healer Miguel Perdomo Neira: Medicine, Ideologies, and Power in the Nineteenth-Century Andes
   By David Sowell
Based on a True Story. Latin American History at the Movies
   Edited by Donald F Stevens
Cuban and Cuban-American Women: An Annotated Bibliography
   Edited and Compiled by K. Lynn Stoner, with Luis Hipólito Serrano Pérez
Patriotism, Politics, and Popular Liberalism in Nineteenth-Century Mexico: Juan Francisco Luca and the Puebla
   Sierra
   By Guy P C. Thomson with David G. LaFrance
A Parisian in Brazil: The Travel Account of a Frenchwoman in Nineteenth-Century Rio de Janeiro
   By Adèle Toussaint-Samson
   Edited and Introduced by June E. Hahner
Argentina· The Challenges of Modernization
   Edited by Joseph S. Tulchin with Allison M. Garland
Cuba and the Caribbean Regional Issues and Trends in the Post–Cold War Era
   Edited by Joseph S. Tulchin, Andrés Serbín, and Rafael Hernández
State and Society in Spanish America during the Age of Revolution
   Edited by Victor M. Uribe-Uran
Disorder and Progress: Bandits, Police, and Mexican Development
   By Paul J Vanderwood
Hacienda and Market in Eighteenth-Century Mexico: The Rural Economy of the Guadalajara Region, 1675–1820
   By Eric Van Young
Latin America in the Middle Period, 1750–1929
   By Stuart F Voss
Repression, Resistance, and Democratic Transition in Central America
   Edited by Thomas W Walker and Ariel C Armony
Vagrants and Citizens: Politics and the Masses in Mexico City from Colony to Republic
   By Richard A. Warren
On the Border: Society and Culture between the United States and Mexico
   Edited by Andrew Grant Wood
Revolution in the Street: Women, Workers, and Urban Protest in Veracruz
   By Andrew Grant Wood